BORN
EXP

BORN TO EXPLORE

HOW TO BE A BACKYARD ADVENTURER

RICHARD WIESE

With illustrations by Kimberly Wiese Lanza

HARPER

This book is for informational purposes only. The author and publisher expressly disclaim all liability for any injury or damages that result from the improper use of the information contained in this book.

HarperCollins books may be purchased for educational, business, or sales promotional use. For information, please write: Special Markets Department, HarperCollins Publishers, 10 East 53rd Street, New York, NY 10022.

FIRST EDITION

Designed by Emily Cavett Taff

Library of Congress Cataloging-in-Publication Data is available upon request.

ISBN 978-0-06-144958-1

09 10 11 12 13 OV/RRD 10 9 8 7 6 5 4 3 2 1

*I would like to dedicate this book to the explorers
who have come before me and to the people
who made this book possible.*

*This would not have happened if I did not play
softball with Scott Waxman who, between innings,
said, "You ought to write a book," and became my
literary agent. He introduced me to Matthew
Benjamin at HarperCollins, who "got me."*

*My sister, Kim, illustrated this book between
hurricanes in New Orleans. My wife, Nicci, provided
much needed guidance and encouragement while
pregnant with our first child, Sabrina. But mostly
I would like to thank my parents, Rick and Marie,
whose unconditional love enabled me to follow
my inner explorer.*

CONTENTS

V Food

VI Weather

VII Exploring

VIII Giving Back

ACKNOWLEDGMENTS AND THANKS FOR RESEARCH HELP

Julio Aguilar, *professional alligator and snake wrangler*
Ed Anderson, *Beretta USA*
Franco Gussalli Beretta, *Beretta USA*
Borden Radio Company
Boy Scouts of America
Wildman Steve Brill, *edible plant expert*
Martin Buser, *four-time Iditarod winner*
Kim A. Cabrera, *educator, tracker*
Kathy Chaponton, *chef*
Joe Conlon, *Spectrum Brands-Cutter Insect repellants*
Paul Cormack, *PCLIX*
Jim Fowler, *animal expert and TV personality*
David A. Francko, *assistant vice president for academic affairs and dean of the graduate school of the University of Alabama*
Lisa Hacken, *editor*
Mark Hemming, *photographer*
Blake Holl, *boat-building assistant*
Rich Hilsinger, *director of the Wooden Boat School in Brooklin, Maine*
Hunter Public Relations
Stefani Jackenthal, *researcher and editor*
Sam Javanrouh, *photographer*
Kirk Johnson, *chief curator at the Denver Museum of Science*
Lloyd Kaufman, *professor emeritus at NYU*
Sean Lambert, *researcher*
Charles Lanza, *crab expert*
Dr. Richard Lanza, *MIT department of nuclear engineering*
Nina Lanza, *planetary geologist*

ACKNOWLEDGMENTS AND THANKS FOR RESEARCH HELP

Wyatt Lawrence, *boat builder*
Brian Lang, *University of New Hampshire*
John Loret, *explorer*
Leah Lyon, *outdoor chef*
Christopher Mangun, *researcher*
Jim Mason, *Buck Knives*
Del Morris, *tracker*
William Needham, *Hiker's Notebook*
Bryan Norcross, *meteorologist*
Oleg Novikov, *photographer*
Ben C. Oppenheimer, *curator of astronomy, American Museum of Natural History*
Porters and Guides of Mt. Kilimanjaro
Mathew Pittman, *Snow maker*
Chris Roddick, *curator, the Brooklyn Botanical Garden*
Sue Purvis, *survival expert*
Jim Reid, *outdoor spokesman, Coleman*
Steve Resler, *research diver*
Lorie Roach, *outdoor chef*
Paul Schurke, *arctic survival expert*
Ian Scott, *GSI Outdoors*
Stephanie Shore, *researcher*
Robert Smith, *boat-building assistant*
Michael Smith, *boat-building assistant*
Tina Smith, *tracker*
Josh Schneider, *director, Wollemi Pine North America*
Carl Sommers, *writer, New York Times*
Nicole Young, *researcher, editor, and cheerleader*
Richard Wiese senior, *celestial navigator*
E. O. Wilson, *zoologist, Harvard University*
Richard Wilson, *physicist*
Inspired by the giant redwood cross section at the American Museum of Natural History
Inspired by the Great Hall of Dinosaurs at the American Museum of Natural History, *New York City.*
The creative people of Africa for all the neat things that they make and recycle
My imaginary friend who taught me about rainbows, *whom I have not seen in years*

FOREWORD

The wilderness has been my playground ever since my mother told my brothers and me to "quit roughhousing and go outside and play." We went outside and began to climb trees, take hikes, and ascend hills. To me, wandering in the great outdoors is as natural as breathing.

On my first real mountain, the Tooth—a fang of rock that sticks out of a jawbone ridge in the Cascade Mountains—I was absolutely terrified of the height. I made a vow that if I got off the mountain alive, I would never climb again. Needless to say, I broke that promise and a fascinating new world was revealed to me.

Throughout my life I have been drawn forcefully to the outdoors, to the forests and mountains, seacoasts and oceans, drawn by both a conscious delight in the grandeur and diversity of the planet and an unconscious spiritual yearning to be in the natural world. It is in the wild places—in the damp, clean air of an ancient forest, on a heaving ocean in unpredictable winds, on a snowy summit at the top of the world—that I enter my own personal cathedral.

When I met Richard Wiese while he was president of the Explorers Club in New York, I found a kindred spirit. He, too, is intimately familiar with wild places—the wonders and beauty to be found in the depths of a forest, on a river, on a beach, in high alpine country amid the snow, ice, and rocks, and on the oceans that connect us all.

Richard's book, *Born to Explore*, is not only a story about adventure and how to survive while exploring the wonders of the great outdoors, but also about exploration and how to find nature everywhere and at any time. He has written this book with fun projects that will immediately get your imagination soaring and have you thinking like an explorer.

Of concern to all explorers are the basic questions of food, shelter, weather, and navigation. Richard deals with all these issues in a modern and unique way. He not only has information on "Starting a Fire without a Match," but also includes chapters on how to use the "Miracle Material: Duct Tape" for just about everything, along with other fascinating projects that will have you counting the minutes till you can get outdoors.

The knowledge gained from this book can give you what is needed to go places that are still waiting for the first human footprint or to make discoveries that you never thought possible in your own backyard.

Those who have lived the adventurous life know that the benefits are many. It is a healthy, vigorous lifestyle that promotes physical and mental well-being. Wilderness experiences can be the seed of positive growth for many individuals. Practical knowledge of the outdoors enables one to feel comfortable while enjoying its beauty and the transformative journeys waiting for all. That is exactly what this book delivers.

Another long-term benefit is what this book can do for our planet. If we can get young adults into the natural world—"No Child Left Inside"—they will learn to love it. When they love it, they will want to take care of it, to preserve it. They will want to pass this magical planet on to the next generation, and the next generation, and on and on.

Richard's book, *Born to Explore*, can help make this happen.

—Jim Whittaker
First American to summit Mount Everest

INTRODUCTION

I was inspired to write *Born to Explore* during a trip I took to Antarctica with a group of 70 high school students in December 2002. The students were mostly from the United States and Canada, and the trip was intended to expose them to Antarctica's wondrous ecosystem in a time of notable global warming.

Aboard a burly icebreaker, we were traveling along the Drake Passage, which separates South America from Antarctica and is considered the roughest body of water in the world, when our ship came upon a pod of approximately 50 whales. The whale biologist onboard nearly tripped overboard as he ran to the rails because he had never seen so many whales in one place at the same time. It was an extraordinary spectacle of nature that none of us would likely ever again witness.

Much to my surprise, about a dozen students did not look up from their Gameboys to catch what probably was a once-in-a-lifetime sight. Their lack of interest in the world beyond electronics saddened and frustrated me. Since then, I have spent a lot of time thinking about my experience on the boat that day and how to reintroduce the spirit of exploration to a new generation.

I created this book not only for those boys on the icebreaker but for those of us who are constantly amazed by the little—and big—occurrences in our daily lives. The title *Born to Explore* is meant to reflect an innate curiosity for discovery that I believe all of us possess. Discovery does not just occur in the Amazon or deep in the ocean but everywhere around us.

I hope *Born to Explore* inspires both the nature enthusiast and the nature-impaired and provides information on the tools needed to discover and love the outdoors. In these pages you will find cool projects to do alone, with friends, or even with the entire neighborhood. This book is meant to be a tool and a companion you turn to for fun and creative ideas. Whether it's building an igloo on a snowy winter day, learning to measure trees and buildings in an innovative way, or creating a species-finding competition, it's all in here, just waiting for you to get busy exploring.

Growing up, I couldn't wait to get home from school so I could hop on my bicycle and spend hours snooping around the neighborhood, digging in the sand for lost treasures, and always looking for the next adventure. I was lucky to have my father, Richard Wiese Sr., as a fantastic mentor who nurtured my interests and challenged my brain. He was a pilot with an affinity for weather and astronomy, which he still shares with me to this day. My uncle, Dr. Richard Lanza, a physicist at M.I.T., was a guiding force as well, and he was (and still is) readily available to answer the goofiest of my questions without judgment.

My passion for exploration ultimately led me to become the youngest president of The Explorers Club in New York City in 2002. Members of the 105-year-old organization for field explorers include legends such as Sir Edmund Hillary, the first man to reach the summit of Mount Everest in 1953 with Tenzing Norgay; Neil Armstrong and Buzz Aldrin, the first people to step on the moon; and virtually every great explorer of the twentieth century.

During the four years I was president of The Explorers Club, I had the honor of working with world-class scientists, explorers, and heads of state whom I had idolized as a kid. Being the youngest president had its advantages, as I was young enough to participate in many of the club's expeditions. One of my most memorable experiences was actually in New York City when I teamed up with E. O. Wilson, who is perhaps the most beloved and respected naturalist in the world. Together with several other environmental organizations, we created two biodiversity awareness projects ("Bio-Blitzes"), which involved cataloging organisms in New York City's Central Park over a 24-hour period. I was also able to collaborate on a number of innovative projects with Jim Fowler, professional zoologist and host of the television show *Mutual of Omaha's Wild Kingdom*.

It is amazing what we can see and find when we know what to look for. Observation is a powerful tool that can turn a simple hike in the woods into an exotic journey. I am frequently asked, what is left to explore. The answer is everything. For example, there are an estimated 100 million living species of organisms on Earth, yet we have identified only about 1% of them. As an explorer, scientist, and educator I look at life as an adventure in progress. When I began writing this book upon returning from a medical expedition to Mount Everest in Nepal, I was physically exhausted but energized by the possibility that I might inspire others to explore. Beginning with the ordinary, each of us has the ability to find and uncover the extraordinary. It's what ignites curiosity and keeps us exploring ordinary life for the extraordinary magic hovering within.

Born to Explore promotes a wide range of skills and activities that draw on science, creative arts, physical and mental challenges, interpersonal skills, and bush craft. This book is as much about learning skills and doing projects as it is about expanding your imagination to see possibility where only obstacles might be obvious.

I was born to explore, and so were you!

PART I

EXPLORER TOOL BOX

1 ALTOIDS SURVIVAL KIT

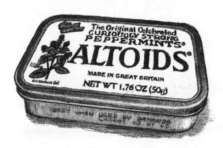

An explorer must be able to adapt to changing conditions and always be a step or two ahead of any situation so as to avoid disaster or unnecessary danger. "Be prepared" is the Boy Scout motto, and it is still the best advice for getting out of sticky situations.

Field and Stream magazine once ran an article about creating small survival kits that fit inside an Altoids tin. It was an interesting experiment that initiated a stir among explorers, raising thought-provoking questions about which safety essentials to pack for an exploration if given only the space of an Altoids tin. It was a terrific exercise in paring down and packing light and smart. We also had curiously strong, minty-fresh breath.

Some of the experts disagreed on particular items to include, such as duct tape versus a fishing hook. (Are you really going to have time to go fishing when you are trying to find your way out of the woods?) But all agreed on two basic elements critical for short-term survival: water purification tablets and a fire-starting substance.

When putting together your own survival kit, choose items that will enable you to perform nearly any minor life-saving task. Think about things with multiple uses. For instance, take duct tape instead of Band-aids. The latter are primarily for covering cuts, whereas duct tape can be used not only to seal wounds and blisters, but also to fix tools and eyeglasses, patch holes in shoes and clothes—pretty much anything (See Chapter 4, Miracle Material: Duct Tape). Instead of toting the entire roll along on your adventure, transfer what you think you'll need—plus a little more—onto a stick by rolling it over itself (shiny side up) around the base of the stick. Tricks like this optimize space and weight.

Being in the wilderness requires a bit of compromising: You should take essentials and leave (most) luxuries home. When packing, bring items that will help in building a fire, constructing shelter, purifying drinking water, gathering food, signaling for help, navigating back to civilization, and administering basic first aid. Let these principles (not necessarily in this order) dictate your gear list.

Survival Kit Gear List

My two biggest priorities are building a fire for warmth and drinking clean water.

Let's begin by stocking our kit with something to start a fire.

Fire

Matches are a waste of space, as they damage easily and are good only for one use. Instead, I'm a big fan of magnesium fire-starting sticks (See Chapter 5, Starting a Fire without a Match) with a sharp metal striker. Give me a good magnesium stick and I'll start a thousand fires. Don't skimp on space by planning to use your knife instead of a separate striker. The magnesium will dull your blade, limiting its ability to cut. Strikers cost about $5 in any camping store.

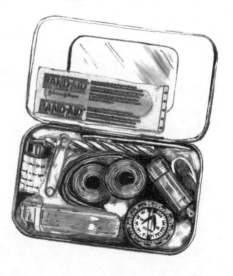

I often include a couple of birthday candles (use the trick ones that you cannot blow out), and I have friends who swear by Tinder-Quik fire tabs, which can ignite even when wet. They are also great for cramming into the extra spaces of a survival tin to keep loose items from rattling.

Water

Drinking unpurified water can result in disease and diarrhea (See Chapter 13, Rumble in the Jungle) or just ruin your trip. Dehydration can lead to muscle cramping and miscellaneous medical nightmares—including death—so what do you do if you run out of water and only unquestionable water sources (streams, rivers, lakes) are available?

That's where water purification tablets come in. Each tablet can purify 1 or 2 quarts of water, depending on the pollution level. These pills are iodine-based, so the water can also be used to sterilize wounds. To use them, add one or more tablets to your water source (water bottle or bladder), let them dissolve for 20 minutes, and shake the container vigorously until most of the chunks have dissolved. Iodine can taste pretty gross, so I like to add a scoop of energy drink to sweeten the flavor and add an electrolyte kick. I recommend including at least 20 iodine tablets in your survival kit. Also, pack a couple of nonlubricated condoms or balloons, which can serve as water containers. But you can also boil water, so you may not need 20 tablets, right?

Tools for Constructing a Shelter

Building a shelter is critical to staying warm and dry in bad weather, and it's easy to do with a couple of basic tools like a sharp knife and sturdy cord. Equipment is no place to skimp, so choose the best equipment to allow for the swift construction of a survival structure. Here are some of my favorites.

GEAR LIST

Suggested Shelter-Building
- Sharp knife with a brawny blade:
    Large: X-acto knife
    Compact: Victorinox Swiss Card or Swiss Army Swiss Card Lite. These amazing kits measure 2$1/4$ by 3$1/4$ inches, about the size of a credit card (they can fit into an Altoids box). They include a letter opener/striker, scissors, ballpoint pen, nail file, screwdriver, tweezers, toothpick, needle, and ruler. Swiss Card Lite also has a magnifying glass and a tiny LED light.
- Parachute cord (550 cord or Paracord). Wrap a wad of cord around an Altoids tin. Paracord (not the cheaper versions) is great because

it is strong, sturdy, and can be split into seven separate strands, which can be used individually for sewing, fishing, and other assorted things.

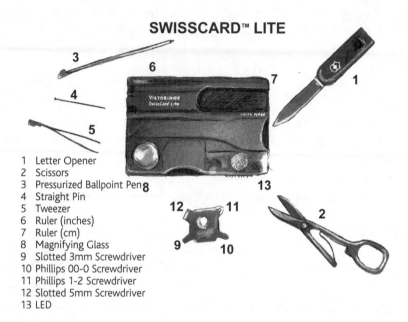

SWISSCARD™ LITE

1   Letter Opener
2   Scissors
3   Pressurized Ballpoint Pen
4   Straight Pin
5   Tweezer
6   Ruler (inches)
7   Ruler (cm)
8   Magnifying Glass
9   Slotted 3mm Screwdriver
10 Phillips 00-0 Screwdriver
11 Phillips 1-2 Screwdriver
12 Slotted 5mm Screwdriver
13 LED

Food

It drives my friends crazy when I say that I think food is overrated—I really only mean this in the context of short-term survival situations. I would put the obligatory fishing hooks, lures, and 50 feet of line (30-pound) in my kit, but realistically I would probably forage for edible insects and plants instead of fishing. While chomping my crickets and berries, I'd use the fishing line and hooks to set snares and construct shelters. Naturally, if it were a long-term situation I would opt for fishing if possible.

The only food I'd pack into my Altoids tin is a stick of wintergreen gum (my favorite flavor, but any flavor works), as it can ward off thirst, give you a quick fix of energy, and kill bad breath. Your buddies will thank you. Or you could opt for an Altoids mint instead.

Signal for Help

If you get lost or are in a serious emergency, use your Altoids can—as you would a signal mirror—to signal for help. Use the sun's refection to shine off the inside of the tin. I also recommend gluing an ultra-thin mirror to the inside bottom and putting a strip of reflective tape across the top of the tin to attract rescuers searching with lights, in case you get lost at night. Reflective tape can be seen from a surprisingly long distance away.

Tiny LED lights (often used on key chains) are great for short durations, when you need to locate items at night. Choose white or yellow (not red), as they are easier to see from a distance. Photon Freedom Micro-Light, a bright LED flashlight that also has variable brightness and three speeds of signaling strobe and an automatic SOS mode that can run for four days and can be seen for a mile, is fantastic.

Navigation

Although I can navigate using the sun and stars (See Chapter 16, Sky), I am at a loss in rain and snow. So I always bring an ultra-thin compass, such as a 20-millimeter, AA liquid-filled button compass.

First Aid

Your first-aid supplies are meant for wound and pain management. Pack pills, which are space efficient, in a small, watertight capsule. Here is a suggested survival medical kit packing list.

GEAR LIST

- 4 anti-diarrhea pills
- 6 ibuprofen or aspirin tablets
- 1 small packet of antibiotic ointment
- A small suture kit
- A small wad duct tape neatly rolled over itself, shiny side up
- 2 safety pins
- 2 feet aluminum foil folded into a tiny rectangle (for making cups, signals, cooking, etc.)

Stranded-at-Sea Altoid Survival Kit

The principles of survival are just about the same everywhere, but being out at sea presents a new set of challenges (and opportunities) that you do not have on land.

Items for fire starting are for the most part unnecessary and in some cases can be very dangerous. The modification to my Altoid land kit mostly reflect differences in obtaining drinking water and preventing dehydration. At sea, the only drinking water available is from rain, dew or, surprisingly, fish. While I minimized the need for fishing hooks in my Altoid land kit, out on the water it is different—a fishing hook and line are vital. Your little micro light may also be useful in catching fish; they have been known to jump into boats because they are attracted to light. To get rid of the temptation of drinking salt water, chew gum or suck on a button, as it will create saliva in your mouth.

To extract water from salt water fish, which have a high percentage of fresh water, you can simply chew on the raw fish and spit out the solids. A variation of this method is to put the fish in cloth and twist and squeeze the water into a container or your mouth. Surprisingly, water obtained this way does not taste that bad, but it is nice to add a little powdered flavor such as Gatorade to sweeten it.

Reflection from the sun can be a real problem out at sea. Sunburn will compromise your skin's ability to regulate your body's temperature and the damage caused by a burn can lead to dehydration. To that end, I would add a fingernail-width amount of waxy sunscreen (I use Neutrogena Stick). Strips of duct tape can also be used to make a sun mask or pin-hole sunglasses.

Here is what's in my stranded-at-sea Altoid kit.

- Tiny LED lights, such as the Photon Freedom Micro-Light, which can be used to locate items at night and can be seen from a long distance.
- Chewing gum to ward off thirst. The aluminum wrappers can be used as fishing lures.
- Small amount of powdered Gatorade to give water collected a better taste and to add some electrolytes.
- Ultra-thin mirror.
- Strip of reflective tape across the top of the tin to attract rescuers searching with lights.

- 3 condoms or balloons for collecting water.
- Ultra-thin compass, such as a 20-milimeter, AA liquid-filled button compass.
- Sharp knife with a brawny blade:
    - Large X-acto knife.
    - Compact Victorinox Swiss Card or Swiss Army Swiss Card Lite.
- Parachute cord (550 cord or Paracord); this may come in handy for boat repairs, although if you have to give up one item, it might be this as fishing line is quite versatile.
- Monofilament line 50 feet (30-pound test).
- 4 fish hooks of various sizes.
- 6 sea-sickness tablets (Dramamine).
- 6 iodine tablets for purifying water.
- 4 anti-diarrhea pills.
- 6 ibuprofen or aspirin tablets.
- 1 small packet of antibiotic ointment.
- A small suture kit.
- A small wad duct tape neatly rolled over itself, shiny side up.
- 2 safety pins.
- 2 feet aluminum foil folded into a tiny rectangle—for making cups, signals, fishing lures, etc.

Packing Thoughts

When making your Altoids mini-survival kit, choose carefully, picking compact, essential survival items. Be innovative in selecting multi-functional items, and don't get discouraged if everything on your first list doesn't fit in the tin. Repack and rethink how to reduce size while maximizing efficiency.

Parting Thoughts

Here's another cool use for an Altoids tin: Make a candelabra by filling the tin with candles. This could score you big points on an outdoor-survival date.

2 YOUR KNIFE, A POINT OF PRIDE

I can tell a lot about an outdoorsman by the condition of his knife. A well-honed knife should be a sharp, shiny point of pride, not a dull, greasy mess. And a sharp knife is safer than a dull one. Not only that, but using a dull knife is not fun! It makes cutting line and opening bags a time-burning struggle and can result in ragged edges, sore hands, and sometimes open wounds.

A sharp edge makes cutting through most anything an effortless pleasure. But all knives, whether used in the field or at home, get dull pretty quickly and need regular sharpening. I prefer using a sharpening stone—as all "real" outdoorsmen do—rather than an electric one-size-fits-all sharpener. Remember, the goal of sharpening is to bring two surfaces—each side of the edge of the blade—together to a fine point.

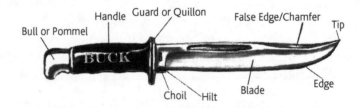

Bull or Pommel · Handle · Guard or Quillon · False Edge/Chamfer · Tip · Choil · Hilt · Blade · Edge

How to Sharpen Your Knife:

STEP 1: Inspect Knife Scrutinize the edge of the blade's condition by holding the knife (edge up) and shining light on the length of the blade.

- A sharp edge will look smooth and even along the edge. Since you can't always see uneven imperfections on a blade, feel for it—carefully! Run your index finger and thumb down the flat side of the blade away from the handle.

> **!** *Don't wet your thumb and slide it down the sharp edge since parts of the blade may still be sharp. Many a man has shown his sad mug in the emergency room after cutting himself this way.*

- A dull knife looks and feels ragged and uneven on the edge. It will be slower to cut and rougher to use than when sharp. Extremely dull and nicked edges require a lot of time to sharpen, which requires a sharpening stone.

STEP 2: Sharpening Stone Sharpening stones, also called whetstones, can be made from any kind of material, including absorbent stone or metal. These use oil or water to float away particles that result from dragging the knife blade across it to sharpen. Many decent ones come from Arkansas and are called Arkansas Stones.

FYI *Sharpening stones can be used dry or wet, but I recommend wet. Use water or honing oil (3-in-1 or WD-40 work well), but do not use vegetable oil, which can turn rancid and stinky.*

1. Secure the stone and use the right grip. Secure whetstone on a stable surface that will not move because you will need both hands on the knife blade. While sharpening, I prefer gripping the knife with my thumb and/or finger resting against the back of the knife blade, with my other thumb and finger on the handle close to the edge.

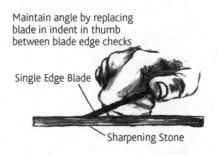

Maintain angle by replacing blade in indent in thumb between blade edge checks

Single Edge Blade

Sharpening Stone

2. Maintain a constant angle between edge and stone. Depending on how it will be used, different knives get sharpened at different angles so before starting, you should know the correct angle. For instance, an axe is used for chopping and is sharpened at a steep angle (30 degrees); a slicing knife, like an X-acto knife or a culinary blade, has a razor-thin edge (5 to 15 degrees); a pocket knife is in the middle (15 degrees). It's nearly impossible to measure a precise angle, but eye it up and know if you hold the blade at too high of an angle against the stone, the resulting edge will be blunt. A masterfully sharp knife should be able to shave hair off your arm, but don't go nuts getting the perfect edge. You'll have plenty of opportunities while resharpening. Most knives come with instructions on sharpening at a particular angle, so read up.

3. "Shaving the surface" off the sharpening stone. To sharpen, push the knife from handle to tip, maintaining the same angle along the stone's surface. When done correctly, water or oil will curl up along the blade. Ed Anderson, a gunsmith for Beretta USA and a fine knife maker, told me the best way to handle a knife is to push it as if you were shaving off the surface of a stone. He recommends keeping as much of the knife's edge as possible in contact with the stone.

4. Keep it on the stone. Sliding the blade off the end of the stone creates a round tip or makes unwanted scratches to the side of the blade. Keep your fingers and thumb behind the blade, while allowing your other fingers or thumb to rest on the stone.

5. Use even control and alternate blade sides. While sharpening your knife, work on alternate blade sides with each stroke to remove equal amounts of burr (roughness) on each side. If

you feel roughness forming on one side, switch to the other side, and frequently (and carefully) check for rough spots. Whatever you do, do not mimic the Hollywood macho men who sharpen their knives by swiping it back and forth swiftly and carelessly. It's purely bad acting and awful technique.

6. Inspect the edge for evenness. Wipe the knife dry. With a soft cloth, buff away any scratches made from the stone grit by making one stroke from hilt to tip. Turn the knife to other side and repeat. Carefully run your fingers along the flat side (not the sharp edge) to check for any remaining roughness. Test it out! If the knife fails to cut as expected, you may need to do a bit more stone shaving.

Knife Tips

1. Maintain the edge and sharpen regularly. A knife becomes dull quicker than you think, so if it's not working properly, chances are it's dull. Sharpen the edge as soon as you notice dullness. With frequent maintenance, a few single strokes side-to-side should quickly bring the edge back to sharpness.
2. Keep the sharpener where the knives are used (shop, tackle box, kitchen). To encourage regular sharpening, I keep mine next to my knives.
3. Use your knife for its intended purpose. Some knives are designed for cutting and piercing, others for opening, and then there are those miscellaneous utility knives that are not worth stressing over. For the most part, a kitchen knife is meant to cut through food only, while pocket knives are meant for the outdoors. Use common sense to keep your knives in excellent condition and avoid injury.
4. Use care in storing knives. Store knives neatly and protect their edges. Don't toss them in a drawer where other metal utensils will dull their blades. Keep kitchen knives in a wood block or on a magnet. Avoid stowing a knife in its sheath as it will tarnish the blade.
5. Wear your knife on your side. In the outdoors, keep your knife in a sheath attached to a belt and wear it on your side (not in front or back).
6. Your mother was right: Don't run with a knife!

Parting Thoughts

Treat your knife with respect. Not only is it good for the equipment, it reflects well on you as an outdoorsman. Make it a point of pride, as your knife may be your best friend in a jam.

3 BACKWOODS BOW AND ARROW

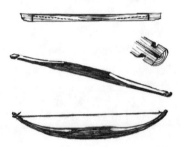

Created some 10,000 years ago for hunting and protection, bows and arrows have been an important part of human existence and advancement. Before this "modern" tool was developed, men and women hunted with their bare hands, heavy rocks, or crude knives. All of those methods required up-close-and-personal intimacy with their prey. The bow and arrow offered precision and much-needed personal space, so there was less chance of becoming a bear's dinner. I often wonder what it felt like in those times to watch your feathery arrow take flight in a beautiful arc, knowing it was a matter of life or death.

While knowing how to build a bow and arrow is no longer vital to survival, it's a fun project that leaves you with a sense of achievement and confidence. Once you turn a tree branch into a bow and learn how to release an arrow from it, you'll want to do it again, and you'll never look at a branch in quite the same way again.

Your Bow and Arrow

Try making a basic backwoods bow with arrows. You will need a few simple things to get started.

GEAR LIST

- One dead, hardwood stick or branch about 4 or 5 feet long and 2 inches thick for the bow. I like white ash, but there are plenty of other kinds of wood. My first bow was made with lemonwood, which worked fine, but many consider it too easy to break.
- Non-stretchy string—you can use sinew, cordage, nylon fishing line, or even hemp to name a few.
- A wood-cutting tool (like a sharp knife or axe).
- Straight, dead sticks about 1.5 feet long for arrows.
- Sharp knife.
- Wood chisel (optional).
- Feathers for fletching. You can them find under bird nests, at chicken farms, duck ponds, or even hobby stores.
- A garbage bag for target practice.

STEP 1: Find a Piece of Wood to Make the Bow

- Find a piece of dry, dead hardwood like elm, ash, juniper, black walnut, or willow (but not pine) for the bow. It should be straight, without twists, twigs, or knots. The branch should be longer than the finished bow as it is easier to remove excess wood than to add it back when carving. It should be about 2 inches in diameter.

> **!** *Avoid green wood, which will bend and lose shape, and wet wood, which makes a slow bow.*

- Cut it down to size with a saw or small axe.

FYI *You can dry wood indoors or next to a warm place like a heater.*

STEP 2: Shape the Wood

- Keep the center and body of the bow thick, but taper the ends by carving off about $1/4$ inch of thickness from both ends (carving inward to about a foot from each end of the stick). This makes the wood flexible for shooting.

> **!** *If you carve one end too much, it will throw it off balance. If this happens, it is probably easier to start over with a new piece of wood.*

STEP 3: Make Notches at Both Ends

- Make a 1/8-inch notch about 2 inches in from each end. This is where you will hook your string to secure it to each end of the bow.

STEP 4: Stringing and Shaping the Bow

- To string the bow, wrap the string around one of the notches a few times and knot it off using a slip knot.
- Bend the bow, attach the string to the other notch, and knot it off. The string should be tight and somewhat difficult to pull back, but not so tight that it feels like it will snap.
- Let the bow sit overnight (24 hours), allowing the wood to settle into its new shape.
- Pull the strings back to create tension to test the bow's strength. Any weakness could result in breakage.

STEP 5: Find Sticks for Arrows

- Select dry, straight branches or sticks for the arrows. Steer clear of green sticks because they will bend.

STEP 6: Making Arrows

- Carve off layers of bark until the arrow is smooth along the shaft. Do this for each arrow.
- Carve a small notch at one end of each arrow. This is where the bowstring will brace the arrow.
- Whittle the tip of the arrows into a point.
- For advanced arrows, find the feather's fletching (arrow's tail), which makes arrows aerodynamic. Cut the feathers in half, leaving only one side of the vain (the hairs of the feather). Glue the rachis (the boney center of the feather) to the ends of each arrow—use three fletchings, spaced equal distance apart on the end of the arrows.

STEP 7: Set Up Your Target

- Create a target by filling a garbage bag with dead leaves, grass clippings, or anything to puff it up.
- Always place targets in a safe location, away from others, and no more than 30 feet away from where you are standing.

STEP 8: Take Your First Shot

- Standing roughly 30 feet from your target, hold your bow vertically. Right-handed people should hold bow shaft with your left

hand and draw back the string with your right hand. The opposite is true for left-handed people.
- Find a comfortable technique for drawing (pulling back) your arrow.
- Draw the arrow back with your string, and take your first shot!

Important Warnings!

- Before every use, examine your bow for cracks (or other obvious faults), and bowstring for fraying or broken strands. A cracked bow can shatter when drawn.
- Never fire your bow without an arrow on the string, as the force will be re-absorbed by the bow causing it to fracture over time.
- Never randomly fire arrows into the air as they can fly a long way and hit (and injure) an unanticipated target!
- Protect your forearm (the one bracing the bow during firing) as the string uncoiling can easily bruise your arm.

FYI *The world record for an arrow shot from a hand-held bow is nearly a third of a mile.*

Parting Thoughts

Bow and arrows can become fatal weapons if used irresponsibly. When shooting, you are responsible for the range and must keep a keen eye for nearby hikers, animals, and others who could be at risk. Remember that an arrow is like words; once let loose, it does not return.

4 MIRACLE MATERIAL: DUCT TAPE

Duct tape rules!

Perhaps the most versatile manufactured product on our planet, duct tape can be used in nearly every situation. Several years ago, I was competing in the La Ruta Maya river canoe race in Belize. The four-day, 170-mile race was good fun, but it turned into a bit of a calamity for my two friends and me. Had it not been for duct tape it might have been a disaster. We started the race with our palms covered in duct tape to prevent blisters while paddling. We also made nifty nose guards to ward off sunburn, and we taped gear to the boat in case we capsized. Most important, though, was using duct tape to patch a hole we incurred on the third day that would have sunk our hopes of finishing, which we did in a respectable time.

I have actually seen guys in the field make clothing out of duct tape, repair leaking fuel tanks, and I once used it to tape the snout of a snapping alligator while transporting him. There are websites, books, films, and even cults devoted to the virtues of duct tape.

Originally developed by Johnson and Johnson in 1942 as a water-resistant sealant to keep ammunition cases moisture-free, duct tape has become a one-stop repair kit for problems big and small. Commonly referred to or mispronounced as "duck" tape, this stupendous, shiny, sticky strip has an uncanny ability to fix things from home to trail. I've listed some of my favorites uses for duct tape here, but don't let my suggestions limit your vision of what this miracle matter can do for you. Innovative creators have discovered literally thousands of duct-tape applications, ranging from elaborate clothing ensembles to delicate works of art. Here are just a few.

Common Uses for Duct Tape

- Patch ripped clothing, footwear, and miscellaneous gear.
- Reinforce belts, straps, and gloves.
- Cover cuts and blisters; or wrap and secure twisted or broken body parts, such as ankles, wrists, or fingers.
- Cover books, maps, journals to strengthen and protect them from the elements.
- Wrap ends of shoe laces, rope, and cloth to prevent fraying.
- Twist lengths to use as substitute twine or clothesline.
- Wrap around handles of camping pots, pans, and cooking implements to reduce heat and ensure a solid grip.
- Supplement or replace webbing in lawn chairs when the original wears thin.
- Secure pant cuffs around your socks to protect against ticks and other nasty bugs when traipsing on and off trails.
- Mark a trail by wrapping duct tape around trees as you go. (Although this doesn't seem very "green.")
- Wrap a length, sticky side out, around your hand and pat down clothing to remove lint, burrs, and animal hair.

Inventive Uses for Duct Tape

- Wrap around your dog's paws to offset frostbitten pads. It's best to wrap the tape around a sock or rag to prevent the adhesive from coming into contact with any hair.
- Use strips on your face to protect against windburn. Rub or rough down the sticky side so it does not adhere to your skin too tightly.

Apollo 13 "mailbox"

- Remove cactus spines and splinters by placing strips over affected area of skin and rip off in one quick motion. Ouch!
- Pull a length of the cotton fiber from the sticky side of tape to make "duct string" and use it as dental floss.
- Apply it to the back of sandpaper before using it with a vibrating or orbital sander—sandpaper will last up to five times longer!
- Never get locked out of your car again: tape a spare ignition key to the rear axle.

- Fold your pants inside out and use duct tape to temporarily hem them to a desirable length.
- Keep matchbooks sturdy and dry by wrapping them in a few folds of duct tape.
- Use strips of duct tape as flypaper in a tent or cabin.

Outstanding Uses for Duct Tape

- The folks at Duck Tape Products offer a $5,000 scholarship every year to a single high school prom couple (judged in five separate categories) fully dressed in duct tape attire. See www.ducktape club.com for more details.
- Entire boats have been constructed using nothing more than cardboard and duct tape.
- NASA has regularly used duct tape for in-space repairs on things from Lunar Rovers to a CO_2 filter modification that saved the lives of the *Apollo 13* astronauts.

5 FIRE

Starting a Fire without a Match

> *"Sticks and stones may break your bones,*
> *but they also make fire!"*
> —Susan Purvis

Fire-building is one of the most important skills a person needs to survive in the wilderness. It's not only critical for cooking up grub and

staying warm at night, but mastering the ability also builds an out-doorsman's confidence. Knowing how to make a fire without matches is even more rewarding.

> **!** It's important to practice all these techniques under calm, controlled conditions at home before taking them into the field. Trying them for the first time in adverse conditions is a recipe for disaster. In addition, fire can not only burn or kill humans, it can destroy habitat and all the creatures that depend on it, so use it wisely.

When I was younger I thought starting a match-free fire meant rubbing sticks together, which, at the time, seemed like an arduous task not worth the time. Years later, however, I was inspired to try it after watching a survival show on TV. While visiting my parents, who still live in the house I grew up in on Long Island, NY, I slipped into their basement and spent nearly two hours desperately rubbing two sticks together. It worked so well on the show, I thought; surely I must be doing something wrong. I was on the verge of aborting the mission when, much to my surprise, I saw smoke. At first it was a mere puff, but that grew into a cloud of smoke, which ultimately set off the smoke detectors and freaked out the entire household. Yet there was still no fire. My mission was officially terminated.

Not only did I learn that day that aloe lotion soothes sore hands, but also that there is a difference between working hard and working smart. My technique was okay, but I was using the wrong kind of wood.

Fire has been used to cook food for nearly as long as humans have walked the earth. As you might imagine, back in the day, there were no matches or lighters. Here's your chance to learn how to start a fire like a primitive man.

There is more than one way to do it and, with a bit of practice, you can be whooping up flames at family BBQs faster than your charcoal-lighter-fluid wielding Uncle Smokey. Before getting into the details, it's important to understand that three things are necessary to start and sustain a fire: oxygen, heat, and fuel. Take any of these elements away, and starting a fire is impossible.

Getting Started

Tinder, such as newspaper in a fireplace, is essential to starting any fire. It's easy to find, and almost any fibrous, dry material that easily ignites should do. I've used everything from feather down to dried moss. Surprisingly, lint from my pocket worked exceptionally well.

Here are four basic ways to start a fire without matches.

Spark-Based Fire Making

Technique 1: Magnesium Steel Fire Stick

This method is so simple that using it almost feels like cheating. Anyone can master this technique the first day out. Magnesium sticks are available at local Army/Navy surplus or sporting goods stores for a few bucks and will last years. They are ideal for wet or windy conditions when matches are difficult to light. Scraping the stick creates sparks that will fall into

and ignite tinder. But properly positioning the tinder is important.

STEP 1: Dig a small hole in the ground or use a flame-proof metal bowl and stack tinder in a pile, creating a "fire nest." It should contain materials as small and as delicate as you can find, things that light easily, like dry grass or leaves.

STEP 2: Grasp the magnesium stick between your thumb and forefinger, and then scrape it against the backside of a knife at a 45-degree angle, away from your body into the fire nest. Do not use the sharp blade side or it will dull your knife. Stoke the fire by blowing into the bowl where the sparks fall. Once the tinder catches, continue blowing on it until the fire is going strong. An easy victory for sure, and no one gets kicked off the island.

Technique 2: Magnifying Glass

Use a magnifying glass to focus the sun's rays on a pile of dry leaves, grass, or tissue paper to start a fire. The more powerful the magnifying glass, the better it works. When the tinder starts glowing, blow on it to get it flaming. The finer the tinder, the better the chances are for quickly lighting a fire. (Resist the temptation to scorch innocent crawling insects with your magnifying glass, as they are a form of life and pound for pound much stronger than you. But we'll get into that in later chapters.)

Technique 3: A Glass of Water

Believe it or not, you can use a glass of water to start a fire! The wider the glass the better and midday, summer sunshine works best. Essentially, the glass of water will be used like a magnifying glass, redirecting and concentrating sunlight onto tinder. In this case, the tinder—such as a piece of paper—must be held and maneuvered into the shifting sunrays in order to ignite. Again, blow on the sparks to rev up the flames. It's a bit more challenging than the other techniques but oddly entertaining.

Technique 4: Bow Drill

Starting a bow-drill fire separates the men from the boys. This technique, which seems to be a favorite of most old-school wilderness gurus, essentially creates coal. Considered one of the most challenging survival skills to learn, mastering the method will make you feel like a competent outdoors person.

Identifying the correct materials takes a keen eye, and using them requires precision. But experts can typically get a flame in less than a minute.

STEP 1: Find the appropriate wood.

WOOD (TINDER) SUGGESTIONS

- Balsam (or Fir)
- Yucca
- Cedar
- Cypress
- Tamarack
- Basswood
- Cottonwood

  Note: I've also used the base of sagebrush bushes in Idaho and Colorado.

STEP 2: Make a Bow-Drill Fire

GEAR LIST—THE BOW-DRILL SET

- Drill or spindle
- Bow
- String
- Fireboard
- Coal catcher
- Socket rock or smooth board
- Knife—to make notch in fireboard

MAKING BOW DRILL

1. *Drill or spindle.* Use a piece of wood resembling a pencil with sharp points on either end that can spin, creating friction and heat with another piece of wood (fireboard). It should be about the diameter of a hot dog, 12 to 15 inches long, with smooth and straight sides (without notches or cracks) to ensure consistent, uninterrupted strokes with the bow.

Note: Carve a sharper point on the end of the spindle that will drill into the fireboard. The point where the spindle meets the socket rock (used to protect your hand) should be duller to provide minimal friction.

2. *Bow.* There will be a lot of pressure on the bow, so make it from bendable yet stiff wood such as oak or pine. It helps to have a bow that has a natural curve on both ends, which keeps the bowstring away from the bow. Beginners should make a lightweight bow 1.5 to 2 feet long, as it will be easier to control and takes less strength to push back and forth.

3. *Stringing your bow.* The bowstring should be the diameter of shoestring or a little thicker. (Avoid smooth ropes made of nylon that will slip and not catch drill.) Tie the string at the end of your bow.

4. At the other end, wrap the string around the end four times, but do not tie it off. Remember, you are not making a bow and arrow. You will need to wrap your spindle with the string, so leave some slack in the string.

5. The block board or fireboard. Find a piece of wood that the spindle can rub against to create friction and ultimately spark coals to make a fire.

The fireboard should be uniform, smooth, dry, and large enough to be easily controlled, yet thin, about .25 inches, which will save you time in carving out the notch. The best wood will be sap-free, light, dry, and soft enough to easily dent with your thumbnail without gouging.

STEP 1: Using the spindle, create a hole in the fireboard with the tip of your knife. Make a tiny groove, just big enough for the spindle to fit into without slipping and sliding while rotating.

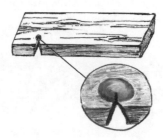

STEP 2: Carefully cut a narrow triangle-shaped notch into the edge of the hole with a knife. This will allow air in and coals to drop down on the tinder. The notch should be on the side of the board that faces you.

1. Coal catcher. The coal catcher is essential for catching and protecting the coals that drop through the notch on the fireboard. Use a dry leaf, sliver of wood, piece of paper, or bark.
2. Socket rock or board. A socket rock is a smooth, fairly flat rock that can serve as a hand piece that will protect the palm of your hand from heat and abrasion while you are pushing on the spindle. On my first try, I used a crushed soda can and quickly rediscovered how metal transfers heat. Ouch! Take my hot-hand advice and use a pine knot or a hard, smooth stone with which to drive your spindle. Be resourceful!

TURNING WOOD INTO FIRE!

This part of the operation is the most crucial and has to be completed within seconds to start a fire.

STEP 1: Once you have your complete bow-drill set assembled, line up all the supplies in front of you in a wind-free and dust-free area.

STEP 2: With your right hand, grab the end of your bow where the bow string is wrapped several times around the end of the bow. Use your left hand to twist the spindle into the string so that the spindle length is perpendicular to the bow. Place the drill in the bow so that the loop is on the outside of string, away from the bow. This prevents the drill from rubbing against the bow. Move the spindle toward your right thumb to secure the spindle while preparing the remaining items. Now, take a deep breath!

STEP 3: Place the fireboard under your left foot, making sure it is flat and steady. Kneel on your right knee while bringing the spindle to the fireboard with your right hand. Then, with your left hand, put your socket rock on top of the spindle.

Now you are ready to heat things up!

STEP 4: Brace your left hand firmly against your shin bone to prevent the spindle from slipping out of the notch. Apply firm downward pressure by keeping shoulders over socket and spindle.

STEP 5: Make long, even strokes against the spindle, using the entire length of the bow. I like keeping my right thumb in the action by adding or subtracting tension on the bow string. Rhythmically, move the bow perpendicular to the spindle. Use the entire length of the bow to create firm, steady strokes. Increase speed and pressure until you see smoke. Remember to breathe.

Don't stop yet! After you see smoke billow from the fireboard, continue for 20 more strokes. Phew! Carefully stop and remove your spindle from the fireboard, and take your foot off the fireboard. Expect to see black soot scattered all over; it's coal.

STEP 6: This is the motherlode. Lift the fireboard off the glowing coal. I like to use my knife blade to pick up the embers and drop them into the tinder bundle. Cup the nest in your hand, and lightly blow on it until it catches fire.

TROUBLESHOOTING: If the spindle squeaks, push it down harder while maintaining the speed of the bow!

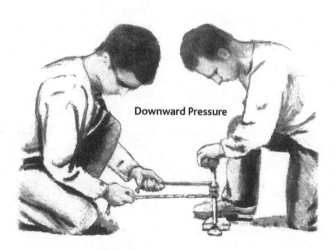

Use thong to rotate spindle

Technique 4: Fire-Plow

Rubbing two sticks together to build a fire generally refers to using some type of a fire-plow. Since that hand-cramping day in my folks' basement, I have actually grown to love this technique. It was pretty easy to do once I had the right wood and technique.

The fire-plow is a friction method of ignition that requires rubbing a hardwood shaft against a softer wood base, such as cedar. The method works by cutting a straight groove into the base and forcefully scraping (or plowing) the blunt-tipped hardwood shaft along the groove. Plowing releases small particles of cedar-wood fibers that ultimately ignite from the friction.

I like using cedar, ash, or walnut for the shaft because they are dense and steady. While experimenting to find your favorite wood combination, try rubbing a piece of cedar shingle and a cedar base and see what happens. You should quickly see smoke but probably no fire.

Parting Thoughts

In 1669, a German chemist named Henning Brand was intent on making gold. He theorized that since his urine had a golden hue, it must contain the mineral gold. Talk about a golden ego!

To prove his theory, he peed in his bathtub for a few days and let the urine stand for a few more, until it dried into a solid, pasty material (do not try this experiment at home!). I hope he was wearing nose plugs when he took this putrefied material and heated it to a high temperature. Much to his surprise and disappointment, he did not excrete gold-laced pee. Rather, his stinky, sticky specimen mutated into a white, waxy substance that glowed in the dark. He had discovered phosphorus, commonly used today in the flammable tip of matches. In Greek, *phosphorus* means "light bearer."

There Is a Fungus among Us: The Incredible Chaga Fungus

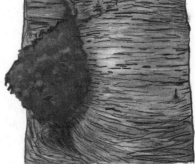

While the word *fungus* is more likely to evoke thoughts of mold or something between your toes than of fire, it's truly a fire-starting gem from Mother Nature with a fascinating history beyond its flammability.

In 1968, the wonders of the chaga fungus were brought to light by Nobel Prize–winning author Aleksandr Solzhenitsyn. In *Cancer Ward*, a Russian country doctor named Sergei Maslennikov notes that cancer was nonexistent in patients in Muzhik who drank chaga tea daily. Research over the last 20 years has confirmed that chaga fungus can be used to treat numerous diseases, including uterine, breast, lung, cervical, and gastric cancers.

How to Use Fungus as a Fire Starter

Chaga fungus is commonly found on birch trees that have sustained injury to their bark. It is generally pretty easy to remove with a knife, and it dries quickly. When I first discovered chaga I was on a group canoe trip in the Adirondack Mountains in upstate New York. On our way to

our lodge after a fun, exhausting day of paddling, we came across a huge, black bulge sprouting on a birch tree. I pried it off the tree with my pocket knife. The hardened black outer layer gave way to a crumbly reddish-brown clumpy material, resembling tightly packed coffee grounds. Back at camp, it lit immediately with a strike of a match.

It had a pleasant forest-like aroma as it started to glow, but after about an hour of being stoked by a strong wind, it grew and blazed like molten lava. The harder the wind blew, the more it radiated. We were drawn to the glowing fungi, but when bedtime rolled around, I couldn't extinguish it. Safety first! I turned it over, expecting it to smolder. Instead, it flared and flames shot out from the belly side. This thing was possessed! Try as we might, we were unable to douse its mighty flame. So we surrounded it with a tall pile of rocks, removed all flammable items from the area and went back to our cabins.

To this day, I have never found an organic material as flammable or as durable as the chaga fungus.

Starting a Fire with the Chaga Fungus

Talk to ten outdoors people and you will hear ten different ways to use chaga fungus. These are two of my favorites:

- Scrape the fungus with a knife to produce a powder. The powder is used as tinder to catch the spark.
- Hold the entire fungus off the edge of the flint or fire striker. Let the sparks hit the fungus.

Fungus 101

In 1991, the body of a well-preserved Neolithic man who died more than 5,000 years ago on an alpine glacier in Italy was found in the melting ice by a climber. Among the "Oetzi Iceman's" possessions was a leather pouch filled with well-preserved tinder fungus (in this case, *fomes fomentarius*), commonly found in the surrounding lowlands. From this extraordinary find, scientists speculated that fungus was used as natural tinder well before our time.

Really Alternative Campfire Fuels

I bet you did not know that, in addition to the chaga fungus, animal dung is another natural source that can be used for heat and warmth.

I once traveled on a medical expedition to Mount Everest Base Camp, where the stunning peaks were immediately visible upon beginning our trek, whetting our appetite for what lay ahead. The higher we hiked the more barren our surroundings became,

and by the time we reached 13,000 feet there were no more trees—only shrubs growing near to the ground. Instead of camping out, we decided to stay in tea houses along the trail. The houses were, of course, warmer and more comfortable during rain or snow. What became immediately apparent at high altitude, however, was that oil was not readily available to heat these dirt-floored huts. The main fuel source was dried yak dung. Cracked and brittle, it was collected in fields and piled like bricks outside houses to dry and ultimately get loaded into a wood-burning stove like barbecue briquettes and doused with a bit of kerosene. And voilà—we had a fairly decent fire with a little extra smoke.

Animal dung has been used as a heating source in just about every part of the world for millennia. You don't have to go to Nepal to find and burn dung. Any grass-eating animal's poop will suffice. Whether it comes from a camel, goat, cow (cow patties), buffalo (buffalo chips), or horse (manure), the dung needs to be dried before it is burned. Because it burns a lot cooler than wood, it maintains a steady low flame that radiates as much heat as wood, so it's best to surround the fire with rocks or metal (as in a wood-burning stove) to transfer the warmth efficiently for space heating or cooking. Thankfully, it doesn't smell as bad as you might expect; it's akin to burning grass, which it mostly is.

In Egypt, local villagers make "camel dung cake" fuel using palm fronds for initial tinder. Similarly, dry grass and twigs are used for the starter. Obviously, camel dung may not be available, but this method can be adapted to use with your local brand of poop.

FYI *Camel dung as more than fuel!*

One of the better stories that I have been told regarding animal poop had to do with an unusual use of animal dung during World War II. The British Army hid land mines in piles of camel dung because German tank drivers thought it was good luck to drive over camel dung. Personally, I would not have wanted either job! But wait, it gets worse.

During the war dung was also used for medicinal purposes. Many German soldiers fighting in the Middle East contracted dysentery (diarrhea) from consuming bacteria-filled local food and water. Since antibiotics were not readily available in those days, finding an alternative cure was essential to keep soldiers active.

Looking to local customs, German scientists noted that the regional Arabs were not immune to the deadly bacteria, either, but at the first stomach flutter, they would do the unthinkable. They sought out the nearest pile of horse or camel droppings, scooped the poop, and ate it. Yuck! But the dysentery would be gone overnight. It was an ancient tradition passed down through generations. Imagine the first one to experiment with this technique. What was he thinking?

Initially, scientists did not understand why this worked, just that the feces needed to be fresh. After thorough examination, they found the dung was chock-full of powerful bacterial microorganisms, eventually identified as Bacillus subtilis, a super bacterium capable of cannibalizing the harmful microbes.

During the war, the Nazis produced vast amounts of Bacillus subtilis cultures for their troops in the field. It ultimately became the leading treatment for dysentery and similar intestinal illnesses throughout the world, and was sold in the United States and Mexico under the brand name Bacti-Subtil.

Windproof Candle Holder

Recyclable, resourceful, and even a little romantic!

Are you an environmental hero? In the know on what's hot and what's not? Perhaps you are looking for a low-key, bang-for-your-buck way to wow your girlfriend with a romantic candle-lit dinner on the beach. Check this out! Here is an easy (and cheap) way to make a wind-proof candle-holder out of a simple plastic bottle.

GEAR LIST

- Plastic bottle
- Scissors
- Candle
- Matches or lighter

STEP 1: Cut

Using scissors cut off the upper quarter of any plastic bottle.

STEP 2: Insert

Turn the upper part of the bottle upside down and insert it into the bottom part of the bottle, pushing it all the way to the bottom.

STEP 3: Create the Mood

Place a candle in the neck of the bottle, and fire it up!

If your candle is too wide, whittle it down to size with a sharp knife.

Clear bottles give off the most light, but those with contours—like a Coke bottle—refract light, creating cool designs. Try both!

Parting Thoughts

Although western culture is in its infancy when it comes to reducing waste and recycling, folks in developing countries have been crafting goods out of what we might consider "trash." Often, their "make-do" creations for essential needs—food and shelter—become works of art that inspire me toward greener ways.

6 CHOPPING DOWN A TREE

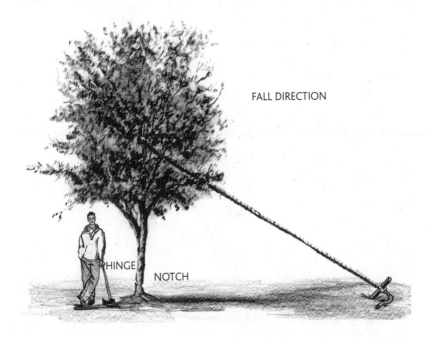

FALL DIRECTION

HINGE NOTCH

On a hiking trip in Adirondack State Park I was talking to a park ranger about campers chopping firewood, when out of
the blue, he said, "If trees could scream do you think these people
would be so willing to cut them down?" Remembering an old Jack
Handy quote, I said sarcastically, "I might if they screamed all the
time without good reason."

All kidding aside, chopping down a tree is not something just anyone can or should do. It's important to have a good reason and a plan
for chopping down a tree. If you are in a state or federal park check out
the regulations, and if you are on someone else's land, get permission
first. Never chop a tree down just for fun, unless it is dead. In any case,
there is a right and wrong way to chop down a tree. Let's first look at
the wrong way.

The Wrong Way to Chop Down a Tree

I don't have enough fingers and toes to count the times I have been in a friend's backyard or at a campsite watching some guy wielding his chopping axe like he is trying to hit a home run or kill a scurrying rodent. Not only is he expending a ton of energy with little to show for it, but he is a danger to himself and those around him.

So, what could go wrong while chopping down a tree? Lots! You could miss hitting the trunk with your axe and slash your foot instead. This is a frequent mishap, especially after about 15 swings of a ten-pound axe head. Accidents typically occur when you are tired and shift to autopilot, not thinking and just swinging away. Sometimes an axe blade gets stuck in the tree trunk, causing the tree to tip in the wrong direction, potentially crushing you or your neighbors. That would suck!

Another devastating axe act would be chopping down a hundred-foot tall tree in your backyard and miscalculating the trajectory when it's rooted only fifty feet from your home. You do the math.

Having a plan and taking a few simple steps will lead to safe tree chopping.

The Correct Way to Chop Down a Tree

So, what is the right way to chop down a tree?

GEAR LIST

- Axe
- Rope
- Strong spike (to tie off rope)

STEP 1: Set Up

After gathering the materials, stand in front of the tree and estimate its height using the shadow or sexton method (See Chapter 16, Sky—Getting to the Height of Things). This is a critical measurement, because you must be sure that the tree does not hit power lines, homes, or people as it falls.

FYI **WARNINGS**

- *Take into account uneven ground, which may affect the tree's lean and where it may "naturally" want to fall.*
- *Accommodate for extending branches and wind direction.*
- *Do not allow tree to fall into ditches or muddy areas where it will be hard to remove later.*

STEP 2: Rope It

Tie the rope around the tree trunk at about three-quarters of the tree's height or as high as possible. This will later help direct the falling tree. Make sure the rope is significantly longer than the fall zone, and have a plan for creating tension on the rope when the tree is ready to topple, such as wrapping it around another tree or using a trailer hitch to pull the rope tight.

STEP 3: Clearing for Safety

Trim away any excessive growth at the base of the tree that may interfere with a clean axe swing. Then choose the direction the tree should fall, and make a small notch. The is the place where you will be aiming the axe for another 20 to 50 chops.

> **!** Before swinging your axe around, make sure you are standing on firm ground and that nobody is standing within a 10-foot radius of where you are swinging.

STEP 4: Chop a Clef

Chop a clef, a notch axed into the trunk, on the falling side of the tree (see illustration). Make this groove roughly 1/8 the depth of the trunk.

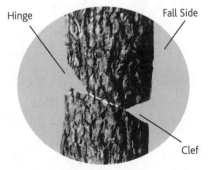

Hinge

Fall Side

Clef

> **!** *If you make it too deep, the tree may fall before you want it to, and you will be unable to control its fall.*

STEP 5: Make a Hinge Cut

Make a cut on the opposite side of the tree from the clef cut, allowing you to pivot the large tree, and have it fall in the selected direction.

STEP 6: Controlling the Tree Fall

When the tree shows signs of giving way, create tension on the rope by either wrapping it around another tree or using a trailer hitch to pull the rope tight. When the tree falls, remember to yell "Timber!" Don't forget to roll your R's!

> **!** *Be wary of the back kick and splintering from the butt of a falling tree, which can cause serious injuries.*

STEP 7: Trimming and Making Firewood

Collect thick branches, and chop the tree trunk for valuable firewood. Before trimming, examine the tree to see if it is resting awkwardly on any branches and if it's likely to move while you're working on it.

HELPFUL HINTS

- When standing up hill, remove the supporting branches by knocking them out with the axe and bring the tree to a safe rest.
- Trim the small braches first.
- Cut with the grain—upward.
- Cut larger branches by working upward from the butt.
- Stack brushwood and butts together.
- Cut wood into convenient lengths for carrying, and stack it in neat piles.

Parting Thoughts

Chopping down a tree should be well thought out for personal safety and with consideration to the surrounding forest and ecosystem. On the flipside, you may consider planting a tree for a special occasion. Contact the Arbor Day Foundation (www.arborday.org) for more information on planting, nurturing, and celebrating trees.

7 FLOATING ART: THE SIX-HOUR CANOE

For as long as I can remember, I have wanted to build my own boat. No manmade object can match the radiance and grace of a finely crafted wooden boat. It's not only a thing of beauty but practical, "functional art," if you will. While building a boat seems like the quintessential do-it-yourself project, I was overwhelmed by the thought of attempting something so mammoth.

I had read about Native Americans who had crafted canoes from materials grown in sustainable boreal forest, using things like birch bark, cedar, and spruce root. But I was just a suburban Long Island kid without a stitch of boat-building know-how. How could I ever do it? Besides, I certainly didn't have the time to wander forests harvesting necessary materials.

Michael makes the Maiden Voyage.

Just Do It!

Curiosity got the better of me when I heard about the six-hour canoe, a small, inexpensive, and easy-to-build plywood canoe. It can be assembled with simple hand tools and costs about $400 for materials.

I called Rich Hilsinger, director of The Wooden Boat School in Brooklin, Maine, to get his advice about which type of boat would be best for a novice to build. Although he invited me to the school, I decided to go it alone (I traveled to Maine later and learned to build a sailboat) armed only with his encouragement and a book called *Building the Six-Hour Canoe* (Tiller Publishing, 1994). The title is a bit misleading, as the project may take a day or two to complete. Still, that was a lot better than foraging forests for a month.

With a little convincing, my father and two twenty-something-year-old nephews agreed to help me fulfill my dream. We decided to dedicate the third weekend of August to the project and would build our wooden canoe in my parents' garage.

Although the plans were simple, getting materials cut to specifications was a bit more complex. If you do not have wood-cutting skills or the right material, you may consider spending a few extra dollars and having most of the wood pre-cut.

On August 14, 2007, we built our boat and launched its maiden voyage in my parents' swimming pool the following afternoon, which happened to be my mother's birthday. After an off-key chorus of "Happy Birthday!" and candles and cake, partygoers—including my 100-year-old grandmother—turned their attention to my guinea pig, oh, I mean, my nephew Michael Smith, as he gingerly slipped into the vessel. He tipped and topped and then plopped onto the seat. His fist-pumping success inspired everyone, except Grandma, to give it a try. No store-bought boat could rally that kind of excitement.

Build Your Own "Six-Hour Canoe"

GEAR LIST

BASICS

Two sheets of plywood, $1/4$ inch×4×8 feet (fir or marine grade) OR

One sheet of plywood, $1/4$ inch $\times 4 \times 16$ feet

Two boards, $2 \times 4 \times 28$ inches (stems)

One board, $3/4 \times 2 \times 36$ inches (frame bottom piece)

Two boards, $3/4 \times 1^{1}/2 \times 13$ inches (frame side pieces)

Two boards, $3/4 \times 2$ inches $\times 16$ feet (gunwales)

Two boards, $3/4 \times 2$ inches $\times 14$ feet (chine logs)

FASTENING AND GLUING

One pound 7/8-inch bronze ring nails

Fifty $3/4$-inch no. 8 bronze flathead screws (for fastening the gunwales)

Four $1^{1}/2$-inch no. 10 bronze screws (to secure each end of each gunwale)

One pint marine epoxy adhesive (this is a two-part glue)

One hundred $3/4$-inch no. 6 or 8 particle board or drywall screws (for temporary fastening)

Handful of 10-penny finishing nails (for laying out the lines on the panels)

Scarfing jig materials (used only if you are scarfing your panels together)

Two pieces of wood, $2 \times 6 \times 48$ inches (pressure plates)

Twelve 3-inch drywall screws

Plastic sheet (to be used as a drop cloth for separating pieces to be glued)

TOOLS

16-foot tape measure

Screwdriver

Sliding t-bevel

Combination square

Framing square

Chalk-line

Hammer

Sharp saw

Low-angle block plane

Electric drill with $1/8$-inch and $1/4$-inch bits

Saber saw

Electric, random-orbit sander

Band saw
At least six 2-inch spring clamps
At least two 12-inch bar or 4-inch C-clamps
Pair of stable sawhorses

Build It!

SCARFING PANELS

If you did not purchase your plywood as a 16-foot panel, you will need to join the two 4×8 foot panels together. This should be done indoors in temperatures above 50 degrees. The following steps describe the process:

STEP 1: Plane a 3-inch bevel at one end of each panel as shown. (You can also use a belt sander to make the bevel.) Thoroughly mix ample epoxy and wet the two surfaces to be joined. Add silica, wood flour, or cotton powder to another batch of epoxy until it is the consistency of peanut butter and apply it to the two surfaces over the epoxy that you have already applied. Lay down the 2×6 inch bottom pressure plate and cover it with a plastic sheet. Set one panel on top of the plate and the other panel on top of the bottom panel so the edges to be joined are properly mated.

SCARFING THE PLYWOOD

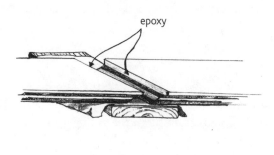

epoxy

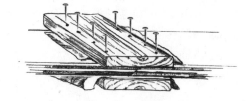

STEP 2: Carefully align the panels using a chalk line. (You might want to temporarily nail the sheets to the ship floor so they won't slide apart.) Put a piece of plastic sheet on top of the joint, and then screw the top pressure plate down through the plywood into the bottom plate. Use only enough pressure to compress the two pieces to be joined. I was pleasantly surprised by how strong the epoxy joint was when it dried. If you do not feel comfortable scarfing the panels together, there are many ways to build a wooden sleeve to hold the sections together.

LAYING OUT PANELS

1. Mark a line down the center of the 4×16 foot panel, lengthwise.
2. Mark one end of your panel as the bow and, starting at that end, mark lines perpendicular to the centerline at 1-foot intervals as shown in the illustration on page 47. These will be your layout lines. Starting at the bow end, number these lines 1 through 17.
3. After line number 16, draw another line 5¼ inches from number 16 and parallel to it. (This is the stern end of the panel.)
4. Locate and draw position of the frame 8 feet 5½ inches from the bow.
5. At bow end, mark points 16 inches from each edge.
6. At the frame line, mark points 11 inches from the edges. (These points indicate the top of the sheerline at the frame position.)
7. At the stern end of panel (5¼ inches aft of number 15), mark points along the line, 15 inches from each edge.
8. Lay out angle of bow end by marking a point 16¾ inches aft of bow end along each edge of the panel. Connect these points with lines running to the points where the sheerlines end at the bow (see Step 5).
9. Mark another set of points along edges of the panel 3½ inches aft of line number 14. Connect these points to the points where sheerlines meet at the stern (see Step 7).

LAYING OUT SHEER

1. Drive finishing nails lightly into the following points: (a) where the sheer ends at the bow; (b) the frame position on the sheerline; (c) where the sheer ends at the stern.

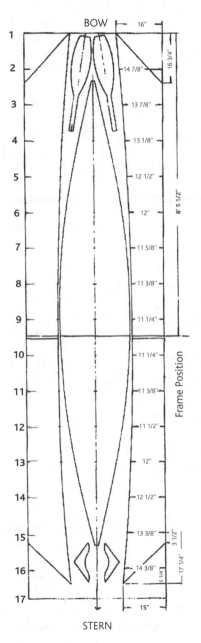

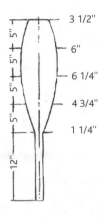

PADDLE DETAIL

SIX-HOUR CANOE PLYWOOD LAYOUT

Station No.	Height to nearest 1/8"
1	16
2	14 7/8
3	13 7/8+
4	13 1/8
5	12 1/2
6	12
7	11 5/8
8	11 3/8
9	11 1/4
10	11 1/4
11	11 3/8-
12	11 1/2+
13	12
14	12 1/2+
15	13 3/8
16	14 3/8+
17	15

2. Using one of the gunwales as a batten, bend it over nails and draw the sheerline as shown for each side panel.

LAYING OUT THE SHEER

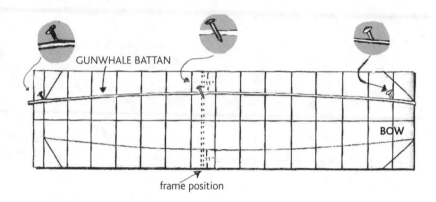

GUNWHALE BATTAN

BOW

frame position

CUTTING OUT PANELS

You should now have the sheerline and bow and stern angles clearly marked on your panels. Using a saber saw (or circular saw), cut about ¼ inch outside the lines marking the outlines of the side panels. Clamp the two panels together, and plane them to the lines with a block plane.

CUTTING THE PANELS

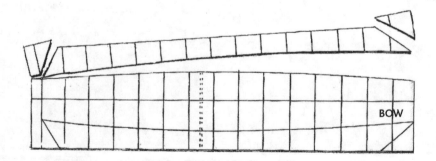

BOW

CUTTING OUT STEMS

This is one of the tougher tasks that you really want to think through as it will affect the shape of your boat.

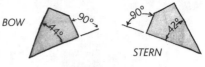

1. Mark one end of each stem "A" and the other end "B." Draw a line down the center of each stem end, the long way.
2. For the bow, set the band saw table to a 68-degree angle and attach a fence as shown.

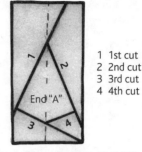

1 1st cut
2 2nd cut
3 3rd cut
4 4th cut

Cutting sequence as seen from End "A"

3. With end "A" facing you, make the first cut as shown.
4. Reverse the stem so end "B" faces you, and make the second cut as shown.
5. Reset the table to 90 degrees, and realign the fence. Make final two cuts as shown.
6. For the stern, follow the same steps, but set the table to 66 degrees for the first two cuts and 90 degrees for the third and fourth cuts.

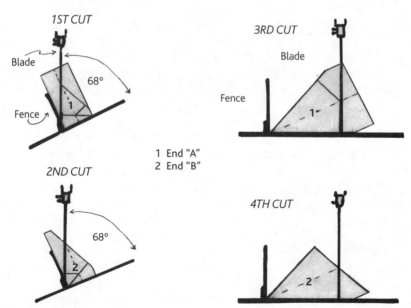

1 End "A"
2 End "B"

MAKING THE FRAME

1. Using the pattern in the plans, cut out two frame gussets from scrap plywood. Clean up the edges with sandpaper and/or a cabinet file, if you have one. Mark nail hole locations and drill 1/8-inch holes.
2. Using a gusset as a guide, mark the angle for the bottoms (heels) of the frame sides and cut the angle with a handsaw.
3. Using gussets again as guides, cut angles for the ends of frame bottoms shown on the plans. Remember that the assembled frame measures 24 inches across the bottom edge.

Cut the gussets from scrap plywood running the grain as shown. Predrill holes before assembling

4. Epoxy and nail gussets to the frame pieces with bronze ring nails.
5. After the epoxy cures, mark the outline of your chine logs using a scrap of chine log on the frame assembly, and cut out two notches.

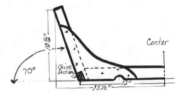

ASSEMBLING SIDE PANELS, STEMS, AND FRAME

Before using epoxy to assemble boat (it's best to assemble it when dry), use particle-board (or drywall) screws. This allows time for careful alignment, while giving you the opportunity to check measurements and positions before gluing them together.

1. Lay side panels on floor with inside facing up.
2. Mark the positions of the stems, and attach them to one side panel with 3/4-inch particle-board screws. Drive in eight screws for each assembly.
3. Cut a short (3-inch) piece of chine log and clamp it to the bottom of one side panel at the point where frame will be located. Then position the frame so its notch fits over chine log

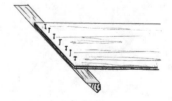

piece, and screw it into place. Orient the frame so that the gussets face forward. Use four evenly spaced particle-board screws. (Note: The frame is located abaft the frame line.)

4. Unscrew the frame, and repeat this process on the other side panel. Leave the frame in place this time.

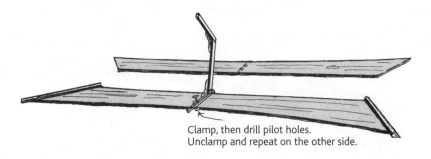

Clamp, then drill pilot holes.
Unclamp and repeat on the other side.

5. Now, get some extra hands, and attach the panels together at the stern. Be careful to line everything up. Drive in the eight particleboard screws.

6. Pull the panels sufficiently close together to permit attaching the frame to the other panel. Remember to drive the screws into the existing holes.

7. Pull the bow ends together and attach them to the stern with eight particle-board screws.

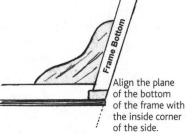

8. Now, stand back and look at the boat from all sides and ends to check alignments and positions. Refit if necessary.

Align the plane of the bottom of the frame with the inside corner of the side.

9. When the pieces are properly aligned, take them apart, apply epoxy, and reattach.

INSTALLING AND PLANNING CHINE LOGS

1. With boat upside down, cut protruding ends of stems flush with the bottom of boat.

2. Using a sliding t-bevel, take angle of bow to the bottom edge. Use this angle to scribe a line on one end of each chine logs (the 14-foot-long pieces of the 1×2 inch boards). Cut the ends off, and mark each one "bow."

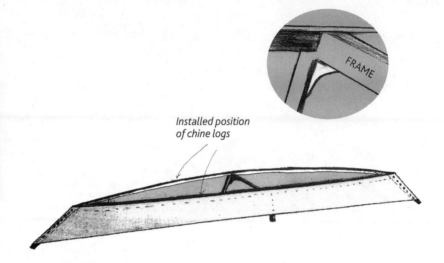

Installed position
of chine logs

FRAME

3. Do the same for the stern angle, and mark the other ends pieces "stern." (Although both ends of the pieces will now fit in the boat at one time, the chine logs are too long. The following steps will adjust them to the proper length.)

4. Bend the chine log into the boat, and fit it into the bow and frame notch. Make sure the edge of the chine log and the boat's bottom edge are flush. Clamp with spring clamps and mark a line across the chine log where it intersects the forward edge of the frame.

5. Remove the chine log and bend it into the stern and frame notch. Clamp with spring clamps. Again, mark a line across the chine log where it intersects the forward edge of the frame.

6. Remove chine log. The distance between the two marks is the amount of stock to be cut off so the chine logs will fit into the boat. Transfer this distance to one end and carefully cut off the excess stock to maintain the correct angle.

7. Repeat this process for the other chine log.

8. When both chine logs are properly fitted, glue them in after coating mating surfaces with epoxy. Use particle-board screws, spaced at 4 inches, to hole them in place. Use spring clamps to close any gaps that remain.

9. After the epoxy cures, plane the chine logs and heels of both stems so they are perfectly flush with the bottom of the panels and a straight stick laid across the boat will bear fully on the planed surfaces. It's necessary to true or plane bottom into a

flat bearing surface for gluing and water tightness. We glued 30-grit sandpaper to a 30-inch long 2×4 foot board and used this "sanding board" to true up the bottom edges after they were rough planed.

Once the epoxy is cured, you can remove all the particle-board screws.

ATTACHING GUNWALES

1. Turn the boat right-side up and attach one 16-foot gunwale to one side with spring clamps. Mark screw positions every

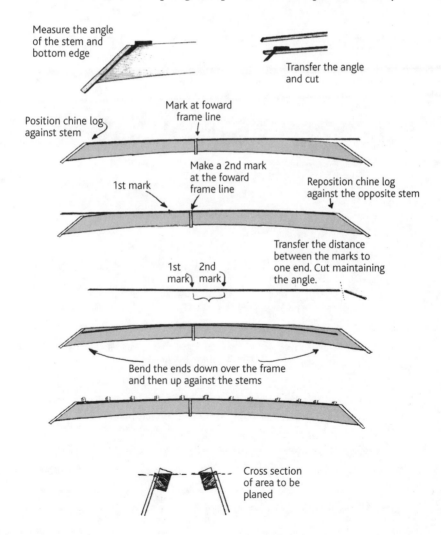

Measure the angle of the stem and bottom edge

Transfer the angle and cut

Position chine log against stem

Mark at foward frame line

1st mark

Make a 2nd mark at the foward frame line

Reposition chine log against the opposite stem

1st mark   2nd mark

Transfer the distance between the marks to one end. Cut maintaining the angle.

Bend the ends down over the frame and then up against the stems

Cross section of area to be planed

4 inches and, beginning at center, drive the particle-board screws, moving toward each end.

2. At each end of the gunwale, predrill and drive 1½-inch bronze screws into the stems through the gunwales.

3. Trim the ends of gunwale to match angle of the bow and stern.

4. Remove the gunwale, apply epoxy to both surfaces and reattach.

5. Repeat this process for the other gunwale.

6. When the epoxy is cured, trim off the upper ends of the stems and the tops of the frame, and plane the gunwales flush with the sheer edges.

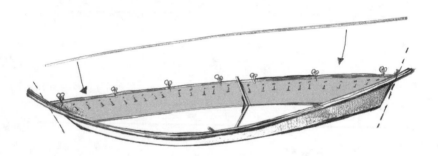

MEASURING AND MARKING BOTTOM PANEL

1. Turn the boat upside down. Lay the bottom panel on the boat and attach it temporarily with a particle-board screw at each end (driven into the stem bottom).

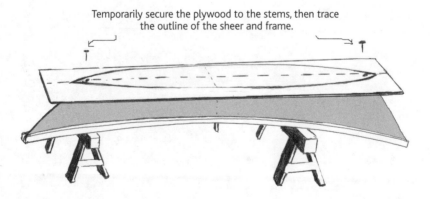

Temporarily secure the plywood to the stems, then trace the outline of the sheer and frame.

2. With a pencil, draw a line on the bottom panel around the outside of the boat where the sides meet the bottom and on the inside where the chine logs meet the bottom. Also draw lines on the bottom panel to show the location of the frame. These lines will show you where to trim the panel and where to apply epoxy after the panel is trimmed.

3. Take the bottom panel off and cut it along the outside line, leaving about ¼ inch excess.

Trim bottom 1/4" to 1/2" larger than the trace line. Epoxy along the edge and frame line. Nail 2" apart into chine logs and frame.

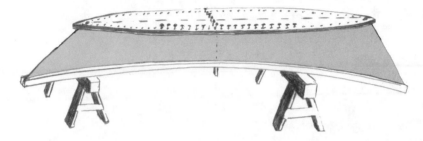

ATTACHING THE BOTTOM

1. Put the bottom panel back in place and use a marking gauge to mark nailing line. This line should lie about ⅜ inches in from the side panel.

2. Remove the bottom panel, apply epoxy to mating surfaces, and put it back on with two particle-board screws.

3. Beginning near the middle of the boat, drive in bronze ring nails about every 3 inches on the nailing line. Work toward each end. After you have hammered in a couple dozen nails, remove the particle-board screws at the ends. Don't forget to nail the bottom into the frame.

Rob putting on some final touches.

4. When the epoxy has cured, trim off the excess plywood along the chines. (We used a router with a flush-trimming bit for this purpose, and finished off with the plane.)

FINAL DETAILS

1. Clean up the ends of the stems with a block plane.
2. Use plane to trim the ends of the gunwales, and then finish them off with a sanding block or cabinet rasp.
3. Use a cabinet rasp or sanding block to round over the tops of the frame ends.
4. Using a block plane, radius the corners of the gunwales, the inner corner of the sheer, at the bottom corner at the chine.
5. Sand all surfaces with a random orbit sander or sanding block.

FINISHES

1. Seal all plywood edges with epoxy. After they cure, sand them lightly.
2. Apply plywood sealer to the entire boat.
3. If you are varnishing the gunwales, apply one coat of thinned varnish now.

The launch is made by Robert and Michael on August 14th, their Grandma's birthday.

4. When the varnish is hard, apply marine primer to all surfaces to be painted.
5. When the primer is hard, lightly sand all primed surfaces.
6. At this point, you can apply marine paint or ordinary house paint. We like a semigloss finish on boats, so we used Sears latex Weatherbeater. Give it a few weeks to harden up, and it's as good as anything we've tried—and the cleanup is a breeze.

SEATS

This boat is intended for one adult. The paddler sits facing forward, just abaft the frame. It's nice to sit up off the bottom about 1 inch. We used caned canoe seats laid on the chine logs as a quick solution, but you can get innovative and use old chairs with the legs cut down. In any case, keep the seat low in the boat and locate it just abaft the frame.

FLOTATION

Positive flotation is a good idea. You can install bulkheads and decks and fill the voids with foam, or purchase kayak flotation devices and secure them to the chine logs with bungee cords. Always wear an approved life vest (PFD) when on the water.

Contact Info: Building the Six-Hour Canoe

Although this canoe can be built from the directions given here, more detailed advice is offered in the book *Building the Six-Hour Canoe* (Tiller Publishing, 1994), which can be ordered from The Wooden Boat Store; www.woodenboatstore.com, 800–273–7447.

Parting Thoughts

Building our boat was more satisfying than I could have imagined. Not only was it fun, but creating something so graceful out of raw materials and completing the project was quite grounding and rewarding.

Most special was spending quality time with my dad and nephews—and now we have a functioning boat!

Talk Like a Sailor

Even if you don't build your own boat, some day you may get invited onto a boat, and you will want to talk the talk and say, "Ahoy, matey!" upon embarking. Get to know a thing or two about "ship-speak" if you want get invited back—and we're not talking the plank!

Sailors have a special jargon that has evolved over centuries to provide clear and concise communication. With roots in ancient Greece, the Roman Empire, Scandinavia, and England, the vocabulary and sayings have developed over time and been adapted to particular needs.

Essential Terms

These five terms are vital to the foundation of your sailor vocabulary.

- Bow: Front of boat
- Stern: Back of boat
- Starboard: Right side of boat

AAARH!! ?

- Port: Left side of boat
- The Head: The toilet

Talk the Talk!

Here's a vessel-friendly vocabulary primer, with enough words and terms to get you started on your way to speaking like a sailor!

CRITICAL TERMS

1. *Head.* The toilet.

   The term *head* comes from early boat etiquette—aka, the pre-toilet era. According to the U.S. Navy, sailors commonly relieved themselves from the bowsprit, where the figurehead was fastened.

   Today, most vessels have heads, but in the event you find yourself bladder-full and head-free, try this hassle-free pee solution.

   Don't even think about that soda bottle! We're talking drippy disaster on rolling seas. Instead, get a five-gallon plastic bucket and line it with a trash bag. If you're feeling extra special, you can even top it with a toilet seat and have your very own inexpensive, portable head.

2. *Coming about (or tacking).* This is the method for turning a sailboat through the wind, ultimately changing the side that the wind is blowing onto the boat.

   When turning a sailboat with a low boom (the wood or metal pole at the bottom of the sail), the skipper will shout, "Ready about!" to prepare the crew to tack, or swing, the boom to maneuver the boat. Upon the acknowledgment of the crew, the skipper announces, "Coming about!" Verbal cues like these are critical to safety at sea by keeping everyone aware of upcoming action.

3. *Underway.* When the ship is no longer at anchor or attached to a dock or the shore.

4. *Adrift.* When the boat is at the mercy of the wind and tide. In naval slang, it can also mean "being late" or "absent from place of duty."

5. *Weigh.* To raise something, as in "weigh anchor" or "raise anchor."

6. *Rope versus line.* A "rope" comes from a manufacturer neatly coiled. However, as soon as that rope is cut to a particular length and used in a specific nautical task, such as tying a boat to a dock or adhering an anchoring, it becomes a "line."

There are a few exceptions: The line on the ship's bell is called "the bell rope" and the line tied to a bucket to retrieve water is called "bucket rope."

DIRECTION

When pointing out an object on the water, call its position as if you were reading a clock. It's helpful to think of the ocean, sea, or river as a great big splashy clock face—the bow represents 12 o'clock, the starboard beam 3 o'clock, the stern 6 o'clock, and the port beam 9 o'clock.

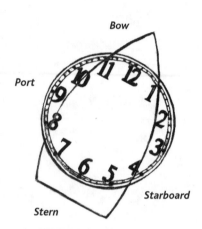

WIND BAG

1. *Windward.* The direction from where the wind is blowing. For instance, a "west wind" means the wind is generating in the west, that is, blowing from west to east.
2. *Weather side.* The side of the boat facing windward.
3. *Leeward.* The side of the ship facing away from the wind. It is often called the "sheltered side."
4. *High side.* The side of the boat farthest from the water when vessel tilts due to bad weather and water conditions—or an aggressive turn.
5. *Low side.* The side of the boat nearest the water when vessel tilts due to bad weather and water conditions—or an aggressive turn.

BOAT VERSUS SHIP

Any vessel shorter than 40 feet in length and weighing less than 40 tons is designated by the Historic Ships Committee as a "boat." So, with a couple of exceptions, all vessels longer than 40 feet and weighing more than 40 tons are "ships." Submarines and fishing vessels are exempt from this rule and are always identified as boats regardless of their size. This is from the early days, when submarines were small enough to be carried aboard ships on long journeys.

FLEET FEET

Take my advice, please! Always wear shoes on a ship or boat. You may be thinking that pirates didn't wear shoes, so why should I? Decks are peppered with splintered wood, metal cleats, and dropped fish hooks, which become potential foot flatteners when the boat rocks and rolls over choppy water, making crossing the deck as challenging as walking a tightrope. Under duress or excitement it's easy (and common) to stub toes or slip on the wet deck and possibly tumble headfirst overboard. Not recommended!

While deck shoes may not be your fashion choice for a night out, they should be your choice for days at sea. You need thick soles that grip and don't slip on wet surfaces.

MEASURING DISTANCE

The measurements of distance on land are close but not quite the same as on the water. Land distance is measured in *statute miles*, and water distance in *standard nautical miles*.

1. One statute (land) mile=1 mile=5,280 feet
2. One nautical (water) mile=1.15 miles=6,080 feet

We use different measurements because the earth slightly flattens at the North and South poles and is not a perfect sphere. Taking this Earthly imperfection into consideration, land and sea measurements vary 1/60th of a degree of latitude, which varies from 6,046 feet at the Equator to 6,092 feet at latitude 60°. It sounds confusing, but don't go crazy over the numbers. Just remember to use nautical miles for water.

MEASURING SPEED

On land, our cars clock speed in miles per hour, but at sea speed is measured in knots. One knot equals one nautical mile per hour.

To measure ship speed back in the day, sailors tied a heavy wood panel, called a "chip log," to a reel of line that literally had knots tied in it about every 50 feet. With the boat in full forward motion, the chip log was tossed overboard into the bouncy water behind the ship, allowing the momentum to madly unwind the sturdy rope. The higher the speed, the faster the rope unwound. As the rope passed through a sailor's burly hands, one of his mates timed the operation with a 28-second hourglass timer. In theory, the number of knots overboard in 28 seconds equals the ship's mile-per-hour speed. So, if 10 knots hit the drink in 28 seconds, then the ship was cranking at 10 knots—or 10 nautical miles per hour. To landlubbers like you and me, that's 11.5 standard miles per hour.

Parting Thoughts

Our ability to navigate one of Mother Nature's most humbling forces played a huge role in colonizing our planet. Traveling on water isn't something we do every day, so whenever you have the honor of embarking on any seaworthy vessel, view it as a special treat. Observe and listen closely.

8 BUILD A WORLD WAR II FOXHOLE RADIO

It's not quite an iPod, but in the field it will make you feel very civilized!

Believe it or not, it's easy to build a working radio that doesn't use electricity in less than an hour. Offering instant gratification, World War II foxhole radios are simple, ingenious gizmos that reflect sound moving through airwaves. Best of all is the pleasure of listening to music under starry skies on an apparatus you built!

I did this project with my uncle, Dr. Richard Lanza, a nuclear engineer at MIT's Nuclear Engineering Department. Rolling out antennae wire attached to a toilet paper roll in the halls of one of the most prestigious institutions was beyond comical. Oddly enough, many of the scientists who walked by smiled and made comments like, "I remember making one of those when I was a kid." Who knows—making this radio could be your first step toward MIT.

During World War II, GIs were often isolated from hearing the day-to-day news of what was happening beyond their barracks. A few clever radio-deprived GIs figured out that they could use miscellaneous scrap metal and junk to construct a simple radio. Word spread, and soon scores of soldiers were creating their own radios. Amazingly enough, these radios did not require electricity or any other power source. Here is a chance for you to take a step back in history.

Making a World War II Foxhole Radio

GEAR LIST

- Vintage-style fahnestock clips or paper clips
- 10 wood screws or thumb tacks
- 10 washers for the screws
- Needle-nose pliers
- Wire hanger
- Wooden board (a $1/2$-inch-thick pine board is best)
- Coil form (you can use a cardboard toilet paper roll that's at least $13/4$ inches in diameter—2 inches is best)
- Number 2 lead pencil
- Single-edge safety razor (preferably "blued"; see step 13)
- Geranium diode—1N34A (from Radio Shack), optional
- 40 feet of #22 AWG coil or magnet wire
- 1 foot of #26 wire
- 100 feet of antenna wire or an antenna kit
- Sand paper
- Crystal earphone
- Safety pin
- Screw driver
- Spray lacquer

STEP 1: Cut the wooden board to which your radio will be attached. The exact size is irrelevant, but it should be at least 6×6 inches to accommodate all the parts.

STEP 2: Create coil form. This is the tube around which you are going to wrap about 40 feet of copper wire. A toilet paper role will do, but it might be a bit flimsy. If you can get your hands on thicker tubing, such as the type used for gift wrapping paper, it will be more solid. In my set I used a 4-inch wide tube.

STEP 3: Punch four tiny holes in the tube. The two holes at each end should be about $1/2$ inch from the end and about $1/4$ inch apart. The two holes on each end should run width-wise to the ends. (See illustration on page 65.)

STEP 4: Wind the wire tightly around the coil form. This may be accomplished in many ways, but ultimately wrapping it by hand is best. It is very important that the coils be wrapped neatly next to each other.

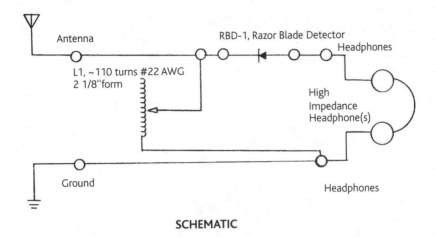

Antenna

L1, ~110 turns #22 AWG
2 1/8"form

Ground

RBD-1, Razor Blade Detector

Headphones

High
Impedance
Headphone(s)

Headphones

SCHEMATIC

Allow for about 6 inches of excess wire on the right side of the tube. I used magnet wire, which is a copper or aluminum wire covered with thin insulation. If you go to a place like Radio Shack, ask for #22 AWG (American Wire Gauge). It should be between 100 and 125 turns.

STEP 5: Tighten the coil manually by gripping it between both hands and rotating your hands in opposite directions.

STEP 6: Spray the coil with lacquer to help keep the form wrapped tight. Allow it to dry.

Turn the tube in this direction with left hand while guiding the wire with your right thumb

START HERE

END HERE

STEP 7: Attach the coil to the board. Use either two thumb tacks or two small screws. The excess coil wire should protrude from the front side of the tube, closer to the board, rather than from the top of the tube (see illustration).

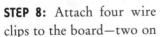

COILING THE TUBE

STEP 8: Attach four wire clips to the board—two on each side of the board below the coil. They should be about 4½ inches apart from each other width-wise along the coil and about 1½ inches apart from each other on each side of the board (see illustration). The top clips should be about an inch below the coil.

TIP: You can substitute paper clips for the clips and thumb tacks for the screws. The idea is to be as innovative as the GIs in the field!

STEP 9: Make the tuner slider by cutting 7 or 8 inches of wire from a wire coat hanger. If the hanger has any type of coating on it such as paint, lightly sand it to improve contact points and reception.

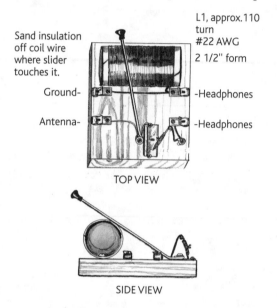

Sand insulation off coil wire where slider touches it.

L1, approx.110 turn #22 AWG 2 1/2" form

Ground- -Headphones

Antenna- -Headphones

TOP VIEW

SIDE VIEW

STEP 10: Using needle-nose pliers, bend a loop around the bottom end of the tuner slider. This loop will be wrapped around a screw and washer, so bend it accordingly. You may want to attach a knob or ball of tape at the top end of the slider as this is where your fingers will move the slide later for tuning. About 3 inches below the coil, in the middle of the board, attach the slider to the board by placing it on top of two washers. Then screw it to the board firmly but not so tight that it inhibits the movement of the slider. The hook-up wires should go under the washers for all contact points. (See illustration.)

STEP 11: Attach the safety pin, which will be the detector contact, to a 2-inch piece of bare lead by bending the pin open about 90 degrees (on the clasp side—see illustration) and wrapping the pin side with #26 wire. Sharpen the end of the lead with a razor.

STEP 12: Attach the safety pin to the board, using a washer and screw, in the lower right-hand corner. Attach a wire between the safety pin head and board with a washer and screw and wrap wire to the lower right clip, which will ultimately be one of the headphone attachments clips. The tip of the lead will ultimately come in contact with the side of the razor. (See illustration.)

STEP 13: Attach the razor blade, which will act as the radio's crystal. If you use a standard single-edged razor, it will need to be "blued" or heat treated. To do this, attach it to some pliers in a vise and heat it with a torch. (If you don't have a torch, you can purchase one that's ready to go from a hobby shop.) Bend the safety pin so that the tip touches the razor's surface.

FYI *During World War II, standard-issue razors were blued because they remained sharper longer.*

The crystal is the trickiest and most important part of this set. If you want better reception, you might consider purchasing a Germanium crystal detector from Radio Shack or from a radio hobby store like Borden's (Borden Radio Company, 138911 Kensington Place, Houston, TX, 77034, www.xtalman.com).

I found that it was easier to work out the kinks in my set by using the crystal detector before trying out the razor blade crystal.

STEP 14: Attach the rest of the wires according to the illustration. If any of the connections or contact surfaces are lacquered or painted, sand them lightly.

STEP 15: Attach a long wire to use as an antenna to the lower-left clip. The longer and higher, the better—use between 50 and 100 feet of wire of any type. Radio Shack sells some really great antenna kits for very little money. I have found that it works fairly well to attach the antenna high up on a tree.

TIP: If you want it really high, attach a weight and toss one end as high up in the tree as possible.

Your radio must have a ground wire. Plumbing pipes work as do flag poles. Experiment with different metal contacts. Attach the ground wire to upper-left clip.

You are now ready to operate your foxhole radio! Don't be frustrated if it does not immediately work. I found that I had to experiment a lot with gently moving the tuning slider back and forth along the coil. The antenna and grounding wires made a big difference in how they were placed and how well they were connected.

I remember the first time I actually heard an AM station being tuned in. It was a bit of a mind-blowing experience listening to a radio on a device with no electrical parts.

I felt like I was listening to the propaganda DJs Tokyo Rose or Axis Sally as the GIs did during World War II. It was the most fun I have ever had with a radio. Enjoy listening to your new set.

PART II

SAFETY

9 HOW NOT TO BE A VICTIM OF INSECTS

*"We hope that, when the insects take over the world,
they will remember with gratitude how we took them along
on all our picnics."*
—Bill Vaughan

I was attending the National Boy Scout Jamboree in 2005 as a guest of honor and as I was sleeping in camp I was woken by a terrible iching on my backside. At first it was itchy in a small area, but soon my entire caboose was on fire. I immediately knew I was in trouble, since I had had this condition before. It was chiggers! These gnarly microscopic six-legged hairy creatures can bring a heavy-weight boxing champ to his knees. Their bites produce small, reddish bumps or welts on the skin accompanied by intense itching even more irritating then an acute case of poison ivy or poison sumac.

I jumped out of my sleeping bag, zipped closed my tent and trotted to the medical tent, knowing there would be no sleep that night. Much to my relief, the nurse was still on duty and I awkwardly explained my predicament as the screen door slammed behind me. As he rustled through the medicine cabinet, I remembered hearing about the triple secret chigger solution during my previous attack. Apparently, applying nail polish to each bite suffocates the mite, so the rash won't spread. I was so itchy I would try anything. So I asked if he had nail polish. The nurse dug around the cluttered shelves a few more seconds and miraculously, pulled out a small glass bottle of fire-engine red polish. Red! An incredibly embarrassing moment, but the nail polish worked. Live and learn.

Insects, the Ultimate Warriors

Insects may be the most successful group of living organisms on our planet. Every outdoorsy person has his "favorite insect story." According to journals dating back to the 1800s, long before bug repellant, there were times that renowned explorers Lewis and Clark were unable to hunt while investigating the uncharted American continent because the countless insects were so thick they couldn't aim their rifles.

Nature enthusiasts need an insect-proof strategy to minimize their impact, and that often requires knowing what drives these miniature creatures.

When I was 15, my father took me to Alaska during my summer vacation. It was a fantastic trip, but the insects were out in the zillions. I learned a lot about how not to be a victim of insects from the fishing guides who lived and worked in bug-infested environments. They introduced me to insect repellents and to the importance of wearing preventative clothing.

More recently, I learned about living with assorted bugs from Joe Conlon, an entomologist (a person who studies bugs) for Cutter insect repellants, who has studied mosquitoes for more than 25 years. Joe is such an expert that he has even taught tribes in South American jungles about surviving among deadly insects. Insects, he says, are attracted to some people more than others for a variety of reasons, such as the amount of glandular secretions, skin odors, and activity levels.

Here is some handy info to help ensure that you are a happy camper in the outdoors. Following these basic precautions will likely protect you against mosquitoes, the most common enemy of the happy camper, and against many other insects as well.

Do Mosquitoes Find You Attractive?

Although much insect research is in its infancy, we know the following:

- Mosquitoes are drawn to lactic acid and carbon dioxide, which is why large people, who give off more of both, get bitten frequently.
- People with fair complexions are more attractive to mosquitoes than those with dark skin.
- Men tend to be bitten by mosquitoes more than women as they are larger and tend to give off more heat. However, pregnant women, who produce more body heat and carbon dioxide, are more prone to mosquito bites than women who are not pregnant.

Does Diet Affect the Likelihood of Being Bitten?

My father used to give our dogs garlic cloves to eat to protect them against ticks, but aside from making your breath stink, there is no evidence that garlic or any other food does anything to ward off ticks, mosquitoes, or other bugs.

Is There a Time of Day That Increases Your Chances of Being Bitten?

Most insects are more active at dawn and dusk, which unfortunately is also the best time to go fishing or do wildlife photography.

Why Do Mosquitoes Bite?

All mosquitoes feed on plants' nectar for nutrition, but only female mosquitoes bite humans and animals—not for food, but to use the blood for egg development.

Do Clothes Make a Difference in Preventing Bug Bites?

Clothing is a protective barrier to your skin. Here are some tips on choosing insect-repelling clothing.

- Wear loose-fitting clothing versus tight-fitting, which bugs can easily penetrate.
- Studies have shown insects are more attracted to dark clothes than to light.
- Clothing that is pretreated with a chemical called Picaridin—often labeled "Buzz Off"—is a great investment.
- Wear hat-netting to cover your head, face, and neck. It may look dorky, but it's better than being swarmed by buzzing, biting bugs.
- Tuck your trousers into your socks to keep bugs from biting your ankles.
- In the Australian Outback, many ranchers dangle corks from their hats, which swing and sway, shooing flies from their faces.
- In the New York Adirondacks, many hikers tie a soft pine branch to the backs of their hats, which moves as they hike, similarly shooing away insects.

Are You Allergic to Mosquito Bites If You Get Welts When Bitten?

While some people are allergic to mosquito bites, it's a rare condition. If you get welts after a bite, you're most likely sensitive to the enzymes and anticoagulants that mosquitoes inject when they bite. These substances keep blood from clotting and destroy some dermal tissue, causing itchy skin.

Here are three key methods:

- Remove any nearby standing water every five days. When conditions are right, mosquitoes can breed in 7 to 10 days in as little water as a bottle cap.
- Trim overgrown bushes and debris around your house, which are cozy places for mosquitoes to breed and rest. Frequently check window screens for holes.
- Most important, wear an approved repellent when outside.

How Important Is Repellent Use?

I don't wear repellents all the time, but it's like going out into the sun. If I know I am going to be out in a high exposure area or time of day I will put it on. Repellents are your last line of defense.

What Type of Repellent Should You Use?

There are basketfuls of effective repellents on the market, such as natural plant oils from geranium, lavender, or peppermint. Lemon eucalyptus oil is the only plant-based active ingredient recommended by the Centers for Disease Control, but commercial repellents with Deet or Picaridin work best. (Try to use products that are 25% to 35% Deet or 15% Picaridin.) If I know I am going to be along the coast, where there are more gnats or chiggers, I use Cutter Advanced with Picaridin. If I'm in an area with a lot of ticks, I use a repellent with Deet.

BEWARE OF INSECT REPELLENT PITFALLS!

- Insect repellent sweats off, so reapply frequently.
- Rub the repellent over your skin after spraying to ensure even coverage and wash your hands thoroughly, so you don't accidentally rub your eyes or touch your mouth.
- When spraying the front of your ankles, don't forget to rub repellent around to the back of ankles.

Finally, here are some key mosquito facts from my conversation with Joe Conlon:

- Lifespan varies by species.
    Most adult females live 2 to 3 weeks.
    Some species that spend winters in garages, culverts, and attics can live as long as six months.
- There are 176 species of mosquitoes in the United States.
    While more than 60 species have been found to carry the West Nile virus, only a few are capable of transmitting it to humans.
- When allowed to feed to repletion, mosquitoes imbibe anywhere from 0.001 to 0.01 milliliters of blood.
- Mosquito activity increases during a full moon.
- Not all species of mosquitoes feed on blood.
- Mosquitoes use the blood for egg production and receive nutrition from plant nectar.
- Some mosquito larvae are cannibalistic.
- Some Native American tribes migrated into the mountains during the summer to escape mosquitoes.
- Salt marsh mosquitoes breed at staggering rates and can travel 40 to 70 kilometers to feed.
- Different mosquito species have varying biting preferences, from the time of day to the part of the body. (Asian Tigers go for the ankles!)

Mosquito Dangers Beyond Itching

Aggressive insects can turn outdoor fun into a prickly experience. Remember that using the appropriate protection from mosquitoes and other insects is just as important as sun protection and preventing dehydration. With the prevalence of the West Nile and other viruses carried by mosquitoes, these little pests can leave you with more than an irritating itch.

10 AVOID BECOMING WILDLIFE FOOD

Approaching Wildlife

I am always excited when I see big predators, especially if it is a rare species. Although predators actually have more to fear from humans than humans do from them, they are strong, unpredictable wild animals who need to be approached (or avoided) with respect. With growing competition for land and drastic climate changes, it is more important than ever for us to become ambassadors of nature.

How to Approach Wildlife: The General Principles

- Know the environment, including the habits of potentially dangerous animals inhabiting the area you are entering.
- Bears and moose don't like to be surprised, so let them know you exist by wearing a "bear bell" on your pack, clapping hands, or singing. Be creative!
- Never run when you see an animal! Running makes you seem like prey, and it often triggers the animal's attack mechanism. Instead, steadily back away.
- Stay clear of an animal's "fight or flight zone." Wild animals get freaked out when humans enter their safety zone (or personal space) and will often go on "attack mode" if you get too close.
- Do not touch or pet an animal's offspring. Animals often abandon offspring if they smell of humans.

- Do not feed wildlife in the forest or from a car. Animals that associate food with automobiles frequently get run over.
- A big, firm hiking stick can be a fine weapon against vicious dogs, mountain lions, and other animals.

Protecting Yourself in the Wild

Dogs

I love dogs perhaps more than any other animal, but some can be nasty nippers. According to the American Medical Association dog bites are

the second most common childhood injury requiring emergency room care (bicycle accidents are the first). In fact, about half of all children under the age of 12 have been bitten by a dog. This might be because of their smaller size as well as how they behave around the dog. It's frequently said that dogs can smell fear, meaning they can also sense strength and confidence. Dogs can be territorial and might judge humans as members of the pack and test their dominance over them, even if they're domesticated.

DOGGIE DOS AND DON'TS

- Do avoid direct eye contact with unfamiliar dogs.
- Don't pet a dog without letting him see and sniff your hand first. Keep your fingers tucked into your palm, so they don't dangle like little sausages. Slowly placing a hand close to the dog's nose is a great way for him to get to know you quickly.
- Don't turn your back to an agitated dog and then run away. Dogs will instinctively give chase.

- Don't disturb a dog while it's sleeping, eating, chewing on a toy, or caring for puppies.
- Be cautious if a dog is growling with ears pinned back.
- Allow non-aggressive dogs to check you out visually while pretending to ignore it. This is a good time to evaluate whether he is relaxed and approachable or to be avoided.

WHAT TO DO IF ATTACKED

- If an aggressive dog is running toward you, stand your ground, throw rocks to deter (not hit) him, stomp your feet, yell and in turn become the dominant attacker. Do not run away.
- If the dog continues on attack, keep yelling and find something sizeable to get between yourself and the pissed off pooch.
- If a dog attacks and you fall, cover your ears and face. Seek medical attention immediately because the dog might have rabies.

Bears

Bears are among nature's most majestic creatures, and seeing one in the wild is a uniquely unforgettable experience. The movie *Grizzly Man* provides a good example of what not to do around wild animals. Primitive carnivores, bears are driven by smell, hunger, and a need to protect their young. In Alaska during the salmon runs, bears are busy feeding, and for the most part they tune out nearby humans. But when the feeding season ends, their inhibition ignites and they go into "protection mode." While they are immense, powerful animals, bear attacks on humans are rare.

GENERAL BEAR BEWARES

- Before going camping or hiking, know what type of bears you may encounter such as Brown Bears or the more common Black Bears. Be versed in their habits and respect their natural habitat.
- Bears have an adept sense of smell (many times better than humans), so food in your backpack, pockets, or even car can trigger their hunger. Seal all food in sturdy plastic baggies or air-tight containers, and never keep food in your tent.
- Stay far away from bears with their cubs or when they are near

food (even a carcass), as they will be protective and potentially aggressive. If you happen upon the situation, slowly back away and keep an eye on the bear.

- Grizzlies are known to be the most aggressive bear. If one charges you, play dead! Immediately drop to all fours with your belly on the ground, curl into a tight ball, and cover your vital organs (no not just that—your stomach and chest too) by keeping them against the ground. Upon realizing you are neither a threat nor food the bear will typically leave you alone.
- Grizzlies and Brown Bears can climb trees, so knock that out of your head as a survival tactic. Standing on the ground, most

Grizzlies can reach their claws nearly 12 feet high. They can also knock over huge pine trees by pushing them. So stick to playing dead!

- Black Bears are the smallest, and under extreme circumstances they can be fought—but only when no other options exist. They usually stay away from humans, but if one approaches, use heavy pots or pans, logs, or sticks to shoo it away.

FYI *Brown Bears and Grizzlies are in fact the same species, but Brown Bears live on the coast, and Grizzlies live in the interior.*

Snakes

Snakes are incredible evolutionary survivors. Because their remains are fragile, it is difficult for scientists to determine exactly how long snakes have been around. It is speculated that they have been on Earth for at least 100 million years, possibly as many as 275 million. The main evolutionary advantage is their uncanny ability to unhinge their jaws to swallow animals much larger than their own size. Snakes can also go long periods without eating; some species have been known to survive for nearly two years without a meal. Remember that the next time dinner is served late!

Known for adapting well to their surroundings, assorted snakes live throughout North America. However, widespread building and commercialization of parks and wilderness have had a huge impact on their survival. The four deadliest snakes in North America are the American copperhead, coral, cottonmouth, and rattlesnake. Know your snakes and where they like to hide!

NORTH AMERICAN SNAKES

- Between 85% and 90% of snake bites occur when people are trying to kill a snake.
- Snakes are sneaky and hide while hunting prey, and people often obliviously enter the strike zone.

> Copperheads, found in the Eastern Gulf states and parts of the Midwest, like to hide in tall brush, around dead logs, and under dead leaves.
>
> Coral snakes, found in the Eastern Gulf states and as far west as Arizona, usually live underground or under leaves.
>
> Cottonmouth snakes, found throughout the Gulf states, usually around bodies of water and swamps, are particularly aggressive and should be avoided if seen.
>
> Rattlesnakes are found throughout the United States and are characterized by the rattle at the end of their tail and the rattling sound they make when they are ready to strike.

FYI *North American rattlesnakes, such as the Eastern and Western Diamondback rattlesnakes and cobras are just some of the snakes that warn humans when they are about to strike. Rattlesnakes coil up and rattle their tails, and cobras raise their heads and fan out their faces.*

SNAKE BITE PROTECTION TIP

- To prevent snake bites, wear thick boots when traipsing through tall weedy areas and avoid walking or exposing your skin to places where snakes might be resting, such as under rocks, fallen logs, or other protective enclaves.

Alligators and Crocodiles

Virtually unchanged since dinosaur times, alligators and crocodiles are ancient survivors, and their stillness, camouflage, and patience make them excellent hunters. They wait for extended periods of time before attacking fish, birds, and mammals (including humans) wandering close to the water's edge. They may seem slow and clumsy, but I have seen a crocodile snatch a bird sitting in a tree eight feet off the ground.

Found primarily along the Gulf Coast, alligators and crocodiles live all the way up through South Carolina. But the Florida Everglades is the only place in the world where both creatures cohabitate.

Boasting the highest bite pressure within the animal kingdom, an alligator's jaw grip measures over 3000 pounds per square inch (PSI). A lion's bite pressure is about 800 PSI, while human's is 200 PSI.

According to Julio Aguilar, a friend and gator expert, alligators and crocodiles are most dangerous during mating season, in the spring, which is when about 90% of the rare attacks (20 or so per year) occur in the United States. They fiercely protect their young, creating camouflaged nests in the brush and mud near river banks, so always walk carefully through such areas. If you unexpectedly come up on an alligator or crocodile, give it space and create a barrier between you and it, with a canoe, tree, or river bank. In most cases it will scamper away, but remember, striking range is around 8 or 10 feet and it moves quickly. Steer clear of its powerful tail, often used to smack prey toward their mouths.

FYI *When trying to determine the difference between alligators and crocodiles, look at their noses. The snout shape is the biggest visual give-away. Alligators have round noses, and crocodiles' noses are pointy. Also, alligators tend to be almost black, and crocodiles are brown or gray.*

Moose

One of the most curious sights I have witnessed was at the Alaska Conservation Wildlife Center in Girdwood, Alaska, just south of Anchorage. Mike Miller, the owner of the center, had rescued an orphaned baby moose, Seymour, the year before my visit. This hulking, hoofed beast had bonded with Mike as if he were family, and during Mike's morning jogs and afternoon bike rides Seymour followed him like a dog. Upon meeting, Seymour gently lowered his antlers and let me rub his head. Heartwarming, yes, but Mike said, "Make no mistake, if Seymour wanted to kick you to death he could." Seymour was not sleeping in my bed!

Moose attacks are actually more common than bear attacks. They are often more dangerous because a Bull Moose can weigh more than 1500 pounds, while the average Brown Bear carries a svelte 900 pounds or so. Attacks in the fall mating season are most common.

MOOSE ON THE LOOSE TIPS

- Keep a safe distance of at least 100 yards between you and the moose.
- Steer clear of Mother Moose at all costs when she's guarding her young. She uses her antlers and hooves to protect her calves from threats—grizzlies, humans, or packs of wolves. Moose often kill other animals by stomping them to death.
- If you are in the vicinity of a moose, watch its body language. If it suddenly stops feeding or moving to stare at you, you might have a problem. Beware if its ears point straight up and shoulders square off in your direction. If this occurs, and you are not in a car or near a building, get behind the largest tree you can find. The moose may try to bull you around the tree, but since a moose is much larger and longer, you can out run a moose while circling a tree.
- If somehow a moose gets on top of you, protect your face and head with your arms and curl into a ball. Once you sense it is gone, wait a few minutes, allowing it ample time to leave. And when you are certain it is gone, seek medical attention immediately.

Mountain Lions

Mountain lions live throughout North America and are agile predators known to attack people. As society builds and encroaches on animal habitats and the wilderness, mountain lion attacks are increasing annually.

MOUNTAIN LION TIPS

- Never hike in mountain lion territory alone. Dogs are great alert buddies!
- Mountain lions usually attack the smallest in the pack, so protect little children (or dogs).
- Never run away because mountain lions will instinctively give chase.
- If you get close to a mountain lion, make lots of noise and try to back away, allowing them ample distance.
- If a mountain lion stares at you while crouching, it means he is getting ready to attack, so you must stay calm and react swiftly. Do not run. It can out run you.
- If attacked, use everything available to fight back—throw rocks, swing hiking sticks, pepper spray, appear bigger by throwing hands in air—and remain standing.

Parting Thoughts

Seeing animals in the wild is an amazing treasure, and for the most part, they will stay away if you respect their natural barriers. The suggestions in this chapter are meant to enable you to feel confident in the wild so you can have experiences in nature that are safe, fulfilling, and fun. Every time you see a creature in the wild, remember that you have just witnessed something magnificent that may not be around for very long.

11 TAMING AN ELECTRIC FENCE

More and more of our world is being fenced in. If you have traveled to a state park with cattle or farming nearby, chances are you passed an electric fence.

You may have even unwittingly passed one of these metal beauties en route to your campsite or mid-hike. Until recently, when I came across a fence that I thought might be electric I would quickly swipe the back of my fingers across it to test if it was active. It's kind of like drinking old milk to see if it's spoiled. It works, but I don't recommend it.

If the fence's voltage was high, I got a big shock. Very unpleasant. If the wire had a small amount of current running through it, I wouldn't feel anything—that is, until I grabbed the wires to climb over and unexpectedly got zapped! Again, very unpleasant.

Did you know that when you grab something electrified with your palms, an involuntary reflex kicks in that causes hands to contract strongly around the object, making it hard to release? A strong current can electrocute you—and potentially kill you.

After a scary run-in with an electric fence I sought expertise from a cattle rancher from Texas. He taught me a neat trick, so that if I needed to touch an electrified wire it would be a whole lot safer.

Taming the Volts

Instead of using your hand, touch a blade of green grass to a potentially active electric fence. Since grass contains water, which conducts electricity, the grass will tingle if there is voltage. If only brown or dried grass, which has little or no moisture, is available, put a drop of water or spit on it before touching to the fence.

> **!** *If you have to test a fence with your hand never use your palm because the electric current will trigger a reflex that closes your hand which is not a good thing if it is around an electric wire.*

12 NINJA T-SHIRT SUN HOOD

"Necessity is the mother of invention."
—Plato

It may seem like a drag to have to cover up from the sun. Come on, who needs more than a baseball cap, T-shirt, and long shorts in the summer? You do! While I'm a big fan of ball caps—I have a wall of hooks full of them—on explorations in extreme climates, they do little more than cover up your head in the sleeping bag. If you are going to be an explorer, no doubt you'll spend ample time in unpredictable elements such as whipping wind, raging rain, shredding snow, searing sun, and beyond.

I have spent many days at sea and on glacial mountains where the pounding sun felt like it was eating through my clothing. There are even times when I wear what some may consider to be a dorky wide-brim hat to protect my face, ears, and neck from the sun. While I'm all for better to look good, than to feel good, in certain urban situations (e.g., any situation that requires me to wear a suit and tie), on explorations, fashion and ego get a boot out the door, and safety takes priority.

Several years ago, I competed in a multi-day canoe race in Belize with two friends. Much of the course was along intermediate rapids (classes II and III), but several big sections proved too much for amateurs like us and we tipped more than once. In addition, there were a lot of race boats on the narrow river, and some were capsized by an out-of-control competitor's boat. By the second day, all of us had lost our baseball caps. The scorching March sun was brutal by 10 A.M., and we knew we would fry like eggs on a griddle without covering up. Thus, the Ninja Sun Hat was created.

Here's how you can imitate a Ninja—and save your skin!

Imitating a Ninja

STEP 1: Get a T-shirt (white is the best color because it reflects heat).

STEP 2: Turn T-shirt inside out and tuck your head through top hole, as you would normally, but let the rim hug your head and chin, so that only your face is exposed.

STEP 3: Draw the sleeves out and then behind your head and tie a single knot.

STEP 4: Pull the top section of the neck opening near your hairline down and fold it so that it covers your forehead and eyebrows.

STEP 5: Pull the tag—the section of the neck opening that is on your chin (see illustration)—up and fold it in the same manner, except pull it up over your mouth and nose.

Make any modifications for comfort, and you, my friend, are set for a day on the water, snow, sand, or whatever you can imagine.

Parting Thoughts

*"Most important, remember a Ninja is trained for stealth, so
strike a fearsome pose and prepare for fun adventure!"*
—The Ninja Warrior

13 RUMBLE IN THE JUNGLE: AVOID MR. POOPY PANTS

"It only takes one bad sip to make a bad trip."
—Alicia Stevens

Diarrhea sucks!

You can call it "the runs," "Montezuma's revenge," or "Traveler's Diarrhea." Whatever! I just call it nasty. With all the traveling I have done, I've spent more time getting acquainted with the local toilets or bushes than with the natives. And I've seen diarrhea turn the strongest expedition member into a head-hanging, foot dragging, whining wimp.

Okay, this is a gnarly topic, but it's an important one if you

want to start globetrotting and filling your passport with cool stamps. Every year, 20% to 50% of international travelers—that's about 10 million people—develop diarrhea. Diarrhea is also the most common illness affecting long-distance hikers. While there are many causes, contaminated food and water are the most common. Bad water shouldn't happen to good people.

One of the biggest rookie mistakes on the trail is underestimating how much water to bring on an expedition or hike. Instead of anticipating the worst, novice trekkers look at a beautiful mountain stream and assume it's clean and drinkable. Well, it's usually not.

Water can be contaminated with animal (and sometimes human) feces. Gross but true. There is a wicked parasite known as Giardia that lurks, undetectable by the human eye, in feces. It can infect food, dirt, water, and most surfaces. That's why antibacterial gel is number one on my packing list. When I'm in the field, I'm like an antibacterial gel maniac—dripping and rubbing before I eat anything or put my hands near my mouth and eyes. It kills most of the bacteria that can slip into your system and crush you.

Causes of Giardia

- Consuming, swimming in, or accidentally ingesting contaminated water from tainted lakes or ponds
- Eating infected food
- Touching your mouth with contaminated hands

Symptoms of Giardia

It can take up to a week or two to develop symptoms after ingesting the pesky parasite. Symptoms include the following:

- Diarrhea
- Excessive gas
- Dehydration
- Stomach cramps
- Nausea

Prevention

Prevention is all about preparation, so bring tools to follow some safety rules. There's a saying I like to follow, "boil it, cook it, peel it, or forget it."

- Bring bottled water.
- Use antibacterial gel or wash hands often and diligently with antibacterial soap and fresh water.
- Wash and/or peel raw fruit and vegetables.

Anti-Giardia Techniques

- Boil water until it reaches a rolling boil for 1 minute or more.
- Chemically treat water with iodine or chlorination (but be aware that this will not kill Cryptosporidium or Cyclospora).
- Use a test-proven water filter.

Make Your Own Solar Still-Desalination

Using a solar still is a basic technique for distilling water and removing contaminants using the sun's heat. A solar still basically uses plastic to create hot air that will condense moisture and drip pure drinking water into a cup, leaving the contaminants in the still. Knowing how to make one is a good survival skill to have in the wilderness.

There are several types of solar stills. A few simple models are shown here.

SOLAR STILLS

- Cone shape
- Pit
- Boxed

CONE SHAPE

Using this method, contaminated water gets added to a clear plastic container, where it gets heated by the sun's rays. Distilling occurs as water condenses on the top and drips down along the sides, where it gathers and gets removed for consumption. The contaminants remain in the container.

PIT SOLAR STILL

The pit solar still is often used at sea or in desert conditions. To create this solar still, start by digging a hole about 7 inches deep and covering the base of hole with a piece of plastic. Fill it part way with water and place an empty cup in the center of the water, so it will catch the condensation. Place another piece of snug-fitting plastic over the hole to create an airtight seal. Essentially, it is a hot house. For dripping accuracy, place a rock in the center of plastic to push the roof into a point, which will become the prime drip spot. You can crush fresh green leaves into the surrounding water to increase condensation.

FYI *You can also use a solar still to make drinking water from saltwater. As water evaporates, the sodium chloride (NaCl) is heavier than the water (H_2O) and gets left behind.*

BOXED SOLAR STILL

Making this basic solar still starts with an airtight box. Place water in the box and cover the top with glass (or Saran Wrap) to cause condensation. This method requires that one side of the box be higher than the others to allow condensation to drip. The water vapor will condense on the angled glass and gravity will force it to travel down, gathering in a trough. Simply tilt the trough toward a pot, making sure the good and bad waters remain separated, and you get drinkable water.

FYI

- *A cubic foot of water weights 63 pounds.*
- *Most compounds expand when heated and contract when cooled. Water is among the few exceptions—although it does expand when heated and contract when cooled at most temperatures, water expands when cooled and contracts when heated between 32° F and 39° F.*

If Infected

Dehydration is the most common health concern if you have diarrhea, so drink plenty of fluids such as water, juice, tea, and sports drinks, which are great for replacing lost electrolytes. If it's more serious than basic diarrhea, seek medical help immediately.

Parting Thoughts

It's cool to ponder that if all the water that ever existed were still around today, some of the water molecules that dinosaurs drank could be the same that you are drinking.

PART III

NAVIGATION

14 MAPS

Your Friend the Compass

I'll put my compass against any GPS any day! Sure, GPS devises are high-tech, concise, and quick, but they are not wholly reliable, as certain surroundings and circumstances can zap their zip. Dead batteries, heavily wooded areas, canyons, city buildings can all make a good GPS go bad. Compasses continue to be critical equipment and are often more reliable than electronic gadgets. Compasses are self-contained and require zero energy.

A magnetic compass is a simple device that consists of a small magnet balanced on a pivot point. The magnet is usually called a needle. Since the earth's North and South poles act like magnets, the poles of all magnets are attracted in a north-south line. Therefore, one end of the needle is typically marked "N" for north, or colored in some way to indicate that it points toward the north.

The Anatomy of a Compass

The primary directional indicators—north, east, west, and south—are called "cardinal points," or directions. North is the most important one. Compass needles will almost always point North, even in the dustiest corners of Earth. The one exception is the North Pole. When I was at the North Pole, my compass needle went a bit wobbly and pointed to the magnetic north pole, which is south. But, then again, everything is south of the North Pole.

CORRECT ALIGNMENT   **INCORRECT ALIGNMENT**

North is aligned with the needle.

Using a Compass

Hold the compass base plate flat in your hand (in front of you) so that the needle moves freely and points to magnetic north. The only thing an unobstructed needle can do is rotate to magnetic north. The needle is usually color coded to indicate north from south, so make sure you are reading the right end of the needle.

FYI *It is a common mistake for beginners to forget to orientate their position before using the compass. Novices see the needle is pointing west and think it must be facing west. It's a sure recipe for getting lost. You must turn the compass or your body until it or you are facing north and the needle is aligned. Make sure the compass face is level and the needle is not being obstructed by touching the top or bottom of the case.*

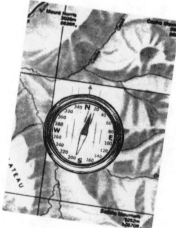

North is not properly aligned with the needle.

Using a Compass with a Map

Now it's time to learn how to use a compass with a map. It's simple, fun, and probably the most important use for a compass.

- Hold the map horizontally or place it flat on the ground.
- Place the compass base plate flat on the map.
- Rotate the map or compass until the "north lines" on the map (a series of equally spaced parallel lines drawn across the map, all running to magnetic north) are aligned with the compass needle.

By orienting a map, you are positioning it so its north is pointing north. When you orient a map and know where you are, try looking for a real landmark and test your map-reading savvy. For example, lay out the map and turn it until the ocean and mountains are in positions that correspond to your location.

The map should now be oriented to the terrain.

North Is Not Always North

Once you get a heading in which you want to travel, you will have to compensate for the earth's magnetic variation. Your compass needle points toward magnetic north and not absolute or true north. In order to understand magnetic variation and how you should apply it, remember this little saying "East is least and West is best." This means that you will either add or subtract magnetic variation to get an accurate heading. For example, in my home state of New York, the magnetic variation is approximately 14 degrees west. This means that I have to add 14 degrees to any compass heading to get my intended direction. This may not sound like a big deal especially for something like a hike but think about it. If your magnetic variation is 10 degrees (Chesapeake Bay) and you hike ten miles, your offset will be almost 2 miles.

FYI *True geographic north and magnetic north (where compasses point) are not the same. While geographic north is a constant, magnetic north—located near Resolute Bay in Canada—is slowly moving west, toward Alaska, due to geographical factors. Scientists say the magnetic pole moves at an unpredictably variable rate. So while the pole may skip around each day, it migrates on average between 6 and 60 miles a year.*

Making Your Own Compass

You can create your own compass much in the same way people did in the old days. There are many ways to make a compass, but they all use the same principle: Earth is a huge magnet with magnetic poles that influence the compass needle's behavior.

GEAR LIST

- Sewing needle
- Magnet
- Glass of water (with enough water to float a cork)

STEP 1: Turn the needle into a magnet by rubbing a magnet in one direction (not back and forth) along the length of the needle 30 to 50 times to create weak magnetization, which will react to the earth's own magnetic field. If you don't have a magnet, which is likely if you're out in the wilderness, you can substitute a piece of steel.

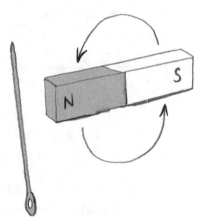

FYI *Standard sewing needles contain trace amounts of iron and can be easily magnetized.*

STEP 2: Place the needle in the middle of the water glass, getting it to float on the surface (the water's surface tension enables buoyancy). Be patient if your needle is float-challenged. Adding a drop or two of oil will help the needle float. It takes a while to find the right touch. If the needle just won't float and frustration gets the better of you, lay the needle in the center of a piece of cork or styrofoam and place them in the water. Avoid any kind of wind because it will affect your results. Since there is very little resistance on the surface of the water, the needle will slowly rotate toward north. Congratulations! You made your first compass. Pretty cool, huh?

A variation of the preceding experiment can be done without water by tying one end of a thread to the middle of a magnetized needle and the other end to a pencil. Balance the pencil on the rim of an empty cup with the needle hanging freely. The needle should move to point north no matter how the cup is turned.

How to Use Your Watch as a Compass

As an explorer, people expect me to know where I am at all times. If I make a navigational mistake in a car or while trekking, I usually get some good-natured ribbing from my friends.

Once I was hiking down a volcano in Ethiopia, a few thousand feet above a desert floor, on what was meant to be a four- or five-hour excursion. Our group of 40 international hikers and 16 local camels split into two groups. The smaller group left about an hour ahead of my group. When we finally set off, we got stuck behind a caravan of camels and I became quickly frustrated by how slowly they were moving and how badly they smelled—the camels, that is, not the people. Staying

true to my hyper New Yorker inner child, I decided to go ahead alone (not a good idea).

It was early morning and the desert sun was still at bay; later, it reached 115° F. I was moving along at a fast put comfortable pace, checking out the beautiful scenery along what seemed to be a well-marked trail. It felt good to be alone in the wild. As the day progressed, the sun heated up and the trail became a bit confusing. I searched for and found what seemed to be the freshest tracks of western boot prints. As I was plodding along the lava-, scree-, and obsidian-strewn trail, it soon became apparent that I was not on the same trail that I used coming up, and I got a sinking feeling that I might be lost.

Although it was just me and the African Desert Warblers rustling in the flora, I blushed with embarrassment. I didn't know what was worse: having to retrace my steps back up the mountain to see if I could find either my group or the right trail, or having to suffer the verbal abuse I was sure to receive upon walking into camp late, otherwise known as "the walk of shame."

I took a deep breath, calmed down, and although I did not have a map, I remembered the general direction of our meeting point, which was almost due south from the summit of the volcano I could see from where I was standing. Using my wristwatch to point me exactly south, I re-oriented myself and journeyed to the set meeting point. I arrived an hour ahead of the group and waited at the base. Of course, when they got there I was tapping my foot, looking at my watch and busting their chops with a sarcastic, "What took you so long?"

How to Use Your Watch as a Compass

After my brush with the walk of shame, this has become one of my favorite ways to find direction. It is a life-long skill that is easy to learn and will truly take you places.

GEAR LIST

- Analog wrist watch (with hands—not digital)
- Blade of grass
- Short, straight twig—or match

STEP 1: Hold your watch horizontally (in your hand), perpendicular to the ground, allowing the small hand (hour's hand) to point at the sun.

STEP 2: Lay a blade of grass (or a match) halfway between the small hand and 12 o'clock—the grass will point south (in the southern hemisphere, it will point north). This direction will be correct if the watch is set for true local time. For daylight savings time, adjust by using 1 o'clock instead of noon. The farther you are from the equator, the more accurate this method.

It works during any season because although the arc of the sun may be shorter in winter or longer in the summer, high noon (or zenith) will always be due south at astronomical noon. Astronomical noon is defined as the time of day when the sun is highest in the sky. This holds true for any location in the world in the northern hemisphere.

This technique even works in thick fog and clouds that block the sun as long as the sun is able to cast a shadow, which it usually can do even through dense fog. Determine the sun's direction by holding a thin object, such as a stick, vertical, which will create a shadow pointed away from the sun.

I typically wear a plastic watch in the field because they tend to be durable and have lots of neat functions. But these days, most people wear digital watches, which won't work as a compass. A great substitute for a watch—as long as it is divided into 12 hourly sections—is a hand-drawn watch face on a piece of paper. If you don't have a piece of paper you can be a bit creative and take a small flat rock or a piece

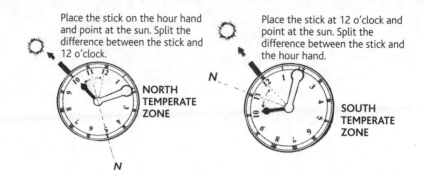

Place the stick on the hour hand and point at the sun. Split the difference between the stick and 12 o'clock.

NORTH TEMPERATE ZONE

Place the stick at 12 o'clock and point at the sun. Split the difference between the stick and the hour hand.

SOUTH TEMPERATE ZONE

of wood and scratch with a knife of sharp stone the numbers of a watch. Rotate the drawn version to the actual time (from your digital watch) and follow the instructions.

Challenge your friends and family by letting them use a real compass while you use only your watch.

Maps: A Love Affair

I love maps and so do most explorers. It's in my blood. When I grew up, we always had a map or an atlas at the dinner table, and a popular game would be to try to stump each other with trivia about distant lands. To this day, my favorite geography trivia question is: What point of land in North America is closest to Africa? Growing up, my Dad would always snap back (without looking at the globe), "It's quite

obvious that it is Newfoundland, Canada. But do you know what island off of Newfoundland is the closest?" Maps today still send my mind swirling. Looking at them always fires up my fantasies and makes me wonder about remote, undiscovered islands. I know many explorers who travel to distant lands and, in the face of unfamiliar surroundings, find comfort in their maps and savvy map-reading skills. Not only can maps guide you to exotic and remote nooks and crannies around the world, but they also tell stories of places you have been and destinations you dream of visiting.

What Is a Map?

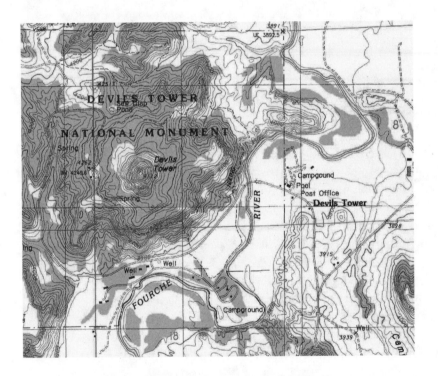

A map is a way of representing any real-world location or object on a flat surface, such as a piece of paper. While most road maps represent only two-dimensional locations—without taking into account their elevation—topographical maps add a third dimension, using contour lines to show elevation changes on the surface of the earth (or below the surface of the ocean).

Orientate Yourself

To be geographically "oriented" is to be familiar with a location. When I was 14 years old, my parents finally let me take our small motor boat to go fishing on my own in the Long Island Sound. I was excited, but admittedly a little anxious to go solo. During most of my outings, I kept land in sight, using it to guide me to the channel of our harbor. But on foggy mornings when I was barely able to see land, I used the Stony Brook University Medical Center as a landmark. Standing 19 stories (288 feet) high, which is 140 feet above sea level for a combined height over approximately 428 feet (attained by using formula below), this building was my beacon and was visible from miles away.

FYI *The formula indicates how far you can see an object on the horizon (remember, the earth is curved). Assuming you are of average height, if an object is 100 feet tall, then you can see 12.25 miles to the horizon. So if I knew Stony Brook University Medical Center was approximately 400 feet high, then I could see it from more than 50 miles away on the water, which makes it a very good landmark.*

Finding Stony Brook University Medical Center on my map was my way to get "orientated" and find my way home. Selecting a simple landmark is a terrific tool to identify your location on a map. In a city, it may be a skyscraper or an apartment building. But nature offers more interesting options. There are mountains, rivers, hills, and so much more.

I sometimes become disoriented when I am bushwhacking through thick, tall brush. Instead of freaking out and wandering aimlessly, I take a deep breath and look for a landmark that I can find on my map in order to get back on track. Sometimes it's as simple as keeping near the banks of a river or knowing there is a big mountain on my right. Using a compass or the sun's position in the sky is another great way to get oriented with a map.

The Key

The *key*, typically located in the bottom right corner of a map, is a box that lists the pictorial symbols used on the map and their meaning. It's not necessary to know all of the symbols, being familiar with the ones related to your route is important and will streamline your journey. There is also a graph of north, south, east, and west in case you space out in the fresh air.

Scale

Maps are drawn to scale; that is, there is a direct relationship (ratio) between a distance or unit on the map and the actual distance that same unit of measurement represents on the earth's surface. It refers to how much "real distance" (miles) was reduced to accurately represent the space on a map's micro version. For instance, a city map scale of 1 inch on the map may represent 1 mile in the real city. Some map scales are presented as a fraction. For example, a map noted as 1/2000 or a ratio of 1:2000 means that a 1-inch measurement on the map would equal 2,000 inches in the real world.

Always look at the scale before starting your journey. The scale of maps, the relationship between distance on the map and distance on the ground, greatly varies. An inch can equal a mile or even a hundred miles, depending on the map's purpose. On a local city map, which is considered "large scale," Lake Michigan (which is 307 miles long and 118 miles wide) may look like a very large blue area, but on a world map, which is considered "small scale," it looks like small blue spot.

Topographical Map

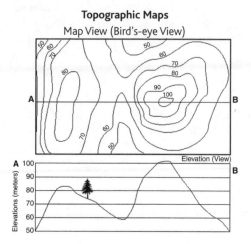

Topographical maps are essential maps for outdoorsmen as they offer a three-dimensional image of the landscape. The contour lines on these maps detail important features such as the steepness of hills and mountains, indicated by the closeness of the lines. Whether you are hiking, biking, hunting, or fishing, being familiar with your surroundings is critical for fun and safety.

Elevation

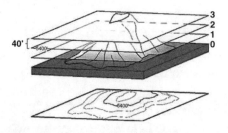

Contour lines on a map represent lines of equal elevation above (or below) sea level. The closer the lines, the steeper the elevation; the wider the spacing, the flatter the terrain. Keep this in mind when determining the kind of trek you want to take.

Looking at the map above, sea level is 0. So, if you put a quarter on the table and stack a nickel, a penny, and a dime on top of one another, each layer represents an elevation zone. Pushing one coin to the side allows a better view of how these layers show up as lines. To visualize what these contour lines look like on a topographical map, picture a mountain and imagine slicing through it with a perfectly flat, horizontal piece of glass.

Project: Sketch Your Own Custom Map

Being able to customize your own map will not only help you get somewhere more quickly, it will also help you to better understand maps. During this project, imagine you are a pioneer—and that Google Maps is not available.

Your job is to create a map of a route from your home to your school—including landmarks and shortcuts. This shouldn't be just a drawing with two lines, but rather a detailed map that someone who has never visited your town could use to find his way around. Include in your map reference points such as gas stations, unusual trees or ditches, and so on. You can even note shortcuts through parks or fields. Try to give details that only your local knowledge can provide.

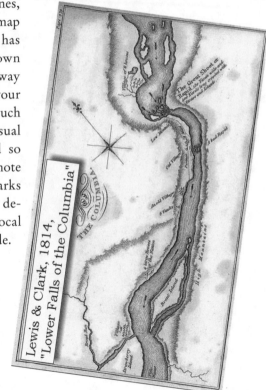

Lewis & Clark, 1814, "Lower Falls of the Columbia"

GEAR LIST

- Paper
- Compass
- Pencil

Parting Thoughts

I am always amazed by how often I look at the same map and discover a new destination to visit. Ultimately, I use maps much like others use a photo album, to rekindle memories and make each point on a map more than just a dot on a page—a potential adventure with a story waiting to be told.

A Handful of Measurements

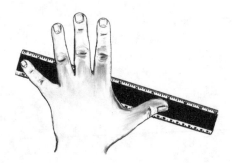

The Human Body—Nature's Measuring Tool

I often use my own body parts to measure things. For example, my hand span (from the tip of my middle finger to the first crease in my wrist) is nearly 8 inches. Knowing this allows me to quickly measure things in stores, like computer and television screens. In the wild, it comes in handy measuring snow depth, the size of animal tracks, and so much more. It's the single most useful measurement you will ever use— just measure and round it off to the nearest whole number. I suggest you momentarily put down this book and measure your own hand span.

ARM SPAN MEASURING

Almost everyone's arm span—fingertip to fingertip with arms spread out like wings—is nearly the same as his height. That's a great FYI for campfire banter. By knowing the length of my arm span (73 inches, which I round down to 6 feet, or 72 inches), I can conveniently measure lengths of rope or fishing line, or figure out if an object will fit in the back of a trunk.

Does your wingspan match your height? If it doesn't, it may mean that you are still growing.

LET YOUR FINGERS, HANDS, AND ARMS DO THE MEASURING!

Knowing that the distance from my elbow to the bone on the inside of my wrist is 12 inches (which corresponds to my foot length), from my elbow to the pad just below my little finger is

"Vitruvian Man"
by Leonardo da Vinci

15 inches, and from my elbow to the tip of that finger is 20 inches, I am able to guesstimate the size of lots of things.

I use these known measurements when I go fishing to measure my catch, so I will know if it is of legal length (every state has different size requirements). To do this, I rest my elbow on the side of the boat, near the fish. If the fish is less than x number of inches, you are required by law to release it back into the water.

Measure the length of your forearm to your wrist, then to your pinky, and then to your finger tips. Now write them down, and you have good measurements to use for estimating sizes and dimensions in the outdoors.

Throughout this book we discuss pacing the distance of an object (See Chapter 16, Sky) by using your stride length. To find yours, wet the bottom of your feet or shoes, take a normal step and measure the distance between each footprint or step. That's your stride length. You can use it to mark off a room or a football field.

Fill in your body distances.

_____ inches=width of my pinky nail

_____ inches=width of my index finger nail

_____ inches=width of my first 2 fingers together

_____ inches=length of my pinky finger

_____ inches=width of my palm

_____ inches=length of my thumb to the wrist

_____ inches=length of my pinky to the wrist

_____ inches=span of my index finger and thumb

_____ inches=span of my middle finger and thumb

_____ inches=span of my pinky and thumb

_____ inches=length of my elbow to the wrist

_____ inches=length of my elbow to the top of palm

FYI *Since most of us know our waist measurement, it's a great tool to use when a measuring tape is not available. Wrap a piece of string or cord around your waist, using your bellybutton as the middle point of reference, and mark the length. If your waist is 32 inches, you can fold that string in half and refold it to get various somewhat accurate measurements.*

- Full string=32 inches.
- $1/2$ string=16 inches.
- $1/4$ string=8 inches.

Measuring Angles

Here are some great ways to measure angles.

Hold your arm out in front of chest, with hand palm down, at eye-level. Close one eye while using your hand and the horizon as your sighting spot to determine approximate angle degrees.

ANGLE DEGREES

- 1 degree is approximately the width of a pinky finger nail at arm's length.
- 10 degrees is approximately the width of a closed fist at arm's length.

- 20 degrees is approximately the width of a hand-span at arm's length.

Using Common Objects as Measuring Tools

Use these household objects for measuring almost anything.

- A dime turned on its side with a quarter placed perpendicular on top of it equals an inch from surface to top.
- A standard business card is two inches wide.
- An AA battery is just shy of two inches long.
- All U.S. paper money is six inches long and two and half inches wide, so folded in half it becomes a three-inch measuring stick.
- A standard sheet of computer printer paper is 8 ¹/₂ × 11 inches.
- A 2-liter bottle of soda is almost one foot long.

Making a Measuring Wheel

Measuring a relatively short straight line with marked tape is pretty easy. But how about when you need to find the length of a field or a pear-shaped swimming pool? That's where the handy measuring wheel enters the picture. This gizmo, resembling a one-wheel, one-handle wheel barrel, has a disc wheel that's clearly marked with a line used to measure each rotation. The line represents a measured distance, or circumference, that is used for measurement. Calculating the number of rotations gives you an accurate measurement. It's sort of like a tape measure that never ends.

FYI *The circumference of a basketball is about 30 inches.*
You can determine the circumference of any round object if you know its diameter.

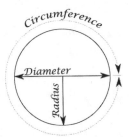

Circumference = Pi × Diameter
$C = D\pi = 3.14\pi$

GEAR LIST

- Large piece of cardboard
- Ruler or tape measure
- Pencil
- Craft knife
- Nail
- Small bolt and nut
- Marker

STEP 1: Work out the unit of measurement. For our purposes, we will use inches and feet. Those of you with an international flair can use the metric system.

STEP 2: Cut a disc wheel from cardboard or use a paper plate. For example, a plate with an 11 1/2-inch diameter would have a circumference of 36 inches or 3 feet. Mark a dot at the center of your cardboard and take a tack tied to a string with a pencil (tied close to the point) and use it as a compass. Or, you can use a dish or circular object to trace and draw a circle.

STEP 3: Measure and cut a wooden handle of a comfortable length so you don't have to bend over too much as you walk, about 3 or 4 feet long.

STEP 4: Attach the circle/cardboard to the handle by cutting a hole in the center of the disc and along the bottom of the handle. Punch a small hole in the center of your circle that is slightly larger than the bolt which will be inserted. Cut another hole of equal size near the end of the handle. Line up the holes, pop in the bolt, and tighten the nut. Make sure the wheel is centered and able to turn easily.

STEP 5: Mark a large visible line for a reference point to count revolutions. From start to finish, your total distance will be the number of revolutions times (x) the circumference of your wheel. For example, if your plate's circumference is a foot and it revolves 10 times, then the distance would be 10 feet (1 foot circumference×10 revolutions=10 feet distance).

NOTE: A paper plate will take you only so far. Sometimes you need to measure a distance that is hundreds of feet long, such as a soccer field, so you'll either need a super-sized paper plate or a sturdy industrial wheel measurer.

A Bigger, Bolder, Better Idea

Since we know that a wheel is an essential component for measuring, why not use the same method as an odometer? An odometer is commonly found on the dashboard of your car and is used to measure distance traveled.

Measure the circumference of your bike wheel and mark this measurement in one spot on the tread with white chalk (my bike wheel's diameter is 28 inches, meaning its circumference is 88 inches or 7 feet 4 inches). Ride slowly and count each revolution to find a set distance. Be sure to look up frequently, so you don't crash!

15 TRACKING

The Art of Tracking

I have been on many expeditions all over the world. And whether I'm tagging jaguars in the Yucatan, climbing high peaks in the Himalayas, or skiing to the North Pole, I am always amazed by the hidden life—animals, insects, and plants—I have discovered by simply getting on my knees and looking around.

I wasn't born an expert nor did I start tracking in canopied jungles, far, far away. I began in my own suburban backyard, armed with curiosity. No matter your level, animal tracking is an ongoing learning process that builds your mental tool box and abilities.

What Is Tracking?

Tracking is the art of following trails and clues in order to find an animal. Its tradition reaches back thousands of years to countless tribes around the world who depended on this critical skill to feed friends and family.

While tracking can be as simple as following paw prints in mud, it may also involve identifying the smell of an animal's fur imbedded in grass. Being a savvy tracker depends on your ability to search for evidence not only with your eyes, but also with your sense of smell, touch, hearing, and possibly taste. But most important is pattern recognition.

Repeated Patterns

In nature there are many patterns. The sun rises in the morning and sets at dusk. Clouds typically move from west to east. Similarly, animals often repeat behaviors. For instance, a lion may always get up at sunrise to search for food, while a deer may bed-down in tall grass during the day and become active at night when it is better able to spot predators. Sometimes, adverse conditions like drought prompt them to move to a new location.

Getting Started

Examining animal tracks is the most obvious and easiest way to find an animal, especially when following tracks along sandy, clear flat lands, like beaches and river banks—or mud.

Think about the last time you strolled along the shore at the beach. You probably walked by a variety of bird prints in the sand. Did you ever stop to think how you knew it was a bird print? Probably you have seen it before or recognize the delicate webbed footprint of a bird versus the heavier footprint of a mammal. Already you are a tracker of sorts if you know this much.

So, what animal should you track? I suggest starting with one that won't be too hard to find or too dangerous when you find it. Some animals are more dangerous than you think, so select your subject carefully. For example, if you live in the mountain states, stay away from North American Moose; they kill a few humans each year by kicking them to death. Instead, try starting with a deer, raccoon, or dog.

GEAR LIST

- Animal track field guide. I like *Outdoor Action Animal Tracking* cards (Princeton Press) or *Peterson's Field Guides*.

- Scat (animal poop) chart. See one of the field guides or talk to your local parks department.
- Measuring tape.
- Notebook.
- Waterproof pen or pencil.

STEP 1: Choose Your Animal

White-tail deer are found in every state, with the exception of Alaska and Hawaii, so it is a good undo-mesticated animal to start with. Once you have chosen your animal, read about its patterns in a field guide or on a credible website. My favorite website is www.bear-tracker.com. I also recommend checking out the International Society of Professional Trackers (ISPT). They have members in every state.

Most important, become familiar with what the animal's foot prints look like and, believe it or not, what its poop looks like. Also, know what the animal does, and when, where, how, and why it does what it does.

Before setting off on your mission, ask yourself these questions:

- What terrain does the animal live in (desert, mountain, prairie, etc.)?
- What and where does the animal eat? For example, bears like salmon, so if you are (carefully) tracking one, look for a salmon stream.
- What do the animal's tracks look like? Carnivores (meat-eaters) typically have claws, while herbivores (plant-eaters) have hooves.

When you feel ready, go out and put your skills to the test in the wilderness.

STEP 2: Observing: Finding a Track Versus a Trail

Enter the forest or your animal's habitat in a nonobtrusive manner, so it does not get frightened and run away. Once in the animal's territory, find a track or trail.

Remember, a "track" is a print from an animal, while a "trail" is either a succession of prints or broken vegetation leading in a direction. Look for slight variations on the ground or vegetation, paw prints in the mud, broken branches, or scat. When tracking, double-check that you are truly on your animal's trail. If you are tracking buffalo and the trail is only a foot wide, then, clearly, it's probably not from a buffalo.

Next, look for prints unique to your animal. If there aren't any prints, look for other signs such as poop. All animals have distinct droppings.

STEP 3: Determine Direction

Study the direction of the print to determine the direction the animal is heading. When the animal is walking, it may leave a scuffmark, which is essentially a track. For example, running on a beach will leave different kinds of tracks than walking. So, play detective and decide if your animal is walking or running—that is, fleeing or hunting. When following a trail, be sure to walk next to it—not on it—so you can find it again if some of the tracks are lost.

Start by choosing a specific set of tracks and use a ruler to measure the size and width of the animal's footprint. Measure the distance from one footprint to the next to determine the animal's stride length, and record them in a notebook. Match the footprint with one in your guidebook to verify the type of animal you're tracking. As your skills improve, you won't need to look these things up as frequently.

Take your time learning everything you can from each track. Notice differences in foot size, stride length, and depth of impression. You might mark each track with twigs so you can see the line of sight of the tracks, to see, for example, if it's curving in a particular direction. This will make it easy to determine where to look for the next print. Study the mark's freshness. Think of your own foot prints in mud. There is a distinct look to fresh tracks; sharp edges, moist surface, and overall new appearance.

There may be another animal's track within your track, as animals commonly use a network of paths to move from one place to another to hunt and gather food. In areas of high animal traffic, pay extra attention. Look for clues like drops of blood to find where and what your animal may be eating.

> **!** Never approach an animal that is eating. Even the most docile animal can become aggressive when food is involved.

STEP 4: Scat ID: The Dirty Methods of Tracking

It is common to be put off by animal poop. But deer, cattle, and moose are herbivores, so their waste consists mostly of grass and plants, placing it on the low end of the nasty scale.

> **!** One should always, however, avoid touching meat eaters' scat, which can contain parasites, bacteria, or other things that can cause illness.

Still, scat is frequently overlooked as a "real" tracking tool, as we tend to think of it as something dirty. But it's a terrific tool for both identifying an animal and determining its proximity. If you hold your hand over a pile of animal poop and it feels warm, you know the animal is still near. Also, every animal's poop is unique. Deer leave little pebble-sized droppings, while horses drop golf-ball–sized droppings that contain clumps of hay. The seeds, plant parts, and berries within scat are good indicators of the animal's health and diet.

For instance, predator scat often contains large amounts of hair and bones from its prey—not such a pretty picture. Herbivores' scat contains only plant material. Online poop ID charts are excellent resources for identifying animals by their scat.

STEP 5: Stalking: Becoming Odorless, Inaudible, and Invisible

Animals have an acute sense of smell and hearing, allowing animals to "smell" and sense danger, so to get close to an animal, a tracker must remain undetectable. Don't wear perfume when you go out tracking, leave your smelly bubblegum and florescent shirt at home, and avoid crushing twigs and dry leaves while you're moving about and approaching animals.

STEP 6: See Your Animal Before It Smells You

Because an animal's sense of smell is more potent than most humans', it is best to stand—or approach an animal—from downwind, where you cannot be sensed.

Become invisible when moving toward an animal by hiding in bushes and crawling on your belly through long grass, if necessary. Make no sudden movements. Keep quiet and still when the animal is looking your way and deliberately creep forward when the animal is not peering in your direction.

Patience is critical. Here are some additional guidelines.

- Move slowly and fluidly, and avoid abrupt or shaky gestures.
- Cover your eyes, teeth, and the whites of your palms when facing the animal. Their light color is easily detected by animals amid nature's brown, green, or gray backdrop.
- Keep your body low and compact.
- Study the animal's alertness to determine if it is watching you or if it is acting "normal" and is unaware of your presence.

Seeing Better in the Dark

After a full day of tracking, it may be dark by the time you approach your animal. Fret not as you don't need night-vision goggles to see in the dark.

OPTIMAL NIGHT VISION TIPS (USED BY THE MILITARY):

- Protect your eyes during the day by wearing sunglasses. My father was a professional pilot for Pan American, and I remember that they recommended pilots avoid being in the sun before night flights.

- In the evening allow at least 30 minutes for your pupils to dilate and to fully adjust to the dark. Avoid looking directly into anything bright.
- Peripheral vision is stronger than direct vision in the dark, so turn your head left and right when searching for something in the dark.
- Avoid smoke from a campfires and cigarettes; it compromises your night vision.
- Scan the area and look for movement in the fore- and background rather than focusing on individual objects.
- If you must use a flashlight, cover it with a red piece of plastic so it will remain unseen by animals and will keep your own eyesight adjusted to the dark.
- Stay lower than your target as an animal's contours blend into the foreground if you are looking down at it. By positioning yourself down low, you might be able to see your target's silhouette against the night sky.
- When moving from light to dark, keep one eye closed so it will remain acclimated to night vision.

FYI *Eat carrots for better vision? Although vitamin A is essential for healthy eyes, eating carrots will not improve your vision. This was a rumor started by Britian's air ministry during World War II to explain their success in shooting down German planes at night, which was most likely the result of a new radar system the Nazis did not know about.*

Tracking People

Many of the skills used in animal tracking are also used in law enforcement and search and rescue. If you spend enough time in the woods, you might have to find someone who is lost. Here are some tips to make that search easier.

1. Find witnesses, perhaps other hikers, who may have seen your lost buddy and be able to give you some information.
2. Determine where the missing person was headed or is likely to be heading.
3. Do you know the missing person's shoe pattern? It does not

do you any good to follow a print of someone else's shoe or boot.

4. Evaluate the terrain by determining natural patterns such as streams or ridges that a person is likely to follow.
5. What is your buddy's frame of mind? Is the missing person someone who is comfortable in the woods or likely to panic?
6. Does the missing person have gear appropriate for the weather conditions—summer or winter, wet or dry?
7. Does your friend have a radio or mobile phone, and will it work in the area?
8. Are you able to search with another person or group?
9. Above all, do not panic! There is a difference between moving decisively and running around like a chicken with its head cut off.

Parting Thoughts

While most of the world operates on ordinary and mundane terms, the tracker lives in the realm of the extraordinary and rare. Tracking is a unique way to see, smell, touch, and hear ordinary things. There is something magical about being able to travel stealthily through the wilderness, revealing a hidden world, absent from most people's eyes.

Animal Autographs

When I was a kid, my mother was always telling me not to track mud into the house. Once in a rare while I'd get caught with mud-packed

sneakers and get a good tongue-lashing. Sound familiar? Somehow, my eagle-eyed mom knew I was the culprit, even when she was not in the house at the time of the crime. She was not formally trained as a tracker, but she sure possessed the necessary instincts!

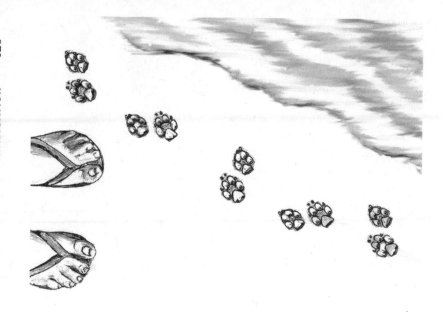

How did my mom know who tracked what into the house? Since my shoes were a different size and shape than my sisters', whose were smaller, and my father's, who were larger, that left me. The mud tracks I left were unique to me.

Animal tracks are much the same. Every animal has a distinct set of prints that tells a story. Identifying animal tracks is like opening up a mystery novel, and each set of tracks tells a different story. Some tracks can date back thousands of years, like those discovered by paleontologists searching for dinosaur tracks in fossilized mud and preserved hardened rock. Their discoveries always send my mind spinning with questions like How fast were they walking? and Where were they headed?

You can make plaster molds of contemporary animal prints to study and analyze. Who knows, one day they may become a prized collection.

Plaster Casting Tracks

Making plaster casts of animal tracks (paw impressions) left in soft ground is inexpensive and easy, provided it's done properly. Casting tracks found in mud or sand are the easiest to preserve, while casting those made in frozen snow prove a bit more challenging.

GEAR LIST

- Plaster of paris or modeling cement
- Mixing container
- Stick or spoon for mixing
- Water
- Thin cardboard strips (optional)

STEP 1: Find an animal's track by looking in wet, sandy or muddy, areas near creek beds, where animals stand on the water's edge and drink. The soft surface provides a deep impression that is clean and therefore easy to cast. I suggest using your dog's or cat's tracks to make your first cast—or borrowing your neighbor's if you are pet-free. For sure, it will be a unique memento of your furry friend.

STEP 2: Upon finding a track, carefully remove debris such as leaves or sticks that have fallen into it. Do not remove things that are stuck in the track, as it will damage the impression—you can remove them from the plaster later. Use an eyedropper to drain any water from the track.

STEP 3: Before pouring plaster into the track, you need to construct a frame about two or three inches high to dam the outside of the track. The material doesn't matter, as long it is sturdy and won't get water logged. Wood and plastic strips are most commonly used to create a square or circular dam around the track. I often use a paper clip or sticky tape to seal plastic strips together. If the tracks are small enough, a tuna-fish can—with the top and bottom removed—works great.

STEP 4: Press the frame lightly into the ground, so it doesn't disturb the paw print. A square, wooden frame can be sealed on the outside corners with modeling clay or wax.

STEP 5: After everything is in place, mix the plaster or modeling cement. In this project, we are using plaster of paris, but modeling cement that dries very quickly can be used for a sturdier cast, but be aware that it is heavier and not as easy to use. Both kinds of material can be bought in most hobby stores and typically come with instructions. Generally, you should use about two parts plaster to one part water.

STEP 6: The consistency of the plaster should be similar to pancake batter or heavy cream. Once the plaster is added to the water, begin mixing immediately. The plaster begins to set upon contact with water, so work quickly. I find it's best to pre-measure quantities, so I can add all the plaster at once and begin stirring right away.

Stir the mixture for 3 to 5 minutes, until it is smooth and lump-free. It's a good idea to tap the mixing bowl on the ground a few times to loosen any bubbles.

If you are casting a print in fine, dry dust, you may need to thin the mixture by adding a little water so the weight of the plaster will not destroy the track's fine details. In this case, you will need to let it set longer to dry thoroughly.

STEP 7: Gently pour the plaster mixture into the impression being careful not to disturb or deform the track in any way. Start pouring onto the ground next to the track and allow it to run into the main im-

pression and the finer details, such as claw marks. Use a spoon or spatula to delicately push the plaster into the finer areas. The cast should be at least two inches above the track, so be careful not to make your cast too thin or it will crumble.

Wet snow is challenging but if you dust a little dry plaster into the track—just a light sprinkling—before you pour the plaster in, it will dry faster. If the snow is fluffy and dry you can harden the track before attempting to cast a mold by using a little water in a misting bottle and spraying it directly into the print and allowing it to freeze before adding your plaster. It's a delicate operation, so go slowly by spraying a little water at a time.

STEP 8: Let the cast dry for about 30 minutes, and then check it for dryness by knocking gently on the plaster. If it has a ceramic ring, it should be dry enough to pick up. If the plaster is still mushy, leave it to dry longer.

After the plaster has hardened, carefully remove the frame (it can be used again) and pick up the cast. Although you can remove large objects such as heavy dirt or leaves, don't clean it too thoroughly at this time. Carefully wrap the cast in paper (newspaper or brown paper bag) to carry it home—never wrap plaster casts in plastic bags because it prevents the moisture from escaping.

Let the cast sit for a few days to harden thoroughly, and then use an old toothbrush to carefully remove any dirt or other unwanted material from it. When cleaning a plaster cast, do not scrub it too hard, because you can erode the plaster and delete details. Use sandpaper to remove irregularities and a pencil to label the back of the cast with the type of animal, date, and location where it was found. You can also paint the track. This is an art for some collectors. Real aficionados will paint the surrounding plaster of the actual track prior to displaying it so that the track stands out from its background.

TURNING CAST POSITIVE

Since your cast is a model of the bottom of the animal's foot, you can make a "positive" cast by filling the track with plaster. Set a plastic

frame firmly around the cast, so is extends approximately an inch or so above, and then seal any gaps between the plastic and the base of the track using plasticene or paraffin.

Using petroleum jelly, grease the original cast and frame, and pour plaster on top of the cast with the

impression side up. Let it set for a few days before carefully separating the two casts. Once the plaster hardens, they should separate easily.

CLEAN-UP

Do not pour left-over plaster of paris down the sink drain. It can plug up your pipes! Instead, wash the mixing container outside and dump the leftover material in the dirt (it is non-toxic). Better yet, use disposable containers and throw everything away when you're done.

Take Home Tracks

Sometimes you will want to collect the animal prints in the field and bring them back home or to a more controlled setting for further observation. Here's how you can take your track home.

GEAR LIST

- Cookie sheet
- Butter knife
- Spatula
- Paper towels

Look for tracks in firm mud that can easily be cut. Those in soft, runny mud will fall apart. Once a track is located, use a knife to cut a square in the mud around the track and carefully slide the spatula under the little mud brick and gently lift it out.

STEP 1: Another way to collect animal tracks is to actually lift them out of the mud much in the same way a fossil hunter would extract fossils from the ground. I have found this works best in muddy sandbars, in mud near rivers, or at the beach. Clay is best. The smaller the track the better, as large prints tend to fall apart.

STEP 2: Carefully slide the mud brick onto a cookie sheet, keeping it as flat as possible on the bottom—to prevent cracking or collapsing as it dries. Put the cookie sheet in a safe place where it won't be disturbed, and allow it to dry completely. This may take several days.

FYI

- *Larger tracks are more likely to crack as they dry.*
- *Mud made mostly of clay is very durable, and mud made from sand is extremely fragile.*

STEP 3: Here's the neat part—preservation! Once you get the track home in good shape, you can make your own animal autograph collection by spraying the mold with clear lacquer or fiberglass resin to preserve it.

16 SKY

The North Star, or Never Saying *I Am Lost*

Imagine you are a contestant on a reality TV show. The show's producers blindfold and fly you in the middle of the night to an unknown location, where you are dropped in the middle of woods with nothing but water, energy bars, and what you are wearing. Your goal is to find your way home. You need a game plan.

Having no idea how you are going to get home, it's best to begin by figuring out where you are. If it's a clear night, you can use one of the most ancient methods of navigation by finding the North Star. The North Star, also called Polaris, is a good guidepost because its position in the sky never changes. It's located almost directly above the northern axis of the earth's rotation, no matter where you are in the world. Two distinct constellations—the Big Dipper and Cassiopeia—can help you locate the North Star. If it's cloudy, you are out of luck. Sorry, game over! Just kidding—but navigating without the stars is a topic for another chapter.

Find the Big Dipper

The Big Dipper is one of the most widely recognized constellations. It is easily spotted by looking for an upside down kitchen pot with a long handle. To use it to find the North Star, pinpoint the outer edge of the dipper (the side of the dipper furthest from the handle) and look to the two stars on this outer edge. They are called the "pointer stars," because if you trace a line straight them they point to the North Star. As you gaze upon these two stars mentally, draw a line from the outer bottom star to the outer top star and then extend this line about five times (or about 2 fists) and look for the North Star along this line. It will always be to your right.

Find Cassiopeia

Using the Cassiopeia constellation is another sure-fire way to find the North Star. Cassiopeia, one of the brightest constellations in the Northern Sky, is located on the opposite side of the North Star from the Big Dipper. Made up of five stars that resemble a "W" or a crown on its side, Cassiopeia's center star (with 2 stars above it and 2 below it) points like an arrow head to the North Star.

But now, back to our reality TV show scenario, which I'll call "Up a Creek without a Clue." Now that you have found the North Star, you have a sense of east, west, north, and south and essentially a compass in the sky. Next, you need to determine your latitude (how far north or south you are).

Using the angle of the North Star compared to the horizon will give you your latitude. Since the North Star is in the northern hemisphere, it will always be at an angle from the horizon that is the same as your latitude. If the North Star is directly overhead at a 90-degree angle to the horizon, you are at the North Pole and the show producers are not very kind. Conversely, if the North Star is on the horizon, you are on the equator. To find places in between, stretch your arm out and set your fist on the horizon with your thumb up. Each width of your fist represents 10 degrees. For instance, New York City is at 40 degrees north, which means that this star will appear 40 degrees above the horizon at all times.

FYI As Earth spins on its axis all of the stars seem to move around the earth, except Polaris. Since there is a slight "wobble" in the earth's axis, Polaris has not always been the North Star, and it will not remain the polestar forever. In 2300 B.C. the polestar was in the constellation Draco; by A.D. 12,000—a long time from now—the star Vega, in the constellation Lyra, will be the polestar.

Simple Sextant—Finding Your Latitude

Help for the Geographically Impaired

I have always had great respect for the explorers and sailors who relied on sextants to navigate land and high seas. One of my all-time heroes is Sir Ernest Shackleton, the brilliant polar explorer who navigated a tiny lifeboat in pitching seas and stormy skies using just a sextant. Despite arduous conditions and the lack of a level horizon and ample stars or sun—two vital elements for using a sextant—his savvy skill and ingenuity saved the lives of his entire 27-man crew.

While the sextant may appear to be complicated to understand and use, it is a simple device that measures the angle of the sun or stars above the horizon. Configured in a half-circle, it has a scope that gets aimed at the sky for locating latitude—the invisible horizontal lines that determine location in relation to the equator. Before there were satellites, GPSs, and accurate maps, sextants were critical to journeymen who depended on the stars to navigate.

At the equator, the angle (latitude) is 0 degrees, while the latitude at the North Pole is observed at 90 degrees north. This is often referred to as "sighting the object," "shooting the object," or "taking a sight." In the northern hemisphere, the "degree of latitude" is equal to the angle at which the North Star is observed above the horizon, thereby indicating your latitude (degrees from the equator).

FYI *On a globe, latitude is noted with thin black lines.*

Make Your Own Sextant

GEAR LIST

- Protractor
- Straw
- Fishing line
- Weight (any object weighing an ounce or two)
- Tape
- Paper

STEP 1: Make a hole in the center of the straight edge of a protractor, or use the tiny existing hole that most protractors have.

STEP 2: Attach with either tape or tie a small weight to a piece of string, and then tie the other end of string to the hole in the protractor. Look at the illustration and pay attention to where you

MAKE A SMALL HOLE

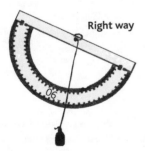

Right way

The line is tied to the protractor correctly.

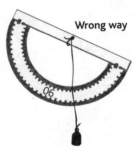

Wrong way

Don't tie the line to the protractor like this.

attach your string. Be sure to tie it around the outer edge, not around the inner edge, which will make your sextant inaccurate. It's a good idea to cut a tiny groove in the top of the protractor to tie off the string.

STEP 3: Turn the protractor so that the straight edge is up. Attach your straw to this section with tape or glue. Cut off any excess straw that may hang over the edges.

Your finished product should look like the illustration. Read the inner set of numbers of your protractor with the 0-degree mark at your eyepiece, and the 180-degree mark away from you.

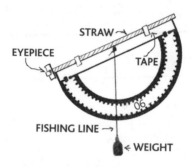

Finished crude sextant

STEP 4: Here's how to find your latitude:

1. Sight the North Star through the straw.
2. Determine where the weight line falls on the protractor (this is called the "plumb line").
3. Subtract this angle from 90 to find the North Star's altitude angle, or its height in degrees above the horizon. This is your latitude.

For example, if you live in New York City, the plumb line will fall on 49 degrees, so your latitude would be 90 – 49=41 degrees.

Other Uses for a Sextant

Your sextant is also a great tool for measuring the height of large objects that cannot be measured by ordinary means, such as with a ruler or tape measure.

THREE EASY STEPS TO FINDING HEIGHT USING A SEXTANT

STEP 1: Measure the distance between your standing or spotting position and the building you want to measure. For example, if you walk 33 paces away from the building, you can say the building is roughly 100 feet away.

STEP 2: Measure the height at which you are holding the sextant in your spotting position. This can be roughly estimated based on your own height. For this example, let's use 5 feet.

STEP 3: While in spotting position, tilt the sextant until you can see the top of the building through the straw. Allow the weighted line to dangle free and then measure the plumb line. Let's use 45 degrees for this experiment.

STEP 4: Use these three measurements (100 feet, 5 feet, and 45 degrees) to determine the height of the object by using a trigonometric chart or graph paper.

STEP 5: Select a scale to use for each square. In this case, we're 100 feet away from the building, so let's have every square represent 5 feet. With that in mind, draw a horizontal line on your graph paper that is 20 squares long and 1 square up (to represent our height of 5 feet).

STEP 6: Based on the plumb line angle of 45 degrees, draw a 45-degree angle from the end of our line to the vertical edge of the paper.

STEP 7: Count squares on the graph to determine the height of the building. In this case, it is 105 feet tall. (Remember, we added the 5 feet for the height of the person holding the sextant.)

FYI *One degree of latitude equals approximately 69 miles, one minute of latitude equals nearly 1.15 miles, and one second of latitude is just about 0.02 miles, or slightly more than 100 feet.*

Parting Thoughts

Globes are fun to spin, but it's more fulfilling to know what all the colors and squiggly lines mean so that you can determine where you are in the world. Mastering awareness of your location and surroundings in the outdoors is an invaluable skill that will build your confidence and self-sufficiency.

The Sun—Nature's Rolex

For as long as animals (including humans) have been on Earth, the sun has been a giant alarm clock in the sky. When the sun rose, it was time to get up; when it set, it was time to sleep. A tidy, simple system, if you ask me. Even before humans had written language, they were using the sun and shadows to determine the time of day.

Because I spent a lot of time outdoors when I was young, I developed a good feeling for time. Instinctively, it seemed natural to get up with the sun and to head home from playing ball with my friends just before sunset. While keeping that schedule now would certainly interfere with my lifestyle, I do use the sun as my rooster on camping trips.

Most people are more instinctual than they realize. Given the chance to spend quiet time in the woods or in your own backyard you can easily learn to tell the time of day, simply by taking cues from your surroundings.

The Lightness of Being

Morning light has less dust than the rest of the day, so sunrise light tends to be yellow or white compared to the red of sunset. Morning air is generally cooler than midday, and the wind is calmer—that's why surfers call calm morning ocean swell conditions "morning glass."

Only the Shadow Knows

Clever outdoorsmen can tell time by observing light and shadows. Long shadows indicate early morning or late afternoon. At midday, the light is harsh, and it washes out colors. Just ask any photographer.

Use It or Lose It

The easiest way to use the sun (in the northern hemisphere) is to wait until it is due South—when it is at its highest point in the sky. This is what people mean when they say "high noon."

FYI

- *Due to daylight savings time, high noon doesn't always mean 12 o'clock in your location, but rather when the sun is highest in the sky (it's typically close to noon, regardless of your location).*
- *Your location and time zone determine the actual Standard Time Meridian, also called Mean Solar Time, which is based on Greenwich Meridian Time (GMT). GMT is 0 degrees latitude.*

Knowing Standard Time Zones

Standard Time within time zones was first introduced in the United States in 1883. Since then, time zone boundaries have evolved considerably, and regions have shifted from one zone to another. Your first step in finding your Standard Time is to determine whether you are in the East, West, Central, or Mountain Time Zone.

Here's a list to help you out. You may want to memorize your exact location in degrees to be able to apply time correction in any global location.

STANDARD TIME

- In the Eastern Time Zone (ET), the Mean Solar Time is 75 degrees west of the GMT (this is often written as 75°W).

- In the Central Time Zone (CT), the Mean Solar Time is 90°W of the GMT.
- In the Mountain Standard Time Zone (MST), the Mean Solar Time is 105°W of the GMT.
- In the Western Standard Time Zone (WST), the Mean Solar Time is 120°W of the GMT.

If you know the longitude difference between two locations, you can use the rate of the earth's rotation (15 degrees=1 hour, or 1 degree=4 minutes) to calculate the difference in time between the two places. For instance, New York City is located 74°W, and Buffalo, New York is 78°W. They are separated by 4 degrees on longitude. So, the sun traveling across the sky would reach Buffalo 16 minutes after it passes New York City at solar noon.

Use the information above to answer the following questions. Understanding and using these concepts will allow you to guesstimate your exact time by calculating it based on noting the sun at its apex.

- Find out at which longitude you live (e.g., Cape Cod is 80°W)
- Find out the Mean Solar Time of your time zone (e.g., the Eastern Time Zone is 75°W, which is the longitude of Philadelphia)
- Calculate the longitude difference between the two (80° − 75° = 5°)
- Your time difference from your Mean Solar Time is 4 times the longitude difference (1° = 4 minutes; e.g. 5° × 4 minutes = 20 minutes)
- Therefore, the time of your solar noon is 20 minutes sooner or later than in Philadelphia. It would be later if your town is west of Philadelphia. Detroit, for example, is in the westernmost part of the Eastern Time Zone.

NOTE: In the summer, we add an hour for daylight savings.

While the sun may be higher in the summer than at other times of the year, solar noon is always on the same vertical plane (i.e., due South) and the shadows always point due North.

For instance, if you are on a summer hike and you know that in your location solar noon—when the sun is at its highest point—is at 1:30 P.M., you won't need to have a watch to know that it's 1:30 P.M. when the sun is overhead. Also, remember that at high noon, shadows always point due North.

If you are practicing your "natural" time telling skills from the same location, like your house or school, select a recognizable landmark that is precisely due south. Because solar noon is always due south, when the sun is aligned with your landmark (on the same vertical plane), you will have a fairly good idea of the time of your solar noon.

Find the Earth's Circumference Using Shadows

Eratosthenes, a Greek geographer (about 276 to 194 B.C.), measured the length of various shadows to first determine the earth's circumference. You can, too. Here's a neat little experiment based on one of Ertosthenes' from more than 2,000 years ago that I learned from our friends at the National Weather Service.

USE SHADOWS TO DETERMINE THE EARTH'S CIRCUMFERENCE

GOAL: Find the earth's circumference by measuring the length of shadows and your distance from the equator.

> Note: This experiment works best on the summer solstice when the sun is in its highest position in the sky for the year.

> Estimated Time 20 Minutes

GEAR LIST

- Meter or yard stick, or a rod 3 to 5 feet long
- Carpenters' T-square to help measure a vertical position for your meter stick
- Tape
- String (at least twice as long as the stick)
- Protractor
- Large piece of paper or cardboard if you cannot adequately mark the ground
- Globe or world atlas
- A sunny day

1. Attach the string to the top of a stick approximately 3 to 5 feet long.
2. Push the stick into a level area of ground or use a stand to achieve a true vertical position.

3. Use the carpenters' T-square to help achieve this vertical position.

4. Find solar noon in your area by consulting your local newspaper or through going to http://solarnoon.com/ on the Internet.

5. At solar noon, pull the string taut to the end of the shadow of the stick, and then carefully secure the string to that point on the ground without tilting the stick.

Measure the length of your shadow. I put a ruler right on the ground and measured the shadow directly.

FYI *You can calculate solar noon for your location and time zone by knowing the exact midpoint between sunrise and sunset times.*

Determine the angle between your string and stick by using a protractor.

If math is your thing, you can use the trigonometry formula of $\cos x^{-1}$ of the length of shadow divided by height of stick.

In my case, in Central Park the angle was 40.5 degrees.

TIP: If you don't know your latitude and longitude, check http://terraserver-usa.com/

Determine the distance of your location from the equator by consulting a globe, an atlas, the Web, or use the math formula that I used for New York's Central Park.

By my calculations, New York's Central Park is 2794.3227 miles from the equator.

Here is the math formula that I used. My mind gets foggy when I hear the words *math formula*, but see if you can plug in your locations to this step-by-step formula.

We know that Central Park's latitude is 40 degrees 74 minutes north

Each degree=60 minutes of arc

1 minute of arc=1 nautical mile

40.74 (latitude of Central Park)×60 (minutes of arc)=2428.2 nautical miles from the equator to Central Park.

1 nautical mile=1.15077945 statue miles

2428.2 nautical miles×1.15077945=2794.3227 statue miles.

• Apply your information to the formula below and you will know the earth's circumference!

Multiply your distance to the equator by 360 degrees, and then divide by the measured angle at solar noon during the equinox. Your answer should be that the circumference around the poles is 24,860 miles.

In my case I multiplied 2794.3 (my distance to the equator) by 360, which yielded 1,005,948.

I divided by my solar noon angle of 40.5 degrees (1,005,948 ÷ 40.5) which yielded my result of 24,838 miles. Not bad, but obviously not as good as the Greek geographer Eratosthenes who did this many many years before me—without a calculator.

FYI *The true circumference of the earth at the equator is actually 24,902.4 miles (40,076.5 km), due to the earth's rotational speed and Earth's liquid outer core and solid inner. Did you know that Earth is the densest known planet in the solar system?*

The Hand of Time

No time to cry over a burnt battery!

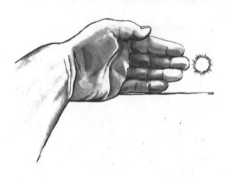

> *"Time is the stuff that life is made of, don't squander it."*
> Sign at Tara in *Gone With the Wind*

Sometimes I'm so intent on checking my packing list not once but twice to make sure I haven't forgotten a critical piece of gear that I've overlooked small items like replacing my watch battery. It's happened more than once. Only hours into the first day of a week's outback adventure and zap!—the face of my technologically genius wristwatch-altimeter goes black. Not only am I gypped of the moment-by-moment altitude and heart-rate updates from its internal wizardry, I also have no clue what time it is and how much trail time we have until it gets dark.

But then I learned a fun and simple trick to figure out how much time is left before sunset using only my knuckles as a guide. It's great for a late-day gag, although it took a bit of trial and error until I perfected this nifty night-predicting trick.

KNUCKLE SANDWICH TIME DIAL

Stand facing the sun with one arm pointing toward the horizon, thumb up and fingers straight. Keeping your fingers together, cup your hand creating a soft 90-degree angle (see the illustration on page 143). Look at your hand while placing your pinky on the horizon with the other fingers together stacked straight above.

Each finger-width represents five minutes. Count the number of fingers between the horizon and sun, and then multiply by five to get the approximate time remaining until sunset. You will amaze your pals at the beach! Good luck, but remember this is only a rough guide to approximate time. Its precision depends on latitude and hand size.

Getting to the Height of Things

Look through your legs to find the truth!

While trekking to the summit of Mount Kilimanjaro in Tanzania, Africa, I met a Chaga tribesman in his late 30s. He was tall for a Chaga, maybe 6 feet 2 inches, and he was eager to teach me an unusual method for measuring large objects like huts and trees. He was indeed a master, and I was honored to be his student. At about 15,000 feet, we came across an old and large volcanic plug called Lava tower, standing nearly 300 feet above the main trekking trail. For fun we used his method to measure it, which required no instruments.

Much to my surprise, his Triple Secret Squirrel system compared well to my GPS height reading (which isn't very good for measuring the height difference of small objects). Here's how his system worked: He stood near an object such as a tree and then strode about 20 feet away. In one fluid movement, he bent over to touch his toes and looked backward between his legs. With toes in tow, he shimmied forward and back, until the top of the object was even with the top of his crotch. Springing up, as if a gymnast completing a handspring, he paced out the distance from where he was standing to the object, and boom! He knew its height. Simply remarkable!

The Chaga tribesman enthusiastically shared his novel know-how, which he had learned from his dad. The secret, he whispered in a hushed tone, was bending over the same way every time and practicing with objects of which you already know the height.

Onward I went, bending and measuring. Not only did I nail this native technique, but my hamstrings were never more limber. With this user-friendly formula, you can practice until you get the feel.

- Find a practice object, with a height in feet that is equal to the number of paces you need to take away from it to accurately view in toe-touching, crotch-viewing, upside down position.

    For example, you could use an official basketball rim, which is always 10 feet tall and get into your position 10 paces away.

Note: You can adjust your position to get that 10:10 ratio. The most important thing is to be consistent in your positioning so you can use this method on other tall objects.

Simple Formula

- This formula applies to objects with a 1:1 ratio—when paces and height are the same. It is similar to using a "sextant" (See Chapter 16, Simple Sextant—Finding Your Latitude), or knowing how a right isosceles triangle works. All of these methods are based on the fact that at a 45-degree angle the height of an object is the same as the distance to its base.

    Number of paces from tree equals Tree height (feet)

Advanced Formula

This formula applies to objects with a disproportional ratio—when paces and height are different. So it may be 6:11 (when you need to take 6 paces to see an 11 foot tall object).

> • *Height of practice object* multiplied by *paces from object to be measured* divided by *pace from practice object* equals *height of object to be measured*

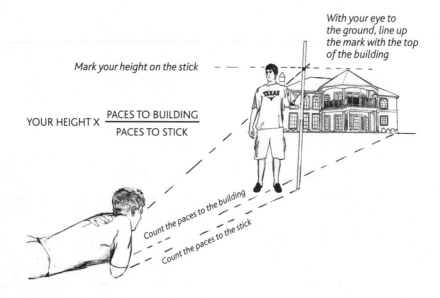

With your eye to the ground, line up the mark with the top of the building

Mark your height on the stick

YOUR HEIGHT X $\dfrac{\text{PACES TO BUILDING}}{\text{PACES TO STICK}}$

Count the paces to the building

Count the paces to the stick

Using a Stick

While I do like the crotch method for its originality and fond memories of my friendly Chaga tribesman, there is a more accurate version of this method.

Say you are trying to measure a building:

- Find an object of known length or height—for example, use a 5-foot stick.
- Have someone hold the stick upright, propped on the ground.
- Lie on your back, resting your head on your fist—knuckles vertical, with thumb down, pinkie up—and feet touching stick.
- In this position, scoot back—away from the stick—until the top of the stick is even with the top of the building you are measuring.

- Stand up and mark the spot where your head was resting.
- Count the paces from the position of your head to the base of the stick and get ready for some math to solve the equation.

    So, How Tall is the Building? To find the height of the building, you will need to calculate the ratio of paces to building, over paces to the stick. And you thought math was just for classrooms!

SIMPLE FORMULA

- *Paces to object to be measured* divided by *paces to object of known length or height* equals *height of object to be measured.*

The Paper Method

Here's a novel measuring method that uses a piece of paper. It combines the methodology of a sextant and our knowledge of a right isosceles triangle.

Say you are measuring a lamp post.

- Hold a standard size piece of paper (8.5 by 11 inches) horizontally and fold the top left corner to form a triangle (this is a right isosceles triangle). Then tear off the extra paper, so you have a clean triangle.
- Hold the triangle with the right angle on the lower side and facing the lamppost, with triangle bottom horizontal to the ground.
- Looking through one eye, back away from lamppost until you can see the tip of the lamppost from the top of the triangle (along the longest edge, or the *hypotenuse*, of the triangle).
- From this position, measure your distance to the lamppost with a measuring tape—or learn the length of your stride and use pacing to estimate.

SIMPLE FORMULA

The distance from your position to the lamppost equals the height of the lamppost.

The Shadow Method

This is my favorite method. Using the length of your shadow to find an object's height requires a strong sun, so it's best to do this one in the middle of the day, when the sun is overhead and shadows are relatively short and more manageable.

Let's say you want to measure a monument. If you try to climb it, you may get arrested, so don't even try. After all, knowing its height wouldn't be all that helpful if you were stuck in a tiny prison cell. Instead, do this.

- Start with an object of known height—yourself, for example.
- Measure the length of your shadow.
- Measure the length of the monument's shadow.

SIMPLE RATIO

Shadow of the monument = object height
    Your shadow   stick height

SIMPLE FORMULA

Height of monument's shadow multiplied by *your height* divided by *your shadow height* equals *monument height*.

Parting Thoughts

I get a kick out of knowing I can measure things any time, anywhere without needing to tote around a clumsy tape measure. Using my shadow as a ruler is one tool I'll never lose. Who would have thought geometry could be fun, useful, and everywhere?

PART IV

SHELTER

17 LEVITATION STATION

During a three-week trip to Ethiopia, I thanked my
hammock every night as I lay in its cozy, deep nest. While our group
relished learning about local culture, visiting historical places, and savoring the flavorful food, finding a clean and safe sleeping place often proved
challenging. In the villages, we often bedded-down on the dirt floors of
schools or beside less-than-sanitary buildings. While there, we occasionally snoozed among snakes and scorpions that were quite visible to the
discerning eye. I chose to sleep suspended above all of this mayhem.

A hammock is an ideal lightweight alternative to toting a bulky
tent or sleeping mat, and it allows you to slumber above ants, curious
critters, and pointy, wet rocks. Hammocks are also great space-savers
in tight quarters with limited floor space. I highly recommend learning how to transform a tarp and rope into a hammock.

Although there are many ways to make a hammock, here is an easy
and cheap method that won't spin, flip, and drop you. It may leave you

wondering why you ever slept on the ground. What better way to enjoy a good book or dream peacefully when camping, than in your very own hammock?

Building a Better Hammock!

GEAR LIST

- One bedding sheet, drape, or painting canvas, 8 feet or longer
- Two pieces of strong rope, 20 feet long and at least 3/8 inch in diameter

STEP 1: Gather Materials and Choose a Tree

With your sheet and rope, find a tree that is at least 3 feet in diameter with a neighboring tree roughly 14 feet away.

STEP 2: Tying a Half-Hitch or Overhand Loop Knot

Cut your rope into two 10-foot pieces. Fold one of the ropes in half. Hold the rope (see the illustration) and make a "bight" (the place where the folded or middle part of the rope bends together). Take the ends of the rope and form a loop over the bight.

Pass the ends around the bight and through the loop as seen in the illustration below.

Pull the end of the rope tight, creating an overhand loop knot.

Repeat this for the other section of rope.

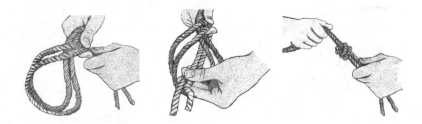

STEP 3: Stopper Knotting Your Sheets

Now that you know how to tie an overhand loop knot, use the same technique to tie a "stopper knot" at the ends of the sheet. The stopper knot keeps your hammock from slipping out of the ropes and dumping you on the ground. First, grab the end of the sheet and gather it together.

While holding the gathered end in one hand, pull the sheet through with the other hand—about 3 feet.

Next, tie an overhand loop knot as shown in Step 2. Pull knot tight and repeat on other sheet end so both ends have stopper knots.

STEP 4: Attaching Ropes to Trees

Hold the rope at one end, forming a small loop to one side of the knot and a long loop to the other side of the knot.

Next, hold the small loop at the knot, placing it against the back of the tree. Bring the long loop around the tree, in the opposite direction from the small loop, and pass it through the small loop.

Pull the long loop tight, creating tension between the bark and rope. Your rope should look like the illustration on page 154, with a 4 foot loop dangling in front of the tree. Repeat this step on the other tree.

STEP 5: Tying the Lark Knot

You should now have two ropes tied around two trees. Both ropes should have 4-foot loops facing one another. Before tying a lark knot on the ropes, fetch your sheet and lay it out with the stopper knots pointing toward the trees. Keep the sheets within reach, so you can grab it as you tie the rope. After laying out the sheet, pick up one of your ropes with a loop, holding it so you have about 2 feet dangling in one hand. Take the other hand and pull the loop up and over, folding the loop back onto itself so it creates two "eye glass" smaller loops (see the illustration).

Next, push the "eye glass" loops down to the sides (keeping a 6--inch hole in the loop center), as seen in the illustration. Hold this loop shape in one hand, while picking up the sheet with your free hand. Then push your sheet stopper knot through the hole, while holding the lark knot.

STEP 6: Connecting Rope Knots to the Sheet Knots

You are one minute away from sitting pretty in your levitation station. All you need to do is slide your sheet stopper knot through the lark knot loop, and then pull the lark knot tight so that it catches on the stopper knot. Your sheet and rope should look like the illustration.

Repeat this step with the other rope, creating an identical lark knot with the other loop. Keep in mind that you want your sheet to be tight and elevated in the air—not sagging on the ground. You may have to play with the length of your lark knot on the other end to properly tweak the elevation. Once you are happy with the length of your lark knot, push the other sheet with its stopper knot through your lark knot. Pull it tight and your sheet should be about three feet above the ground. Congratulations! Climb in and enjoy your hammock.

NOTE: If you are sleeping in a rainy area, make a tarp roof for your hammock by stringing the tarp through the small eyeholes along its edge and around branches above the hammock. Secure the tarp with thin twine rope and angle it so the rainwater slides onto the ground and doesn't pool over your sleepy head. Also, to prevent "flipping," do not over-tighten the ropes. The hammock should be a comfortable nest that gives with your body weight.

If you find yourself in a desert, and you have no trees, innovation plays a big role.

During my expedition to Ethiopia we camped in many places where there were no trees, so on several occasions I tied my hammock between cars (tied to their bumpers) or to metal bars on buildings.

18 HOW TO BUILD AN IGLOO

You don't need to be an Inuit elder to build an igloo.
The small domed snow house most of us have seen in cartoons and
movies can be constructed in a few hours with the right weather and
tools. Believe it or not, an igloo is a cozy, warm place to spend a blustery winter night in the mountains or high Arctic. Igloos are warmer
than tents, less vulnerable to wind conditions, and quieter, too. Because igloos are made from snow, which has a lot of air spaces among
the flakes, they are excellent insulators. The snow also absorbs sound,
unlike wind-whipped flapping tents.

Aside from being fairly easy to create, building an igloo is one of
the few outdoor activities where weather conditions assist in making
shelter. Here are three types of igloos to accommodate a variety of
snow conditions. The amount of snow in your area will dictate which
is the best and easiest igloo for you to construct.

Bucket Igloo

GEAR LIST

- Snow
- Shovel
- Plastic bucket (or garbage pail)

When I was growing up on Long Island, New York, snowfall was typically measured in inches rather than feet, so my chances for making an authentic Eskimo igloo were rather slim. My first attempt to make one involved using a rectangular garbage can to mash the snow into blocks, which I stacked on top of each other. I learned quickly that powdery snow won't stick or clump together. To resolve this, I sprinkled a little water on the snow, making it heavier and easier to "pack."

STEP 1: Fill the bucket with snow and pack the snow down.

STEP 2: Turn the bucket upside down and slam the edge on a paved surface (like road or driveway), until it loosens and falls out, creating a perfectly shaped rectangular snow block. It may initially be too soft to pick up, but after a few minutes in the cold air, it will harden enough to be moved.

FYI *Instead of banging the bucket on the ground, cut a hole in the bottom of the bucket big enough for your hand to fit through and ease the snow out. This will also limit damage to the block. Also, using a tapered container helps with block release.*

STEP 3: Stack the blocks to form a wall. Some tips are given in the following sections.

Artic Igloo

GEAR LIST

- Snow shovel
- Snow saw (or carpenter's saw)
- Ice axe or pick
- Warm and waterproof clothing and snow boots
- Lots of clean snow
- Cold temperatures—(ideally, the temperature needs to be below 32° F for the blocks to harden)

STEP 1: Locate an open area with plenty of snow.

STEP 2: Using boots, snowshoes, or skis, smash down a big circle in the snow (about 15 feet in diameter). This will be your work site.

STEP 3: Mark a circle for your igloo nearby.

STEP 4: Using a shovel or your hands (wear gloves!), dig a couple feet into the snow within the circle to form the lower portion of the igloo.

STEP 5: For the entrance, dig a ditch (about 40 inches) extending from the circle. It should be long enough to lay in and twice as deep, ideally facing away from wind to limit heat loss. Use loose snow to layer the top of igloo once it is built.

STEP 6: Cut large blocks of snow from quarry, using the largest blocks for the edge of the igloo circle. This is the beginning of your sturdy foundation.

FYI *Cutting an arch into the bottom of each block allows it to flatten as the structure settles, creating a tighter bond.*

STEP 7: Use slightly smaller blocks for the next set, which gets placed atop the lower blocks in a spiral formation. Gradually decrease the block size, so the structure leans in, forming a dome. Be sure to leave enough space in the entrance to allow easy access. Build a basic tunnel over your trench.

STEP 8: Upon reaching the top portion of the igloo, it may be necessary to spend more time shaping the bricks to accommodate their smaller size. It can be easier to place bricks from inside, rather than struggling around the contours of the igloo's exterior. Ideally, the final block, which should be cut at a heavily inward angle like the lid of a Jack-O'-Lantern, should be placed directly on top of the igloo.

STEP 9: Fill in cracks and holes with surrounding snow and delicately trim protruding areas inside to prevent dripping as the temperature rises above freezing.

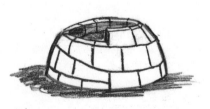

FYI *If you plan to use a torch-lit stove or a gas lantern, make a couple of small holes high up on the igloo for ventilation. Never build a fire in your igloo! The increased temperature could cause it to collapse, and smoke inhalation can be extremely dangerous.*

Your igloo will warm up naturally after a night or two, but to expedite the process, pour a bit of water on the exterior before dark. The water will freeze overnight, creating an icy shell to protect against the elements.

After resting for a couple of days, a well-built igloo should hold firm under your weight—if you are not built like a professional linebacker—when you need to climb atop to see if there's a Marriot or IHOP in sight.

North Pole Parachute Igloo

Not many people own a parachute, but you can buy a surplus military parachute for about $50. Several years ago, while cross-country skiing to the North Pole, I learned about this great shelter technique from my expedition leader, Paul Schurke, and his son, Peter.

Unlike what you may expect, the parachute tent wasn't thick or waterproof. Schurke senior explained that a water proof parachute in a snow shelter creates condensation—your biggest enemy. I have literally seen it snow inside a tent when large amounts of moisture were not allowed to escape. If it's not going to rain, being waterproof is an irrelevant feature. Here's how it works.

GEAR LIST

- Surplus military parachute
- Snow shovel
- Pole (or straight tree branch)

STEP 1: Dig a big ditch in the snow, a few feet smaller than the diameter of your parachute. On our North Pole trip, the hole was about 4 or 5 feet deep, except around the perimeter where it was 3 feet deep so we could build snow benches. They were nice for lunching and sunning like a penguin.

STEP 2: Dig a trench for the entrance on the opposite side of prevailing winds, or at an angle to block incoming wind.

STEP 3: Place the parachute over the main ditch and cover the edges, which are known as the apron, with plenty of snow to keep the parachute from taking off in the wind.

STEP 4: Place a pole (or a solid tree branch) in the center of the dug-out area underneath the parachute and extend the pole, reinforcing the bottom to make it taught. This should raise the parachute, creating an umbrella big enough for people to sit or walk around.

STEP 3: With a shovel, carve a circular snow bench near the edges and pack excess snow against the wall inside of the tent to create a sturdy backrest. Not only will it provide seating, it also adds insulation.

Parting Thoughts

Winter camping can be a wonderful experience. It's magical to be outdoors, with the snow muffling surrounding sounds, hearing only the quiet of nature, and seeing stars in the winter sky that are not visible at other times of the year. Ultimately, it leaves you with a rugged feeling. I often feel like I am a character in a Jack London novel, listening to the calls of the wild.

PART V

FOOD

19 YOUR FIRST MEAL OUTDOORS

Feeding outrageous outdoor appetites!

Although I live in New York City, a metropolis of world-class chefs and exotic cuisine, some of my most memorable meals have been in the wilderness. Going to a fancy four-star restaurant can be a nice treat, but it doesn't compare to savoring a fire-cooked steak while sitting on the edge of a canyon. After a full day of hauling my thirty-pound pack over dusty trails, the colors seem brighter, fragrances are stronger, and food tastes better. Beyond the calories burned, it's the feeling of having earned my meal that flames the flavors and makes the taste so much better than if I had eaten that same steak at my kitchen table or in a great steakhouse. And part of the adventure is making mealtime special.

I try to eat outdoors every chance I can get. When I can't eat in a field in a faraway country, I fill my pack with my favorite food and trek to Central Park in New York City. Sometimes I even make the settings very formal.

The most memorable meals I have eaten have been in the outdoors. I remember being on an ice breaker in Antarctica on a sunny Christmas day, sitting on the deck with friends and looking at stunning views of glaciers and mountains. Another favorite was eating dinner around a campfire (a "boma") after a full day on safari in Africa. The brilliant sunset, the warmth and light from the flames, and the canopy of stars were all intoxicating, and I was mesmerized by the potent roar of lions in the distance. Everything tastes better outdoors.

Eating outdoors doesn't mean you need a banquet fit for a food critic. And although you need to go light, bring things you like, including a few favorite treats. Believe me, it's more comforting than you can imagine. By my third day al fresco, I've had my fill of nuts and berries, and I crave, yes, a nice pan-fried trout or a big slab of beef. After years of going without, I finally figured out how to bring such pleasures with me. Well, sort of.

The big question most people ask is what can I make? The truth is that anything that can be can cooked in a kitchen can be cooked at a campsite.

The Meals

A Big Breakfast

In the backcountry, I always start my day with a belly-filling breakfast, combining carbs and protein, to fuel me up. My appetite seems to grow when I'm sleeping outside, and I wake up with the appetite of a bear after a long hibernation. Some of my favorite starters are breakfast burritos, scrambled eggs and bacon (with toast), and blueberry pancakes. When I want an extra shot of protein, I wrap my pancake around a steaming sausage straight off the griddle. Sometimes, there's no time for cooking, so granola with nuts, raisins, and fruit does the trick. Pack along energy bars, trail mix, and jerky to nibble on the move. It will hold you until you stop for lunch.

A Light Lunch

Keep lunch easy. Bring deli meat, cheese, and PB&J (which is great even when it gets squished) for sandwiches. I sometimes pack along a jar of

Nutella for a chocolate-hazelnut twist. Sandwiches are easy to whip up in the morning and tuck in the side pocket of your pack. I sometimes bring tuna in foil packs. Just rip off the top and dig in with a plastic fork (be sure to bring a plastic bag in which to seal the stinky, empty container). Some chips, fruit, and nuts and will leave you revved for a fun, energetic afternoon. Beware of mayonnaise as it spoils easily in warm conditions.

A Delectable Dinner

I look forward to dinnertime. Not only am I starving from a full day on the go, but it's also fun to rehash the day's events while chopping and grilling alongside my fellow travelers.

On day or weekend trips, I typically prep meals at home to keep it simple. I'll grill chicken breasts or steak, boil some eggs, and stuff sacks with portioned chopped fresh vegetables, fruit, seasoned rice, potatoes, pasta, or couscous. Anything that can be cooked over a flame or in a Dutch oven is ideal. I toss in a few rolls of frozen pop-up bread, and dinner is served.

Jim Read, an outdoor enthusiast and spokesman for Coleman, the world's leading manufacturer of portable stoves, once said that one-pot meals can be a godsend for first-time campers. He suggested that beginners cook or buy hearty stews or chili at home and just reheat them at camp. Boil up pasta or rice, bake bread, and you have a hearty meal. Dried cheeses that are easy to transport and preserve, like Parmesan and Reggiano, add a spark of flavor to your outdoor dining.

Delicious Desserts

There are heaps of desserts that require only a plastic knife or spoon to be conveniently consumed even from the cock of a kayak or on a road trip. Everyone loves S'mores—marshmallows and chocolate melted between two graham crackers—but there are other decadent treats to chose from. Here are some of my favorite camping desserts.

1. *Peanut butter apple s'mores.* Smear a gob of peanut butter on two apple slices, stick a marshmallow in the middle and squish.
2. *Adirondack banana goo.* Make a lengthwise slit in an over-ripened banana (skin on) and stuff with chocolate chips,

marshmallow, and nuts. Cook the banana over the medium-heat portion of the fire. Don't worry if the skin of the banana burns a little because you will be eating only the warm, melted concoction inside.

3. *Baked apples.* Core the top of an apple, leaving the bottom untouched. Fill with equal amounts of butter, sugar, and nuts (optional). Wrap in aluminum foil and let bake near the fire for 15 to 20 minutes, occasionally rotating.

My all-time favorite is an Oreo cheesecake substitute. I call it Oreo cheese naughty.

OREO CHEESE NAUGHTY!

INGREDIENTS

- Cream cheese (soft in tub recommended)
- Oreo cookies
- Jam (red raspberry recommended, but any flavor will suffice)

Hold a plastic knife in your dominant hand, and an Oreo cookie gently in the other. Being careful not to crush the cookie, carefully spread cream cheese on top, add a healthy dollop of red raspberry jam, open mouth wide and stuff in—or go the civil route, and nibble away.

Easy Camp Cooking Tips

There are countless camp cooking tips to be found in books, on the Internet, and from experienced friends. Many of the Boy Scout recipes are geared toward simplicity and hearty appetites. The most important thing is to plan ahead and to prepare simple, filling, daily meals. Remember, your appetite is always bigger on the trail.

Before Hitting the Trail

- Planning is key, so write down a menu for all the meals you'll prepare during your trip. This helps you pack and remember key ingredients.

- Zip-lock plastic bags rule! I use different sizes to store and carry dry ingredients, cereal, sauces, soups, chili, Oreo cookies, and much more.
- Premeasure dry ingredients—such as rice, pasta, potatoes— for each meal ahead of time.
- Prep all veggies—chop onions, peppers, carrots, etc.
- Label each bag with a Sharpie or other waterproof pen, and reuse bags, if possible.
- Wrap food in aluminum foil to make "packet meals" that can be tossed on the fire.

   This is a great way to cook sliced potatoes, onions, carrots, or zucchini. Season them with salt and pepper—and perhaps butter—seal the ends well, and roast. You can use the foil for leftovers, too.
- Repackage just-add-hot-water meals in a heavy-duty zip-lock plastic freezer bag and use for cooking. Their sturdy construction allows them to hold hot water.
- Pack meals that can be precooked at home and survive your journey. Precooked meats last longer in the cooler than raw meats.
- Always bring extra matches (or lighters). Learn to build a fire without matches (See Chapter 5, Fire).

Important Things to Know!

- Block ice lasts longer than cubed ice, but freezing water bottles is even better because you can drink them when they thaw.
- Disposable water bottles have many uses. I have used them as dispensers for sauces, marinates, salad dressings, and oils.
- Cover pots whenever cooking outdoors to allow food to cook quicker. This trick not only saves fuel, but keeps dirt and insects out of your food.
- Before using pots over an open fire, wash them with soap powder paste, soft soap, or liquid dish soap on the outside of the pot to allow soot to easily wash off.
- To evenly cook hamburgers, make a finger-sized hole in the middle of burger. The hole will close during grilling and the center will be cooked the same as the edges.
- Bring no-cook food like granola, cereal, nuts, and dried fruit.

- Pita bread holds up better than sliced bread. Try baking frozen pop-up bread in a Dutch oven or in a bag (See Chapter 20, Baking Bread in a Bag).
- Freeze-dried foods are lightweight, easy, and tasty—and there are hundreds of choices, from chili to lasagna. Another alternative is to buy vacuum-sealed food in supermarkets like tuna fish or salmon. It's basically the same as canned food without the weight and bulk of a tin.

Suggested Cooking Gear List

- Quality camp stove. Propane stoves are the standard and are easiest to use. White gas stoves, which are commonly used at high altitudes and in extremely cold weather, produce more heat.
- Sponge with a scrubber on one side for pot and dish washing.
- Ultrathin plastic cutting board. The roll-up types are ideal.
- Sharp knives for preparing food and cutting meat. A folding (locking) pocketknife is ideal. (The locking mechanism prevents the blade from accidentally opening.)
- Store food in air-tight containers away from your campsite or hang it from a tree to avoid unwanted animal visits.
- Aluminum pots, Dutch ovens, and—my absolute favorite—lightweight aluminum pressure cookers. I use models from an outdoor cooking gear company named GSI. They have really expanded my outdoor cooking horizons. Pressure cookers in particular are probably the most fool-proof. I have found that pressure cookers turn the toughest of meat into a tender treat. During fishing trips when I have been less than lucky, I have thrown a little of this and that into my pressure cooker and have ended up with some nice meals.

HAND THERMOMETER

- To determine the cooking temperature of coals or a Dutch oven, hold your palm over coal or Dutch oven and count "one-and-one, two-and-two . . . ," and so forth, until it starts to feel uncomfortably warm. Use the Boy Scout cooking table to determine the temperature.

Seconds Counted	Heat	Temperature
6–8	Slow	250–350° F
4 or 5	Moderate	350–400° F
2 or 3	Hot	400–450° F
1 or less	Very hot	450–500° F

Bear-Proofing Your Campsite

Bears have an uncanny sense of smell. In fact, a polar bear can smell a seal up to 20 miles away. This sniffing savvy enables bears to detect and seek out your precious edibles. So hide your chocolate bars!

Bears have a sense of smell that is much more sophisticated than that of humans. In fact researchers say that a bear's sense of smell is seven times greater than that of a bloodhound's.

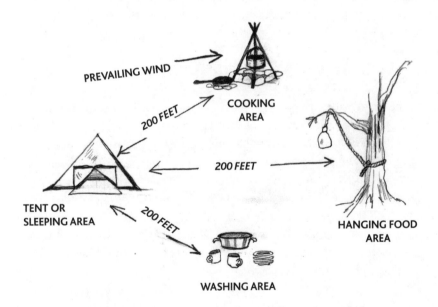

Bear-proofing your camp to minimize odors that might attract bears or other animals is a critical outdoor skill to master. Most important, never leave food and beverages unattended. Leaving strong-smelling fare such as fish, cheese, sausage, and fresh meats unattended is like ringing a dinner bell for bears. These items should be stored in a food cache, a bear-resistant container, hung at least 10 feet above the ground. As much as it may seem like an unpleasant chore, carry all refuse and garbage out! It is also tempting to bury refuse, but with their keen sense of smell, it will attract bears. The idea is to set up safe storage areas for food and garbage that are out of reach of bears and far away from where you are sleeping because you don't want to be considered as an alternative dish. For best results, follow the camp set up shown in the illustration on page 171.

Award Winning Camp Recipes

One of my all-time favorite recipes is Road Kill Moose, also called Happy Trails Hunters Stew. It was created by Kathy Chaponton, the wife of four-time Iditarod Champion, Martin Buser. The Iditarod is the longest dogsled race in the world, covering nearly 1,200 miles across Alaska's unforgiving backcountry, from Anchorage to Nome, with temperatures dipping as low as −60° F. Buser is one tough dude.

In 2004, I was visiting Alaska and was invited to join Martin on a training run. He was going out with 24 dogs, instead of the usual 12, to determine which dogs were performing best so he could assemble his A-team for the Iditarod.

It was a typical brisk December day in Palmer, Alaska. At that time of the year the sun is only around for a few hours, and the dogs were frisky and fired up to get going. Sled dogs are perhaps the greatest creatures of the north. These fluffy, muscular athletes are highly motivated, strong for their size, and extremely affectionate. They make great pals!

Nearly three hours into our training run, upon reaching a huge frozen lake, Martin halted the team. In the blink of an eye, he hopped off the sled, jumped on a snowmobile and shouted "See you on the other end!" as his voice faded into the dry, frigid air. Ugh! It was my turn to go it alone.

My head was swimming with excitement and my body was shaking with nerves. Tentatively stepping onto the driver's ledge at the back of the sled, I took a deep breath and meagerly whispered "Mush." Good things dog have highly sensitive hearing. Swoosh! We were off! Luckily, the dogs seemed to know the way. I held on and hoped they really knew where to go. It was one of the most exhilarating experiences of my life! All I could hear were dogs panting and the blades of my sledge whooshing over the frozen snow and ice. Above us, the Aurora Borealis (Northern Lights) danced in the sky. It was magical. Thirty minutes later, we hooked up with Martin on the other side of the lake.

Later, after the dogs were fed and bedded down for the night, I joined Kathy and Martin at their home for some hearty home cooking and Alaskan hospitality. Kathy whipped up one of the best stews I have ever eaten. No ordinary stew, it was Road Kill Moose Stew.

In Alaska, large animals like moose are frequently hit by speeding cars and trucks as they try to cross highways from behind tall snowy banks. Many highway departments have a list of nonprofit organizations and individuals who are willing to come to the site and haul away the beasts. The rule of the game is that you usually have to pick it up within 20 minutes or the next person on the list is called.

Road Kill Moose is about as healthy a meat as you will ever eat. It's hormone-free, low in fat, and fresh. Kathy's recipe came from Charlie Womack, who was a chef in Tennessee.

Do I feel bad for the moose? Yes. But the best way to turn that frown upside down is to transform a tragic situation into good eating. Here's how you can make your own stew.

Happy Trails Hunter Stew
(Aka: Road Kill Stew)
By Kathy Chaponton, Palmer, Alaska

INGREDIENTS

1 pound carrots, sliced
8 small potatoes
3 ribs celery, sliced

6 medium onions, chopped

6 cloves garlic, minced

2 teaspoons chili powder

2 cups water

3 pounds boneless beef stew meat

1 pound boneless pork

6 slices bacon

3 (16-ounce) cans of tomatoes

1 can of Rotel tomatoes (adjust for taste—these are hot!)

4 ounces Worcestershire sauce

Salt to taste

1 pound frozen peas

1 pound frozen green beans

1 pound frozen corn

1 pound fresh or frozen sliced okra

GEAR LIST

- Large, heavy pot with snug-fitting lid
- Long wooden or plastic spoon
- Sharp knife
- Cutting board
- Can opener
- Paper towels

PREPARATION

1. Slice carrots, potatoes, and celery, and put aside with chopped onions and minced garlic. Stir chili powder into 2 cups of water, until smooth.
2. Cut meat into ½-inch cubes and put aside.
3. Using a large heavy pot, fry the bacon until it is crisp. Remove the bacon and lay it on paper towels to drain off excess fat. Add the cubed meat, and brown it quickly in the hot bacon fat. Reduce the heat, add tomatoes, onions, celery, garlic, the chili powder solution, Worcestershire sauce, and salt to taste. Cover and cook over very low heat until meat is tender, about 2 hours. **Note:** keep the pot covered for the entire cooking time.

4. Add the potatoes and carrots; cook until tender.
5. Add the peas, beans, corn, and okra. Cook another 15 minutes. Serves 8 really hungry men. *Mangia!*

Estimated cook time: 2:30 hours

In 2006, I was one of five judges on the panel of the Redwood Creek Campfire Classic, a national outdoor cooking contest. Sponsored by Redwood Creek Winery, contestants were challenged to create gourmet recipes that could be cooked outdoors. Five finalists were then flown to New York City to go head-to-head at the grand campfire cookout championship, and I was blown away by their creative dishes.

Lorie Roach, from Buckatunna, Mississippi, won with her Sweet Onion, Apple, and Bratwurst Campfire Chili. Thinking about the savory smoky stew still brings a smile to my lips. I have cooked them all, but I have to say none compare to my favorite Road Kill Stew recipe. The event was so much fun that I returned the next year as a spectator, not only to fill my belly, but to learn new recipes to take on my own camping trips.

Here are the two winning recipes from both years. They make savory trailside suppers and are relatively easy to make.

Redwood Creek Campfire Classic Recipes—Winner 2006

Sweet Onion, Apple, and Bratwurst Campfire Chili

By Lorie Roach, Buckatunna, Mississippi

INGREDIENTS

6 slices peppered bacon
6 bun-length Bratwurst sausages, sliced into bite-size pieces (about 1 pound)
1 medium sweet onion, chopped
2 large Granny Smith apples, peeled and chopped
1/2 medium green bell pepper, chopped
1/2 medium red bell pepper, chopped

2 cloves garlic, minced

$^1/_3$ cup light brown sugar

2 (16-ounce) cans of garbanzo beans (chickpeas), drained

1 teaspoon onion powder

1 teaspoon garlic powder

1 teaspoon salt

1 teaspoon pepper

$1^1/_2$ cups shredded white cheddar cheese

Crusty bread, if desired

GEAR LIST

- Dutch oven with lid
- Wooden spoon

PREPARATION

1. At home, slice the sausage, chop the onion, peel and chop the apples, chop the peppers, and mince the garlic. Store each ingredient separately in sealed plastic bags.
2. On a grill rack over a medium-height campfire, cook the bacon in the Dutch oven until crisp. Crumble it and set it aside.
3. Add the bratwurst to the pot and cook until it is brown and crispy around edges. Add onion and next four ingredients (apples, green bell pepper, red bell pepper, and garlic). Cover and cook for about 5 minutes or until vegetables are soft.
4. Sprinkle with brown sugar and continue to cook until sugar melts, stirring well. Stir in the beans, onion powder, garlic powder, salt, and pepper. Cook uncovered for about 10 minutes, stirring often. Remove from the campfire.
5. To serve, ladle into four bowls and top with shredded white cheddar cheese and bacon bits. Serve with crusty bread, if desired.

Estimated cook time: 45 minutes

Coal-Roasted Chuckbox Pazole-Stuffed Onions

By Leah Lyon, Ada, Oklahoma

INGREDIENTS

4 extra-large sweet onions

1 pound thinly cut pork sirloin steak, cubed

2 teaspoons coarse kosher salt

Black pepper to taste

$1/2$ teaspoon ground cumin

1 cup boxed cornbread stuffing mix

2 tablespoons mild green chile powder

3 large poblano chiles, roasted, peeled, and seeded

1 (15.5 ounce) can of hominy, drained

$1/4$ cup sweet red pepper, chopped

$1/2$ cup aged cotija cheese, grated

Cilantro for garnish (optional)

Avocado for garnish (optional)

GEAR LIST

- Measuring cup
- Ice cream scoop or spoon
- Foil
- Sharp knife
- Large mixing bowl
- Can opener
- Small fire shovel
- Meat thermometer (optional)

PREPARATION

1. Slice the tops off the onions one quarter of the way down, and slice the roots from the bottom so they sit without rolling over. Peel the skins from the onions. Cut an X into the center of each onion, using a spoon or ice cream scoop to remove the center portion, leaving walls approximately $1/2$-inch thick. Dice $1/4$ cup of onion from the centers and store the remaining onion for use in another recipe.

2. Mix the diced onion with pork, salt, pepper, cumin, stuffing mix, chile powder, poblano chiles, hominy, red pepper, and cheese. Fill each onion bowl with mixture. Wrap the onions in large squares of heavy-duty foil, bringing the seams together on top by flattening the foil slightly. Keep the wrapped onions upright and nestle each one on hot coals. With a small shovel, top each onion with a few hot coals.

3. Cook approximately 30 minutes, or until a meat thermometer inserted into the center registers between 175° and 180° F. Remove the onions from the coals, carefully open the foil, and serve. Garnish with cilantro and avocado, if desired. This dish serves 4 campers. Enjoy!

Estimated cook time: 30 minutes

Foraging

Central Park Coffee

I enjoy savoring a warming cup of coffee at the start of each day, especially if I'm out in the field. It tastes even better when my brew comes from a few coffee bean pods that I've actually foraged for. I've found Kentucky coffee trees just a few blocks from my New York City apartment.

The red-brown coffee been pods (about 10 inches long), resemble flattened pea pods and can be found scattered on the ground under tall, skinny Kentucky coffee trees. During the American Civil War (1861–1865), war hero George Rogers was craving a cup of java—which was unavailable during wartime—so he planted coffee trees.

Native to the Midwest, the scaly, gray-brown barked Kentucky coffee trees grow to about 60 or 80 feet and in late spring sprout greenish-white flowers. By October, the ripe pods are ready for collecting and roasting. Each pod contains about six seeds (or beans) that are packed in slimy green goo, which easily rinses off.

> **!** *Raw seeds from Kentucky Coffee trees are toxic prior to roasting, so never eat them raw.*
>
> *Industrial coffee producers often air-dry or soak beans in fermentation tanks. I prefer to keep it simple and roast them in a skillet.*
>
> *Roasting makes them edible and flavorful, although "Central Park Coffee" is definitely an acquired taste.*

PREPARATION

Remove the beans from their pods and rinse them thoroughly, until the green goo is gone.

GEAR LIST

- Nonstick omelet pan with lid
- Sturdy aluminum foil
- Long wooden spoon
- Paper towels
- Coffee grinder
- Blender
- Coffee maker
- Coffee cup
- Milk and sugar, optional

Cover the bottom of the pan with aluminum foil and spread the cleaned beans on top of it. Do not worry if they bunch up, but do not pile them too deep or they won't roast evenly. Cover the pan with a snug-fitting lid or aluminum foil.

I like roasting my beans at 450° F for about 70 minutes, or until they turn very dark—but are not burned. These are much thicker than normal coffee beans. You'll know it's working when you hear the beans steaming and crackling. Next, you will smell the wonderful fragrance. Keep a close watch toward the end so they don't burn.

Once done, spread the beans out on doubled-up paper towels to cool and dry. Since the shells of the Kentucky coffee beans are much tougher than conventional coffee beans, you may not be able to grind them in a conventional grinder. I sometimes use a blender to break them up before putting them in the grinder. You might want to use a scoop more than you would of your typical grind, as it's a bit weak. Finally, add milk and sugar, if that's your thing, and savor the flavor of your very own homebrewed decaf coffee.

Many plants such as coffee, cacao, and tea trees have an alkaloid like caffeine to protect them from insects. Trees like the Kentucky coffee tree does not have that alkaloid, so its beans are naturally decaffeinated.

Other Coffee Substitutes

If the devil's brew—coffee—is not your preferred potion, look around. Mother Nature offers countless sassy bean brewing alternatives. Some are as easy to prepare as scoop, spark, and sip.

CHICORY

Chicory, also known as "blue-sailors," is a Mediterranean herb that's popular in places like New Orleans, Louisiana, and it is often added to coffee to enrich it with its notable bitter chocolate flavors. Widely grown in Europe, the blue-flowered herb (sometimes lavender in color) has a long, thick white root (naturally caffeine-free) that can be roasted and powdered.

Chicory grows abundantly along roadsides and in open fields. Its bright-colored flowers open and close precisely at the same time daily, making it easy to spot. I often pull over and pick some on road trips.

Simply dig up a plant and cut off the leaves, and then peel the roots and slice them into thin strips. Place in oven at 250° F for about 4 hours, turning the pan periodically to achieve an even roast. Cool and finely grind the roasted roots.

PREPARATION

Add one teaspoon of chicory to every cup of water and boil for 3 minutes.

GARBANZO BEANS

Generally found growing in central California (or on your market shelf), garbanzo beans are good on a salad or teamed with tahini to make a mean hummus spread. Garbanzo beans also make a tasty sipping treat. Roast raw beans at 300° F until they are dark brown. Finely grind them and brew as you would a standard pot of Joe.

BEACH TREE NUTS

Commonly found across America, with the exception of desert regions, Beach trees produce nuts that can also be made into a rather tart but digestible beverage. They are also used to brew Budweiser beer.

    Remove the nuts from husks with your fingers and roast them until they are dark and crumbly. Finely grind them and brew. Store remaining grinds in airtight container for future use.

BARLEY

Roast barley (leave the husks on) on a cookie sheet in a 425° F oven until the color changes from light tan to dark tan, stirring often. Grind the barley and fix yourself a steaming cup as you would with typical grounds.

SWEET POTATO

Even a sweet potato can be made into a passable coffee substitue. Peel the potatoes and slice them into thin strips. Bake them at 350° F until crisp but not burned. Cut the dried slices into bits and grind them. It's not all that powerful in taste, but it's great to bulk-up a depleted supply of coffee.

PARSNIPS

Chock-full of potassium and closely resembling a carrot, parsnips have been a staple of the Eurasian diet for centuries. The Ancient Romans believed parsnips to have aphrodisiac properties—so choose your sipping partner wisely.

    Although it can be made into beer and wine, the easiest way to turn this vegetable into a drink is to chop a bunch of fresh, unpeeled roots into a coleslaw-like consistency. Dehydrate the bits and roast at 400° F until dark brown. Cool them at room temperature and steep in hot water for a surprisingly flavorful treat.

20 THE PAPER BAG SCHOOL OF COOKING

I have fantasized about taking a camping trip where all my meals were prepared in paper bags. It would be so cool. I imagine arriving at camp after a long day's trek, pulling a premade meal-in-a-bag from my backpack, and roasting it on some hot coals until the entire campsite was filled with enticing aromas, indicating dinnertime. After chowing, just burn the bag. Poof! I could do the same for all my meals and, voilà, go home with zero garbage.

Cooking in paper is a terrific camping technique that dates back to the turn of the last century. Back in 1911, *The New York Times* ran an article about several methods of cooking food in foil and paper—sort of a 101 ways to use a paper bag. The Gray Lady exclaimed, "The day may be coming when our kitchens shall no longer be hung with pots and pans." Suddenly, fancy aluminum pans purchased from the Sears and Roebuck catalog were no longer in vogue, and foil and paper became culinary chic. With aprons in a flurry, Americans and Europeans began cooking anything and everything in ordinary parcel paper—fish and fruit, and poultry and peas, beef and bulgar. Even King George V of England (1910–1936), was served paper bag–cooked meals. I wonder if he knew?

Cooking in paper is still popular in some places and is surprisingly versatile in the wild. I first tried cooking microwave popcorn (that was a no brainer!), which was successful and gave me confidence to forge ahead. Next, I experimented with a Swiss cheese omelet—another winner! Fish was a bit trickier, as it needed to be wrapped tightly in paper or to be stewed in broth. Once I got the hang of cooking fish in a bag it became my favorite paper-bag meal. But then I discovered frozen crescent dough (thank you, Pillsbury Dough Boy). One of my best creations resulted from wrapping dough around butter and raisins, tucking it in a paper bag, and burying it in coals for 15 minutes. It was some of the best bread I ever had. I even know people who have cooked whole turkeys in paper bags. Once you learn how to cook this way, you'll never look back.

- The most important thing to know about cooking paper (brown lunch bags work great) is that the paper always needs to be wet before placing it on hot coals. With many recipes it helps to rub it all over with olive oil. Expect it to smoke and char on the bottom, but it won't burn.

Why Paper Does Not Burn

Paper will not burn until it reaches a temperature greater than 400° F, because it conducts the heat from the coals immediately to the water. Water boils at 212° F. So, if you place water in a damp paper carton and heat it over coals, in theory, you'll have boiling water in a bag. I recommend trying this first at home, outdoors, on a grill, before heading out into the woods.

This is a great experiment to show how water acts as a coolant.

The Great Balloon Experiment

GEAR LIST

- 2 balloons
- Matches

Inflate one balloon and hold it to a lit match. Bang! As expected, it will burst immediately. Take the second balloon and fill it with water. Again, hold it to a lit match, as you did the first. Surprise! The balloon will not burst. Cooking in a paper bag uses the same principle.

Cowboy Bacon and Eggs in a Paper Bag

INGREDIENTS

4 thick slices bacon
2 eggs
1 brown paper lunch bag

GEAR LIST

- 3-foot stick
- Hot coals

PREPARATION

Place the bacon inside the bottom of a brown lunch bag (wipe the sides of the bag with bacon grease) and crack an egg on top of the bacon. Fold the bag down three or four times and cut a hole through it with the stick, so that the paper bag is hanging on one end of the stick (green pine is great because it does not burn easily). Hold the bag over hot coals and rotate it every minute for about seven minutes or until the ingredients look done. Add cheese or hot peppers for an extra zip, and enjoy breakfast! The cooking time depends on the heat of the coals. The more you can coat the inside of the bag with liquid, the better your results.

FYI *The bacon grease prevents the bag from igniting while your meal cooks.*

> **!** *Make sure that the bottom and both sides of the bag are evenly exposed to the coals.*

Bananas con Bacon

This innovative and tasty breakfast (or snack) first appeared as a Boy Scout recipe many years ago and has remained a camping oddball—but tasty—favorite.

INGREDIENTS

6 bananas (very ripe)
Salt (optional)
Pepper (optional)
12 slices bacon
Butter
1 brown paper lunch bag

GEAR LIST

- 3-foot stick
- Hot coals

PREPARATION

Peel and cut each banana in half, lengthwise—or squish them if you prefer—and season with salt and pepper. Put each piece on a slice of bacon and carefully slide them into a well-buttered paper bag (the bag remains in an upright position). Fold the end of the bag over three times securely and bake in a Dutch oven for about 12 minutes. Yum!

This recipe has many variations and can be accomplished by wrapping the banana in aluminum foil or even wrapping bacon around the banana and skewering it on a stick (little toothpicks are great to hold the bacon in place).

Universal Grilled "Steamed" Fish on Paper

Fish is full of natural oils that saturate paper, protecting it from burning while conducting heat to the meat. I first learned this recipe in Hawaii, but the more I talk to chefs around the world, I realize that this recipe is fairly universal.

INGREDIENTS

Cleaned fish
>*Sturdy fish like salmon steak works great, but I prefer more delicate fish like brook trout.*

Oil or butter
Salt (optional)
Pepper
Lemon (optional)
Vegetables (optional)
1 sheet newspaper
1 brown paper lunch bag
Pineapple slices optional

GEAR LIST

- 3-foot stick
- Hot coals
- Grill (or pan)

PREPARATION

Oil or butter the fish, and place it on a piece of wet brown paper. Top it with salt, pepper, and lemon, and add vegetables, if desired. Roll the fish (with toppings and wet brown paper) in newspaper. Place on a grill or in a pan (do not put fish directly on coals unless it is wrapped several times). The wet paper will steam the fish. Cook for 10 to 15 minutes, until flaky or no longer transparent. The cooking time will vary depending on the size and type of the fish and the temperature of the coals.

How to Travel with Eggs without Cracks

Here is a trick I learned when I was a Boy Scout.

It seems ridiculous to carry raw egg into the wilderness. One wrong step and crack! But it's possible, if you think out of the shell. At home, crack eggs into a plastic container that is small enough to fill completely. Cover it with an airtight lid—be sure it's closed—and you're ready to go! Keep the eggs out of heat and direct sunlight. My favorite trick is to freeze them in a plastic bottle or zip-lock plastic bag after they have been cracked and mixed (egg whites freeze better than yolks), and then wrap the bottle with foil.

When you are ready to cook, just pour your eggs and go. They should come out one at a time—or you can use the whole lot at once.

Baking Bread in a Bag

From crunchy toast at breakfast to a turkey sandwich at lunch to a loaf at dinner, bread plays many roles at mealtimes. So, why go without it on adventurous outings? Bread is a great utility food that's packed with carbohydrates to fuel you for a tough day in the wilderness. It is also one of the few foods that you can eat if you get a bad stomach out on the trail.

With the following recipes, you can measure and mix lightweight, dry ingredients and prepack them in little plastic bags. When you're in camp, just add water, heat, and—presto!—you'll have piping hot, savory bread with every meal. I have used a similar recipe in a Dutch oven on my home stove as well as out in the field.

GEAR LIST

- 1 heavy duty gallon-size zip-lock plastic bag
- 1 small (4 to 6 quarts) pot
- 1 large (1 gallon) pot with a snug-fitting lid
  GSI 8-inch and 12-inch Dutch ovens, optional

This recipe was inspired by an article titled, "How to Bake Bread in a Bag," which appeared in the July/August 2007 issue of *Explore* magazine. It requires minimal equipment and is similar to how most of the world cooks bread. For example, in Ethiopia, the locals bake bread on rocks. I found this recipe to be a foolproof way to prepare bread both at home and in the wilderness.

Baking Bread in a Bag

INGREDIENTS

> 2 cups all-purpose flour
> 1 cup whole wheat flour
> 3 tablespoons powdered milk
> 3 tablespoons sugar
> 1 teaspoon salt
> 1 package rapid rise yeast
> 3 tablespoons vegetable oil
> 1 cup hot water (125–130° F)
> Raisins (optional)

PREPARATION

1. Put all of the ingredients except for the hot water into a heavy-duty, gallon-size, zip-lock plastic bag.
2. Pour one cup of warm (not boiling) water, around 130° F (if it's too hot it will kill the yeast), into the bag. Squeeze excess air from the bag, seal it, and knead the bag with your hands to blend the ingredients.
3. Lightly coat your hands with flour and remove the dough from the bag. Knead it on a clean, flat, floured surface.
4. Mold the dough into the shape of a log—or football, if you prefer—and put it back in the bag. Let it rise for at least 30 minutes. It's critical for your dough to have sufficient time to rise, or it will taste gooey.
5. Fill the large pot with 3 to 6 inches of water and put the small pot inside it (uncovered and empty). This water in the large pot acts as a heat diffuser. Next, open the dough bag and place it inside the small pot (still uncovered and empty). Don't worry about the bag melting.

6. Cover the larger pot, bring the water to a boil, and cook until the bread is fully baked—about 30 minutes. Cooking time varies depending on altitude, humidity, and other variables.

7. Remove bread from bag and serve warm. Peanut butter optional.

Bread on a Stick

This fun recipe, pulled from *Legends of American Camping Recipes*, rivals the simplicity of roasting marshmallows! However, it requires coals or a Dutch oven. If you try to roast bread over an open fire, it cooks it too quickly, burning the outside and leaving the inside raw.

To save time, I like using the frozen dough that comes in a pop-open tube. My favorites are buttermilk biscuits, French bread, and dinner rolls. I'm not sure if it's the dough or the fresh air that makes everything taste so good. Whatever it is, it's a treat!

INGREDIENTS

Frozen bread dough
Butter or margarine
Garlic (optional)
Peanut butter (optional)

GEAR LIST

- 3-inch long, pencil-thick stick
- Knife with a sharp blade
- Coals (enough to bury the pot half way)
- Dutch oven (optional)
- Campfire

PREPARATION

1. Clean the stick with a cloth (or your shirt) and whittle off the top layer of bark, using a sharp knife (See Chapter 2, Your

Knife, a Point of Pride). If a you don't have a knife, you can wash the stick vigorously with clean, fresh water.

2. Thaw the frozen dough and roll it into a snake-like shape and twist it around the stick in a corkscrew fashion. The dough should cover the top 4 to 6 inches of the stick.

3. Hold the stick over the coals (or the Dutch oven), turning it slowly until dough is golden brown and puffy. Carefully slide the dough off the stick and fill the cavity with your favorite condiment—butter, jam, honey, butter, cheese, peanut butter, or anything you like.

Parting Thoughts

"Man cannot live by bread alone; he must have peanut butter," said James A. Garfield, the twentieth President of the United States. I cannot agree more. PB&J sandwiches happen to be one of my favorite camp treats. I always bring along my favorite nut spread to put on these championship camping bread recipes, and I recommend you do the same. Bread and peanut butter tastes better under a starry sky!

21 FISHING

Coke-Bottle Fishing

I really enjoy fishing, whether I am fly fishing on a stream or casting off a beach in the North Atlantic. It is an even bigger thrill if I am lucky enough to land one on a homemade rig such as the Coke-bottle fishing rig outlined in this chapter. Sure, in many respects, a rod and reel is superior, but it is so much cooler to be innovative.

So drink up, and let's go fishing!

"Yo, you don't need no stinkin' fishing rod to catch fish in Brooklyn." That's something my pal John Loret, an international adventurer would say in jest. A sailor at heart, he was part of Norwegian explorer Thor Heyerdahl's 1955–1956 Aku Aku Expedition off Easter Island. So when he says you can fish with a Coke bottle, a method he affectionately calls "Brooklyn fishing," who am I to argue?

Line fishing, or fishing without a rod, is more common worldwide than using a rod. In most underdeveloped countries, rods are luxuries that most people cannot afford. Instead, they use sticks or spools to wrap fishing line. A minimalist who's always up for a challenge, John prefers using a Coke bottle. Plastic and glass both work. The smoother the surface, the easier the line moves off the spool.

Line fishing is cheap, efficient and easier than toting a cumbersome rod.

GEAR LIST

- Coke bottle
- Line, at least 40 feet of a 35-pound test monofilament line
- Stainless steel hook
- 1- to 2-ounce lead weight
- Lure or bait (I prefer bait to lures)
    - Clams or squid in saltwater
    - Worms or minnows in fresh water

Go Fishing!

Coke-bottle fishing is similar to using a spinning reel. The line gets attached and wrapped around the center of the bottle, while the momentum of the bait pulls the line off the bottle upon casting. I love watching a local line fisherman who can rival the distances of fancy rod-toting tourists.

Select a strong line, at least 35-pound tested monofilament, to compensate for the leverage lost without a rod and reel. Your line weight depends on surf or current conditions. A one-ounce lead weight should be plenty for small swell, two ounces may be needed to manage big chop.

Use live bait, when possible, but that may have to wait until you catch a few fish. You can grab a pack of frozen squid from the local tackle shop to get started.

Line Set-up

Everyone has a personal style of line set-up or will develop one over time. Decide whether you will be top- or bottom-fishing, and get to work. Whether you fish the top or bottom of the water depends on what type of fish are running as well as your own preference. I find it more exciting to see a fish hit a lure or bait on the top of the water. They are more likely to set the hook, unlike bottom feeders that may nibble on bait. Some people jiggle—move a lure up and down—to attract fish. This is a great strategy for catching mackerel.

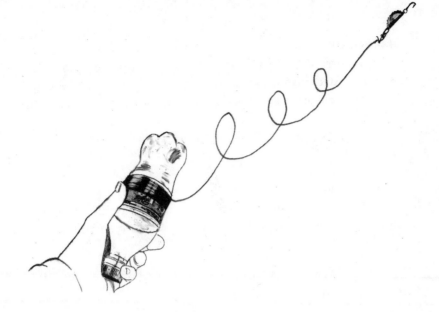

- Tie the line to the middle of bottle using a secure knot.
- Wrap the remaining line around the bottle.

THINGS TO KNOW

- It's important to tie the line around the bottle, in case all the line goes out and you are unable to control it with your fingers.
- Grip bottle the same way you would hold a pistol.
- Use fisherman's knots to tie hook to the line. Any fisherman will show you how to tie this knot.
- If you plan to throw fish back, use a barb-less hook.

> **!** *Never wrap fishing line (or cord) around your hands, wrists, or any other body part because one yank from a strong fish can split skin.*

Tossing Technique

There are countless casting options, depending on the conditions. Here are two of my favorites.

STRAIGHT-SHOOTER

Hold the bottle in your nondominant hand, and aim it at the targeted area. With the weight in other hand, lob the sinker in the same direction using an underhand toss, which is typically more accurate and longer than overhand. Place your forefinger on the spool to control line flow.

LASSOING

Just like a cowboy lassoing a calf, swing a weighted, baited line overhead to generate momentum and cleanly release it toward the water. Ideally, the line should peel off the bottle with as little friction as possible and float through the air. Plunk!

Line Retrieval

The line can be retrieved by pulling it hand over hand, or methodically wrapping it around the bottle. Unlike the old-timers with mega-callused hands, mine aren't so tough, so I wear gloves. Any kind of lightweight glove is good, but I prefer cotton work gloves so I can wash them and wear them again. Gloves also help you grab the fish when you bring them up.

The Coke-Bottle Cap Lure

The best fishing lures don't have to cost a fortune. Fishermen around the world have found that soda bottle caps make great fishing lures. This simple, yet effective lure can be made with a couple of common fishing items or improvisations.

GEAR LIST

- Metal bottle cap
- Hook
- Swivel
- Metal washers (optional)
- Pliers
- $1/8$-inch drill bit and drill or nail punch

> **!** *If you have never used these types of tools, ask for help from some-one who has. Smacking your hand with a hammer or drilling a hole in your hand makes fishing a lot tougher and not as much fun.*

HOW TO MAKE THE LURE

Using pliers, bend the cap until it looks like a taco shell, while keeping the gap wide enough to insert a weight. Insert a weight and squeeze the edges of the cap closed. You can also pop in a small washer to produce a fish-attracting rattle sound that sends vibrations through the water.

Next, drill a hole at the top and bottom of the lure. Clip swivel (to protect metal from cutting through line) from one end of the hook to the other end. Some hooks may require a metal ring to attach a lure—wire is a great alternative.

WHY BOTTLE CAP LURES WORK

Bottle cap lures are shiny and noisy, and they have unpredictable movements, which can excite—or agitate—fish to strike. The key is to keep the lure moving with quick snaps, skipping it along the surface to attract pike or bass, or letting it hover and wobble in the water, mimicking a wounded minnow.

Crabbing: The Poor Man's Lobster Hunt

As a young boy, I loved driving to Freeport, a town on the south shore of New York's Long Island, with my grandfather to spend the day catching Blue Claw Crabs. Toting raw chicken necks, minnows, string, and long-handled nets, we'd trot to the edge of the pier, armed and dangerous. My grandfather had all the patience in the world and was a whiz at meticulously guiding chicken-clutching crus-

taceans to captivity. With polished precision, he smoothly pulled the wet string fist over fist, until the crab appeared under the surface of the murky water. Holding the wad of string in one hand and clutching a net with the other, he'd scoop up the squirming crab with snake-tongue speed and toss it in the plastic bucket.

I was more of a free spirit, preferring to use minnows as bait that I wrapped around my homemade crabbing contraption, which was no more than a twisted metal, weighted coat hanger. Although my average at-crab catch paled compared to that of my Poppy, he had a knack for making me feel proud, no matter how many I caught that day. At night, we feasted on our day's booty, cracking open claws and using their thin legs to pluck out the sweet, juicy meat. Crabbing with my grandfather was as much a part of my summers as going to the beach and hanging out with my friends.

Crabbing is easy to learn and a fun, inexpensive way to spend the day with friends and family—and to bring home dinner. Unlike fishing, crabs are plentiful and hungry so you get a real bang for your buck, and you won't go home empty-handed.

Commonly found all along the coasts of Massachusetts to the panhandle shores of Texas, Blue Claw Crabs—hard-shelled crabs—are cherished fare for folks from the Chesapeake Bay, North Carolina, and Louisiana waters. Naturally aggressive—and a little scary looking—these ten-legged creatures sport powerful front claws, ready to snap at vulnerable fingers, but their succulence and tastiness makes catching them worth the risk. With a little planning, precision, and persistence, you can snag a bucket of these savory swimmers for a well-earned spot on your dinner plate. Here's how.

Getting Crabby

Crabbing can be done off a pier, dock, boat landing, creek, beach, or boat. Saltwater is the main ingredient, and low tide is the best time to go because that's when crabs are feeding close to the shore. Drop lining and trapping are the two most common methods.

Drop Lining, or "Chicken Necking"

This is a simple "active" crab fishing technique using string and bait. It's a terrific fishing substitute done in shallow water.

GEAR LIST

- 10 feet of cotton or nylon string (I recommend braided nylon because it is very easy to tie knots and dries quickly.)
- 1-foot stick
- 1-ounce weight
- Raw chicken for bait (Chicken necks are best, but you can also use fish heads, minnows, hot dogs, and so on.)
- Long-handled dip net
- Cooler or bucket
- Gloves that can get wet

HOW TO DROP LINE

- Tie one end of the string to a stick. Tie your bait to the loose end of the string. Gently toss stringed-bait into the water and quietly wait until you feel a nibble (or light tug) from a crab—it shouldn't be too long. Don't freak out and yank the string, or you can pull your little friend's claw off his shelled body—or, more likely, you'll pull your string off your bait and Mr. Claws will scuttle off with your chicken neck. Instead, gently and steadily pull crab toward you and to the surface, wrapping the string around stick. When you see the crab's shadow, hold your stick in one hand and scoop it up with a long-handled net. It will most likely be holding onto the bait with one clenched claw, so be careful! Drop him in bucket and get back to business.
- You may need to wear thick gloves when coaxing an unruly crab out of the trap to avoid getting pinched. Those suckers can draw blood!
- This is by far the simplest way to catch crabs, but unlike using a metal trap or collapsible net, it allows you to "feel" the hunt. It's like the difference between driving a standard and stick shift car. Both methods produce the same result, but just as the shift and clutch allow you to feel and control the road, crabbing with a line allows you to feel the nibble.

Other Crabbing Methods

There are several other types of crabbing apparatus and techniques. Some are as simple as a mesh basket on a pole, and others are complicated metal mazes of crab doom. Although they all differ in function, each requires tying bait inside the center.

GEAR LIST

1. *Crab pot.* This is a large square trap traditionally made of galvanized chicken wire. Recently, some manufacturers have begun to use PVC-coated wire. This brilliant design is the most commonly used crabbing method worldwide. Designed with crabs' natural instincts in mind, these two-chambered traps have downstairs entrances that let crabs in when they smell the bait in the center bait box. Once in, the crab cannot get out and freaks out. It instinctively swims up toward the surface—or in this case, into the upstairs parlor, where it will stay with his cousins until collection. The top snaps open for easy emptying. It is recommended that you put a brick in the bottom to keep it flush to the floor.

2. *Dip net (scap net).* This is a long-poled net used in conjunction with drop-lining to scoop up the crab. Keep the pole length to six feet maximum because anything longer is hard to maneuver.

3. *Drop net (ring net)*. This simple and inexpensive trap, designed with two metal rings connected by netting, opens flat on the bottom allowing the crab to reach the bait tied to the middle. It closes around the crab like a deep bowl when it's pulled to the surface. It is best used in conditions with a flat, sandy or muddy bottom.

4. *Collapsible basket (folding star)*. This pricey and somewhat complex trap is made of metal, with sides that open flush to the bottom, allowing crab to enter and reach bait. It closes fully, trapping the crab, when pulled to the surface. It's good for moderately strong currents and rocky bottoms.

Clever Crabbing Tips

- Set your trap at the mouth of saltwater creeks as crabs enter larger bodies of water.
- One of my favorite crab baits is bunker, an oily fish that can be purchased at most bait and tackle shops along the coast. Chicken parts (especially necks) are a good second. But your little sister is not a good choice.
- Preserve crabs by keeping them in a cooler or bucket with a little bit of ice. Try using a bushel basket for easy containment of your catch.
- At home, stick crabs in the fridge for a few hours to slow their bodily functions while keeping them alive. Mom may veto this suggestion.
- Keep crabs uncovered and away from heat, like sunlight.
- Never cover crabs in water, as they will rapidly use up the limited oxygen and drown, and you do not want to cook a dead crab (see the warning).
- Check local regulations on size and permits required.

Cooking Crabs

Cook crabs the day they are caught. It is best to steam or boil hard-shelled crabs. Savvy chefs prefer steaming.

Use a crab-steamer or any big pasta pot with a raised steaming shelf or veggie steamer that lifts the crabs above the water while steaming.

- Wash the crabs with running water.
- Fill the pot with 1 cup of water for every dozen crabs plus 1 cup vinegar.
- Cover the pot until it comes to a boil.
- Using tongs or gloves, place the crabs on the steamer over boiling water.
- Generously sprinkle each layer of crabs with Old Bay seasoning or your seasoning of choice.
- Cover and steam the crabs for 20 to 30 minutes, until their shells turn bright red.
- Eat them while they're hot, and savor the flavors!

> **!** *Do not cook dead crabs—throw them away. Shellfish deteriorate quickly, creating bacteria that can be deadly. Also, be sure to wash your hands thoroughly with antibacterial soap after handling live or dead crabs, because they can carry salmonella, which spreads quickly.*

EATING GEAR LIST

- Newspaper with which to cover the kitchen table
- Shell crackers
- Mallets
- Small forks
- Lots of paper towels

Tickle and Noodle a Fish

I have heard plenty of guys argue about what really makes a sport a sport. If you want to try a sport that takes guts and cunning—and one that may put a little extra hair on your chest—look no further than fish noodling. Don't bother bringing your rod and reel. And leave your bait and trusty net behind, too. All you will need is your own two hands and a bit of calm persistence to catch a fish.

You don't believe me? Even Shakespeare mentions the technique in his play *Twelfth Night*, in which he describes the rogue character Malvolio as "the trout that must be caught with tickling." Some less wordy

anglers consider successful tickling and noodling a mystical skill granted to those attuned to the cunning ways of trout and catfish.

"Well, you just go underneath a bank, and sometimes a fish will hang out under sort of a bank where there are some roots," says my friend Jim Fowler, wildlife zoologist and TV personality. "Only trouble is, you might find an alligator or a snake under there, too."

Here's how you can carefully pluck a few big ones out of the river—or at least have fun on the hunt without so much as a hook. Wade slowly up to a big rock, stump, or wherever you think there is likely to be a fish den. Many ticklers prefer to lay down on a flat rock or directly on the riverbank for an improved reach and less exposure to the fish and potentially chilly water.

Beware of getting hypothermia from the cold water, and only stay in for short periods of time. Get out immediately if your extremities begin to go numb.

After getting situated, carefully place your hands below the water's surface with your palms facing up, raising them up and under an exposed fish, and wiggle your fingers. It may be more comfortable to lay on your side and tickle the fish with one hand, leaving your other hand free to pull the fish out at set time.

Regardless, the trick here is to move as methodically as possible so you don't disturb or scare the fish away. Fish will bite if they feel threatened or are protecting a nearby stock of newly laid eggs, so you may want to wear thick gloves (although they can dull finger sensitivity).

Hold your hand steady until you feel the fish just above your hands, then gently massage under its mouth and belly with your fingertips, mimicking the soothing feeling of underwater reeds, until the fish is in a near trance. Wrap your hand around its tail and coolly pull it from the water. When done correctly, the fish will barely move, and you can slip a line right through its gill for easy tethering until you're ready to go. If the fish still has some fight left in it, try quickly tossing it to nearby land, where you can deal with it there.

With a catfish, use your fingers as wiggling bait, and try your hand at noodling by simply grabbing at the fish's mouth or gill cover, or even ramming your hand down the throat of a good-sized fish and forcibly pulling it from its hole. Before you reach into any unexposed area, make sure it is clear of water moccasins or turtles. Gloves won't protect against a vicious turtle bite, and the aggressive moves of a water moccasin will prove even worse. Catfish in the United States can weigh more than a staggering 100 pounds and will put up a good fight before they finish, often leaving amused observers wondering whether you've caught the fish or the fish has caught you. Don't get discouraged if these techniques don't work on your first few attempts. Like all skills, tickling and noodling becomes easier with practice.

Legal Notes

Aspiring noodlers should check their state's fish and game laws to see if the sport is legal. According to the U.S. Fish and Wildlife Services, noodling is illegal in 11 states, and in some cases an infraction could net the angler a fine of up to $500. So before you get started, check with your local wildlife and gaming commission.

In Southeast Asia the Mekong River catfish can weigh up to 700 pounds, which would be a bit difficult to noodle since it could probably swallow you. The electric catfish, native to Africa, is capable of generating up to 350 volts.

22 EAT LIKE THE REST OF THE WORLD

Chopsticks

Long before forks, spoons, or chopsticks were invented, humans had only their thumbs and fingers to pick apart meat, plants, fruit, and perhaps an occasional insect or two. It was simply an unhygienic affair that led to sickness and, often, premature death. I often think about that epoch of man's existence as I douse and scrub my hands with anti-bacterial gel, which is my mandatory traveling companion when I go to exotic locales.

Chopsticks appeared in China sometime around the third century B.C.E. as a means to curtail rampant disease and death. Initially, people used sliced bamboo slivers to pinch food from boiling water. A chop-stick, in theory, is a single-use utensil. It is a stick that's roughly 9 inches long and is used in conjunction with another chopstick. To-gether, the dynamic duo allows the handler to pinch food, while drain-ing excess fat. It is speculated that Confucius, a philosopher ruler of China around 500 B.C., made the utensil popular, promoting it as a symbol of civility.

Today, chopsticks are used around the globe, primarily in Asian cultures. The word *chopsticks* comes from the Cantonese *kap* or *k'wai tse*, meaning "quick little fellows." Both chopsticks and forks can pick up food, but they are not equal in terms of healthy eating habits and taste. Chopsticks may actually help the body stay fit and the palate strong. While the fork's scooping shape encourages a few big bites, chopsticks require many small bites. This is a proven health advantage.

It takes about twenty minutes after you eat to feel full. That's when your brain gets the message and says, "I am full, stop eating!" Leisurely meals to a great extent have become extinct in our fast-paced world, leading people to mindlessly gobble food beyond satiation, which is one of the factors contributing to the obesity epidemic.

Chances are if you live in a Western culture, you use a fork at most meals. Perhaps it's time to slow down mealtime by exploring the joy of chopsticks. Unlike forks, chopsticks require practice. Don't be intimidated. Learn a few techniques, and with a little practice, you'll be trading in your fork for a set of tapered wooden sticks in no time. It only takes a meal or two to get a feel for chopsticks and enjoy the fun. I once heard that a chopstick master can eat a whole bowl of Cheerios in milk without dropping a single one.

Make Your Own Chopsticks

GEAR LIST

- Two straight tree branches about a foot long and about the width of a pencil (Typically chopsticks are made from hardwoods, but I prefer to work with pine since it is easier to find and carve.)
- Pocket knife or wood chisel
- Sand paper (fine grit)
- Nontoxic wood oil

STEP 1: Take both branches (or a wooden rod) and cut them to 10 inches, and then make a mark in each one 4 inches in from the end of the rod. Carefully shave roughly $1/16$ of an inch off each tip, creating a dull point. Carve away any irregularities.

STEP 2: Sand off excessive slivers or roughness, making the ends where the mouth will touch them the smoothest.

STEP 3: Coat the chopsticks with nontoxic wood oil by dampening a rag with the oil and rubbing it over them. Let them dry in a ventilated area for one day and wash them before using.

How to Use Chopsticks

STEP 1: Pick up one chopstick, holding it with your middle finger and thumb while maintaining a light grip. Allow the wide end of the stick to rest on the web between your thumb and forefinger, and rest the narrow end on the tip of your ring finger. Use your middle fingertip to hold the chopstick in place. Imagine holding a pencil. Now lift your forefinger a little to make room for the second chopstick.

STEP 2: Grip the second chopstick with your forefinger, and place your thumb around the first chopstick and over the second. You can adjust your hand position slightly both for comfort and to keep the slim tips even so you can obtain optimal "pinch" (and avoid food-drop mishaps).

STEP 3: Keep the lower (the first) chopstick steady (it should not move when picking up food) and move the top (the second) chopstick up and down with your forefinger. The movement should initiate from flexing the joint that is closest to your knuckle. Straighten your forefinger to open the chopsticks and bend it to close them, while keeping tips aligned. Note that this method is a little different from what is shown in the illustration in how the top chopstick is held. Use whichever method you find most comfortable.

STEP 4: Practice opening and closing the chopsticks, making sure that the wide ends do not cross and make an X, which will make it difficult to pick up food.

23 MINING FOR IRON IN YOUR FOOD

When I was a kid my mother used to tell me to eat my spinach because it contains iron and would make me strong like Popeye. As I miserably munched the mushy green leaves, I would think of the strapping cartoon sailorman who always ate a can of spinach for instant muscles. I ultimately became a spinach fan. Good advertising for spinach, eh?

Studies have shown that our bodies need iron to allow the hemoglobin in our blood to carry oxygen to the tissues. There are baskets of naturally iron-rich foods, like spinach, nuts, and seafood. Recently, cereal companies have accepted the notion that iron is good for us and have enriched their flakes. Did you know you can mine the iron put into certain foods like cold cereal? Here's a cool experiment to prove it.

GEAR LIST

- Cereal that is high in iron, such as fortified corn flakes
- Large container
- Strong magnet
- Plastic bag (gallon size)

- Blender or bowl
- Wooden spoon
- Water (enough to turn the flakes into a doughy consistency)

STEP 1: Put 4 or 5 cups of cereal in large container.

STEP 2: Crush the flakes by grinding them with a large wooden spoon or potato masher or by putting them in a blender. The flakes should be finely ground into a powdery consistency. Don't worry if there are a few large specks. I put them in a blender to save time.

STEP 3: Put the ground flakes into the gallon-sized plastic bag.

STEP 4: Add water while mixing with a spoon until it is the consistency of glue. Securely close the bag over a flat surface, evenly distributing the mush inside the bag.

STEP 5: Run a magnet over the plastic bag—always in a single direction and from edge to edge of the bag—using long, even strokes for 3 to 5 minutes.

STEP 6: Examine the edges of the bag. Do you see fine black material? If not, use the magnet some more. If you do see some particles, use the magnet to push them toward one corner of the bag.

STEP 7: Lift the corner of the bag, and check out the stash of iron particles!

STEP 8: Mine the iron grains with a magnet, your fingers, or a very fine strainer, and put them in a glass vile—or you can just eat them.

FYI

- *Iron is one of the most abundant elements in the universe. The red color of Mars is likely the result of rusted or oxidized iron on its surface, suggesting that there might have been water on its surface at one time.*
- *Most meteorites that survive the heat of entering the earth's atmosphere contain iron. In fact, the first iron tools used by prehistoric men were made from iron mined from meteorites.*

PART VI

WEATHER

24 WEATHER—YOU KNOW MORE THAN YOU THINK

Perhaps nothing affects our planet more than its weather.

Before we had satellites (less than 50 years ago) and sophisticated weather equipment, people spent more time outdoors and were better in tune with what they saw, heard, and smelled. Good or bad weather could determine a pleasant or unpleasant work day—and in some lines of work even life and death. Without consistent forecasts, they had to create quick and clever methods to identify approaching weather. For example, a red sunset foretold of a nice day to come.

This chapter is devoted to common sayings related to our body's ability to sense weather. Many old wives tales or common sayings that we brush off as nonsense actually hold some scientific truth.

The five following sections are arranged by the senses: sight, touch, smell, and hearing. I would have included taste, as it is one of the five senses, but you can't taste the weather, now, can you?

Sight

I often hear people joke that the weathermen should look out the window. Sometimes the weather report is just plain wrong, and sometimes the sky is the best indicator of current conditions.

Simply observing nature can reveal huge amounts of information. For example, the airflow in the United States moves from the west to the east, so if you see a storm in the west you can speculate that it will eventually migrate east.

"Red sky at night sailors delight
and red morn(ing) sailors be warned."

INTERPRETATION:

A red sky at sunset indicates dry weather is on the way. If the air to the east is dry in the morning, dry air is passing and moist air is most likely going to increase. If the sky is red in the morning, chances are there will be a rainstorm later that day. When there is moisture in the air, particles are larger than when it is drier, and the larger particles scatter the blue light, making the sky appear to be red (see Chapter 28, Why Is the Sky Blue and Sunsets Red?). So, red skies at night delight sailors with news of dry weather approaching.

"If a circle forms 'round the moon, 'twill rain soon."

INTERPRETATION:

My father, who was a commercial airline pilot, often pointed out cloud formations and stars after dinner. My earliest memory of learning a weather sign was looking for a ring around the moon.

The ring, my father told me, indicated that bad weather would occur within 24 hours, and a break in the ring showed the direction from which the bad weather came. The ring results from cirrus clouds in the higher altitudes. While the clouds themselves don't create precipitation, cirrus clouds typically precede low-pressure systems laden with moisture. Because these clouds are high in the atmosphere, where temperatures are well below freezing, the moisture occurs in the form of ice crystals that refract the light and appear to us a ring.

If you count the number of stars contained within the ring it provides a fairly accurate prediction of the proximity of the rain or snow. Each star represents approximately 24 hours.

"If the moon's face is red, of water she speaks."

INTERPRETATION:

This saying comes from the Zuni Indians, who live in the American Southwest, and it actually has a basis in science. The red color appears from dust and debris being pushed ahead of a low-pressure front bearing moisture. Dust particles or other small airborne elements are needed to create raindrops, and the more of these particles that are present, the more likely it is that a rainstorm will develop.

The same principle is used in seeding clouds. Without the presence of a nuclei (tiny particles of dust or bacteria), the raindrops have nothing to form around, but when conditions are right and moonlight shines through these moisture-soaked particles, it takes on the appearance of a reddish/orange tone. If you live in an area of high air pollution or dust, the moon will always appear reddish.

*"If the new moon holds the old moon in her bosom
the weather will be fair."*

INTERPRETATION:

This is also referred to as "the old moon in the new moon's arms." The ghosting effect seen in the Moon is actually caused by "earthshine," or a reflection of light off of the earth onto the Moon. This occurs when the weather is clear, stable, and you get a flow of dry air preceding a high-pressure system. This clarity enables illumination of the dark part of the crescent moon holding the old moon. It is usually a good indicator of 24 to 48 hours of fair weather ahead.

"Mare's tails and mackerel scales make
tall ships carry low sails."

INTERPRETATION:

If you look at the sky on a blue, sunny day and see thin, high, wispy clouds (alto cirrus clouds), look closely for the shapes of a mare's tail (a horse's tail) and the scales of a mackerel (a fish).

Typically, these clouds blow off the top of big storms moving from west to east, meaning they bring high winds and rain. In hurricane climates like the Caribbean and Florida, sailors lower their sails in anticipation of rough weather and water conditions when they see cirrus clouds moving from east to west as it means a hurricane might be approaching within 12 to 36 hours. I find that I use this technique more than any other.

"Sun Dogs or Mock Suns"

INTERPRETATION:

"A sun dog" is equivalent to a halo around the moon. It's a relatively common atmospheric phenomenon, mostly associated with the refraction of sunlight by small ice crystals high in the air that result in the formation of a sun dog, or "mock sun." When I skied to the North Pole, I often saw sun dogs. Even on clear days, particles of ice blew in the wind, which felt like tiny pebbles of glass smashing into my face.

Sun dogs appear when the sun is low, such as at sunrise and sunset. This is because the angle of the sun relative to the horizon must be approximately 22 degrees with light passing through the dense moisture in the air for them to appear. The appearance of a sun dog is a predictor of rain or snow. If you see this, look for a drastic change in the weather within 12—24 hours.

Touch and Feel

"If your corns all ache and itch, the weather
fair will make a switch."

INTERPRETATION:
This is what causes your grandfather to complain about an old injury or bones that ache during bad weather. It's not that people with arthritis (or other sorts of inflammation) actually feel weather in their bones, but they do feel painful pressure in their joints. This is because the fluid that lubricates joints when they move creates a small pocket of gas, which builds and recedes with air pressure. When the pressure drops rapidly, the gas in the joints wants to move out of your body, and it pushes against inflamed tissue causing pain.

"Rainy days and Mondays get me down."

INTERPRETATION:
It's a fact that weather can affect health and mood. Some people suffer from migraines on rainy days, while others become depressed. There are many theories about why this occurs but none are fully understood. Almost all of them deal with peoples' sensitivities to air pressure. It has been proven that sunny days make folks happy, and such days typically occur during periods of high pressure. Studies have shown that people are more generous tippers in restaurants on sunny days, so if you need to speak to a teacher about your grades or ask your boss for a raise, don't save it for a rainy day!

"I know ladies by the score, whose hair foretells
the storm; long before it begins to pour, their
curls take a drooping form."

INTERPRETATION:

Bad hair days can be a nightmare for anyone! Unlike other mammals' hair, human hair responds to the amount of moisture in the air. A strand of hair is not solid but rather a combination of different kinds of cells that react differently to moisture. When the air is dry, hair shrinks and straightens out, but if the air is moist (as when it's humid or rainy), it swells and curls up. It's the same process that operates in a thermostat, where two kinds of metal strips are bound together but have different thicknesses and rates at which they expand. So as the temperature goes up, for example, one strip expands more than the other and therefore bends and hits a trigger to turn the heater on. Hair works the same way. Blond hair apparently is the most sensitive to humidity.

"It's not the heat it's the humidity."

I often hear people who live in desert climates like Arizona say, "Oh the heat's not bad here—it's a dry heat." Recently, I was in Ethiopia, considered to be the hottest place on earth, where daytime temperatures approached 140° F in the shade, but the humidity was only 10%. Let me tell you, it was *hot*. But it was bearable. For example, if you were to swim in a pool in Denver (air temp 80° F, humidity 15%) and fly to Miami the next day to swim in a pool there (air temp 80° F humidity 70%), even though the air temperatures were the same, you would feel noticeably "cooler" in Denver. The reason is that the pool water on your skin will evaporate and cool your skin more quickly in the dry mountain air. During the evaporative cooling process, water transitions from liquid to gas, taking heat from the areas around the water molecule and absorbing heat away from your body. So you feel cooler.

Smell

"The smell before the rain"

There is a band called The Smell Before the Rain. I am not sure about their music, but I do know that many people experience this phenomenon before and after rainstorms.

The smell before rain is caused by ozone (O_3). There are three kinds of ozone in the atmosphere:

1. Ozone high in the atmosphere that protects us from ultraviolet rays.
2. Ozone formed as a pollutant, primarily from automotive exhaust.
3. Ozone molecules formed by lightning.

Prior to a rainstorm, ozone is formed by the high voltage that exists within thunder clouds (even if thunder doesn't appear to be present). Downdrafts carry it toward the ground in a thundercloud and blow the ozone out ahead of the storm. This process causes the breeze that often precedes a storm as well as the smell that we associate with rain on the way.

Smell is a very difficult thing to describe, but an approaching storm smells like a photocopier to me. Next time you see a storm approaching, see if you can smell a difference and try to link it to a smell you know well.

"The smell of the good earth."

One of my favorite memories growing up in the country was the smell *after* a rainstorm. After a rain, people often say that the air smells fresh. This pleasant smell results from the rain hitting the dry earth, which was dubbed "petrichor" in 1964 by two Australian geochemists, Richard Grenfell Thomas and I. J. Bear, who published an article in *Nature* magazine (to which I recommend you subscribe). Petrichor, it turns out, is the smell of oils coming out of vegetation after a rain. The oils emit a noticeable musty odor, an odor reminiscent of freshly turned soil.

"It wasn't me . . . was that you?"

Gas can stink! Many people enjoy the scenery of a swamp, but not the stench. Some swamps smell especially pungent during a period of low pressure, when large amounts of gases like methane, produced by rotting vegetation trapped on the bottom of the swamp, get released. But as fair weather approaches and the pressure rises, the smell dissipates.

Hear

"Sound traveling far and wide. A stormy day will betide."

Ever notice that in some rooms your friend sounds like he is screaming, while in others you can barely hear him? This is because of the room's acoustics, or the shape of the room. Materials used on the floor, walls, and ceiling often determine the way sound travels.

This happens in nature, too. Sound becomes clearer and more audible prior to stormy weather, so a dog can be heard barking from a great distance. Instead of sound waves traveling upward and out into the atmosphere, as they do on a clear day, clouds act as a barrier and redirect them to bend back to Earth, thereby intensifying sounds.

Parting Thoughts

These sayings are fun to quote, but they also contain some kernels of truth regarding how we see, feel, smell, and hear the weather. Next time you are at a family party and notice the moon surrounded by glorious optical rings, bring your uncle to the window, point to the moon, and say in your best British accent, **"If a circle forms 'round the moon, 'twill rain soon."** Don't even explain yourself; just walk away.

25 READING THE WIND

> *"Learning to read the wind is to understand*
> *the language of weather."*
> —Peter Burrow

Anticipating the weather by being able to read the
wind is a priceless skill.

People hear weather forecasters talk about high- and low-pressure
systems and become aware that high pressure means clear skies and
low pressure means storms. When you're out in the wilderness, understanding air pressure will enable you to determine if good or bad

weather is heading your way. For instance, a rapid change in pressure over a short distance typically results in strong winds.

It's important to remember that all high-pressure systems rotate clockwise, and low-pressure systems rotate counterclockwise in the northern hemisphere. Knowing this allows you to determine where you are relative to any one system. When the local weather forecaster predicts an area of high pressure to dominate the weather, it generally means you're in for a sunny day, while a low-pressure forecast means rain or snow is on the way. Not surprisingly, high pressure occurs when the pressure of an area of air is higher than the pressure of the surrounding air—and vice versa. I often think of high pressure as a mountain of air and low pressure as a valley of air.

High- and Low-Pressure Experiment

Stand with your back to the wind. Then, turn 45 degrees to your right (a circle has 360 degrees). You are now standing with your back to the wind as it is in the upper atmosphere. This means the high-pressure system is to your right and the low-pressure system is to your left. Keep this in mind, as most weather systems tend to blow west to east. Thus, while one system is blowing away, another is approaching.

Making Your Own Barometer

It is easy to make your own barometer with which you can accurately measure the rise or fall of the barometric pressure and thereby predict upcoming weather.

GEAR LIST
- Empty coffee can (or something similar)
- Large balloon
- Large rubber band (to fit snugly around the coffee can)
- Needle
- Straw
- Glue
- Paper index card, 5×7 inches or larger
- Pen

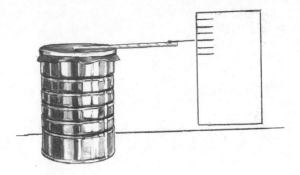

STEP 1: Cut the balloon so that it stretches across top of coffee can like a drum.

STEP 2: Secure the balloon to the can with the rubber band—the thicker and tighter-fitting the band, the better. Air leaks will result in improper measurements.

STEP 3: Glue straw to the top, making sure one end is in the middle of the drum or can.

STEP 4: Attach the needle to the other end of the straw. A couple of drops of glue should work, or you can use a little bit of tape to minimize the weight.

STEP 5: Draw evenly spaced lines on index card.

To calibrate the barometer, get the accurate barometric pressure from a local weathercast and adjust the needle accordingly.

NOTE: This experiment works better outside, but be aware that your readings may fluctuate if your barometer is subjected to excessive heat or cold, which may affect the elasticity of the rubber band and balloon.

Using Your Barometer

High pressure will push the balloon cover in and force the straw up, while low pressure will make the rubber puff up and the straw go down.

Watch your barometer when a big storm approaches and blows out, and use it to predict storms.

26 MOUNTAIN WEATHER

Mountains are important to local and global weather and in many cases they create their own weather systems, which can change with the snap of a twig and can sometimes prove deadly. This unpredictability makes being prepared for hazardous weather conditions the number one rule for anyone heading into the mountains. I'm often amazed by how many climbers are unaware of the real risks posed by weather in the mountains and how frequently they embark on journeys ill prepared.

Be aware that the higher the elevation, the colder and windier it usually gets. A rule of thumb is that for every 1,000 feet ascended, the air cools about 3½° F.

Mount Everest has rapidly changing weather.

It snows on Mount Kilimanjaro.

It snows on the tropical island of Hawaii at the top
of Mauna Loa.

Windward/Leeward

In Hawaii, due to two towering snow-capped mountains, Mauna Kea
and Mauna Loa in the middle of the Big Island (both are just over
13,000 feet), one side of the island is a lush tropical rainforest, and the
other is an arid desert. This crazy contrast is also due in part to the
winds that come from one direction (the trade winds). The mountains
become obstacles, creating windward (wet) and leeward (dry) sides of
the island.

On your next hike or climb, look for these signs on the mountain. Does it have a wet and dry side?

Microclimates

A microclimate is a variation in temperature or moisture in a relatively small area due to local geographic differences in elevation, sun exposure, and proximity to a large body of water. For example, frost may form on your lawn more quickly in some spots than in others, or the front of your house may grow vines whereas the back may not. These are common examples of microclimates.

Mount Baker in the state of Washington is the snowiest place on Earth.

The same thing happens on mountains. The size and shape of mountains creates awkward obstructions for naturally flowing winds, causing the wind at the ground level near the mountains to flow upward. As air rises, it generally cools, and the air's moisture condenses, forming rain or snow-producing clouds.

This explains why there are different temperatures, weather systems, and ecological zones in small pockets of mountains. Mount Marcy (5,344 feet) is the highest mountain in New York state, and although it is small by mountain standards, its summit has a blustery climate that's similar to Northern Newfoundland, Canada.

Mountain knowledge is critical when planning what to bring and

The summit of Mount Washington in New Hampshire is the windiest place on Earth.

wear, because weather can change dramatically in a matter of hours. A classic example is Mount Washington (6,288 feet) in New Hampshire. Many hikers begin the day in the warm valley, wearing nothing more than a T-shirt and shorts. But hours later, they may be donning fleece as they approach the top, where there are occasional snowstorms.

FYI *One of the coolest weather websites is www.mountwashington .org. The weather on Mount Washington is usually dramatically different from the local valleys surrounding it.*

Local Knowledge Is Key

The best strategy for traveling in mountainous regions is to get the local scoop from folks who live or work on or near the mountain. The forecast for valleys or cities in the region may be of little value up high, as mountains create their own weather.

Altimeter watches have become popular with hikers and climbers for their ability to display elevation. But since their technology is based on barometric pressure, they can also help protect you from dangerous weather when used properly.

Most important, use your barometer in conjunction with your

eyes. Get off the top of an exposed ridge or summit if the pressure on your watch starts falling, the wind suddenly picks up, cumulus clouds begin to build vertically, and the bases begin to darken. That means a dangerous storm is brewing. Stay calm and swiftly move to a safe, sheltered area.

Wai'ale'ale, Hawaii, is one of the wettest places on Earth.

Lightning

On mountains and summits you are especially vulnerable to lightning. On hot days warm air gets forced up when it reaches the mountain. As it cools, it quickly loses moisture, forming clouds that can create electrical storms, which can be deadly.

FYI

- *To estimate your distance from approaching lightning, start counting the seconds immediately upon seeing a flash of lightning and stop timing when you hear the thunder bang. Divide that number by 5. For example, if you counted to 15, the lightning is 3 miles away.*
- *Thunder makes that loud noise because of the quick expansion of air molecules caused by the heat of the lightning. Because light travels faster than sound, the thunder is heard after seeing the lightning. If you see lightning and hear thunder at the same time, you're in big trouble.*

Often when lightning is nearby, your skin may tingle or your hair will stand on end. This is a warning that lightning is about to strike nearby. The National Weather Service recommends you get low by squatting on the balls of your feet as you want as little surface area of your body touching the ground as possible. Do *not* lie flat on the ground.

Since the boom or sound of lighting is extremely loud cover your ears with your hands and put your head between your knees. The idea is to make your self as small a target as possible.

Sun

Almost every time I hike a mountain, there's "that guy" who doesn't have a hat or sunglasses who says, "Don't worry . . . I don't burn." Remember, it doesn't need to be hot for you to get fried. As altitude increases, the atmosphere gets thinner and the sun becomes stronger.

The sun's reflection off of snow can literally burn your eyes. It happened to me once while I was on a glacier atop Mount Kilimanjaro in Africa. I was a taking a lot of pictures and went all day without sunglasses. It took my eyes weeks to recover. Sunburn and snow blindness are serious issues, so always wear sunblock and sunglasses when outdoors. You are going to be around a lot longer than that suntan.

Parting Thoughts

Even expert mountaineers can get caught off guard by the weather. To avoid taking unnecessary risks, research and understand updated local weather forecasts and always pay attention to any weather changes. If the forecast calls for sunshine, but it is pouring rain and thundering, change your plans. There will always be another day to hike—if you are wise.

27 WEATHER ANIMAL

Did you ever hear someone say, "The cows are lying down, I wonder if it's going to rain?" While many brush it off as coincidence, some studies have shown that understanding animal behavior may help predict weather changes. For instance, wild and domestic animals alter their behavior before storms, particularly before thunderstorms. Horses have been seen running in circles in their corrals prior to tornados, and dogs are known to repeatedly sniff the air before severe weather occurs.

Animals and insects are also credited with being able to predict earthquakes, and there are many accounts of them acting strangely minutes or even days before large earthquakes. However, there is no "official" research to verify these claims. Much like humans, animals detect changes in atmospheric pressure via a pressurized, air-filled tube in the middle ear.

Precisely what animals or insects sense remains a mystery, but watch birds, cows, or your dog before a predicted storm and look for changes in their behavior. Stay aware of your surroundings and make a note of any behavioral oddities. Observation is a powerful tool, even though there is much scientific debate as to its accuracy. You may make a contribution to this largely unknown field of study.

Birds

When storms approach, birds tend to fly closer to the ground. Prior to a storm, the air pressure becomes low—meaning it is less dense—and that make it harder for birds to fly. They are altitude-challenged and need thick air to take flight. Also, prior to thunderstorms there tend to be cold down-drafts, which may push birds to a lower altitude. Let's face it: heavy, wet wings make it hard to create lift.

Insects, "Jiminy Cricket!"

I can remember being told as a kid, during a camping trip in the Adirondack Mountains in upstate New York, that, by using a simple formula, counting the number of chirps of a common cricket could determine the outside temperature. I was fascinated and spent most of the night tucked in my sleeping bag focused on the sound of one cricket, trying not to confuse his song with others chirping nearby. I diligently counted the number of chirps in 15 seconds and added 37, which should reveal the temperature in degrees Fahrenheit. Jiminy Cricket was pretty square on! He said 52° F, and the thermometer outside my tent read 53° F. Not bad for a green-winged, funky-looking thing!

The snowy tree cricket, whose sound is often dubbed into movie soundtracks to suggest a quiet summer night, is also called the "thermometer cricket." The rule of thumb east of the Mississippi is to count the chirps in 13 seconds and add 40. West of the Mississippi only 38 is added. I was never told why!

So, what is the difference between a common cricket and a snowy tree cricket? Basically, it's color and size. Common crickets are black and relatively large, and snowy tree crickets are whitish-green and lean. Jiminy Cricket from the Adirondacks was probably a common cricket.

Test the cricket-chirping theory with your own thermometer.

Flies Bite

On fishing trips, I seem to get attacked by insects just before a rainstorm. While I have not scientifically documented my torment, I have discovered a plausible explanation. Since the skin's sweat glands release odors and heat when humidity increases, both of which insects love, they gorge themselves on me like sumo wrestlers at a buffet. Scientific studies have found that mosquitoes are attracted to lactic acid and carbon dioxide released in sweat. Another reason could be simply that insects land on more objects, including skin, during moist weather because it is more difficult to fly.

Worms

Worms are known to flee rising groundwater during heavy rainstorms because they and other ground insects can easily drown.

Ants

Some scientists have hypothesized that before it rains, red and black ants build up the mounds around their ant holes to protect their nests from flooding. This has not been proven, so here is an opportunity for you to be a scientist and conduct original field research. Observe and record ant mound-building activities in your own backyard by keeping a written comparison with detailed weather data.

Fish

Fishermen have more superstitions than most sportsmen. The fishermen in my family commonly accepted that fish bite more before it rains. We had no hard evidence, but the theory typically proved accurate.

Air pressure decreases before a storm, so the amount of pressure on the surface of a pond or lake also decreases, allowing gases and debris from the bottom to float up toward the surface. Chances are, fish and insects respond to the sudden availability of food and, thus, do a lot of splashing and jumping before a storm.

Lying Cows

One of the most commonly heard rain-related proverbs is that when cows are lying down, rain is on its way. Although I have never read any scientific explanation for this phenomenon, there are some good reasons for the cows' behavior. It is well-known that being the highest object in a field during an electrical storm increase the chances of getting struck by lightning. Perhaps cows sense moisture in the air and duck for cover, or perhaps they are conserving body heat on the warm ground. Whatever the explanation, the next time you see cows lying down in a field, look for rain clouds.

Me-Ouch!

During cold winter weather, static electricity can build up enough to produce quite a shock when you touch someone. Feline experts have speculated that on low-humidity days indoor cats lick their fur to lessen static charge. Could the moisture from their tongues help dissipate the electricity in smaller charges?

Dogs

Dogs often become restless before a storm, which may be due to their ability to hear thunder long before humans do. Dogs can hear roughly four times better than you and I can, which is why they bark at a car entering your driveway long before you hear it.

Plants as Weather Forecasters

The pimernel opens its leaves in sunny weather; closes tightly when bad weather is approaching.

In addition to animals, plants can also be used as weather forecasters. Recently, I was in the New Jersey Pine Barrens and a pine cone told me it was going to rain. Okay, "told" may be a stretch. But pine cones are one of the most reliable natural weather indicators. Pine cones change shape depending on how wet or dry the air is. In dry weather they open their scales, and in wet weather they close their scales.

Leaves on certain oak and maple trees tend to turn inward to indicate approaching rain. Originally from Asia, rhododendrons are beautiful flowering trees that keep their foliage all year and flower in the spring. Their leaves completely close below 20° F, start to open as the weather warms, and fully blossom at temperatures above 60° F.

Parting Thoughts

Look for nature's language in the signs described here and come to your own conclusions. Remember that Jane Goodall, the renowned primatologist, rocked the anthropology world simply through her observations of chimpanzees. And Charles Darwin helped usher in a new world of science with his theory of evolution, which he developed after a mere three-week observation of birds. Who knows what discoveries your personal insight will bring?

28 WHY IS THE SKY BLUE AND SUNSETS RED?

Have you ever wondered why the sky is blue? Sunlight scattering sunlight off molecules in the atmosphere creates a blue-colored sky. This is known as the Rayleigh Scattering Effect. John William Strutt, (Lord Rayleigh, 1842–1919), an English physicist who won the Nobel Prize for Physics in 1904 for co-discovering the element argon, studied how light waves move from the sun into the earth's atmosphere. He found that all the colors of the rainbow existed in Earth's sky. When looking at a prism as light passes through it, the Sun's white light appears to contain many colors. However, when looking at the sky not all light waves are visible, nor are they of equal wavelength. Rayleigh surmised this was essentially why the sky is blue. Some light waves are short, like blue and violet, while others are long, like red and orange. If you look at a rainbow, you can see the progress of wavelength from violet (shortest) to yellow (longest).

When light from the Sun comes in contact with atmospheric particles, such as water or dust, they are either scattered or absorbed.

Because the sky is vast and filled with gas, there are countless molecules in that area. Thus, violet and blue are scattered most frequently because they have the shortest wavelengths of light. Imagine blue and violet light as billiard balls bouncing around the atmosphere. These colors get caught in our atmosphere while the longer wavelengths of color, like red, yellow, and orange, pass right through.

Some of this scattered blue light reaches you, resulting in a blue sky. Because blue and violet are both short-wavelength light and are scattered more than red or orange, you may wonder why the sky is not violet instead of blue. To some insects that have certain kinds of color receptors in their eyes, it does look violet; but human eye receptors are more sensitive to blue, so that's what we see.

The sky often appears much paler in color on the horizon because it is farther away and the scattered blue light gets diffused because it must pass through more air, so less blue light reaches your eyes. The sky typically appears to be deeper in color when you are riding in an airplane or standing on top of a tall mountain because at higher altitudes, the sunlight has to pass through even less atmosphere, meaning the short blue light wavelengths get scattered even less.

Why Is the Sunset Red?

At sunset and sunrise the sun's light passes through more of the earth's atmosphere than at midday. So the opposite effect occurs: The wavelengths come into more contact with particles, especially at sunset when dust from the heat of the day has been suspended in the air. Because there are more particles to travel through, the blue and violet lights are scattered from sight, and many of the red, orange, and yellow colors become clear.

The most spectacular sunsets occur in dry climates and volcanic regions, where dust and volcanic ash create a particle-crowded atmosphere. The Hawaiian Islands are known for their beautiful sunsets.

Parting Thoughts

Despite my scientific understanding of the Rayleigh Scattering Effect, I still marvel at fiery red sunsets intensely blue skies.

29 THE MYSTERY OF THE FULL-MOON ILLUSION

I am guessing that at some point in their life everyone has looked at a full moon rising over the horizon and commented
on how big or "close" the Moon looks. I remember seeing the Moon
rising over the horizon on my first camping trip and thinking how
huge it looked! But later that night, I was confused when it was overhead and seemed to have miraculously shrunk and once again looked
"normal." Similarly, the Sun often looks red and swollen on the horizon at sunrise or sunset. While your brain may be telling you the large
Moon or Sun you see on the horizon looks very real, it actually *is* an
illusion called the full-moon illusion.

You can set up a series of simple experiments to prove this is actually a trick of the mind, and not reality.

Experiments

- When the Moon is on the horizon, pinch it between your forefinger and thumb, which should shrink it in your view. But when you take your hand away—poof! It blows up like a big balloon. You can also view the Moon through a cardboard tube, like a paper towel roll, or something similar. Both fingers and tube hide the foreground, putting things in perspective and cognitively adjusting the Moon to true visual size.
- Using your pinky nail or calibers, measure the width of the Moon when it is on the horizon (looking big). Wait several hours and repeat this experiment when the Moon is high in the sky (looking small) and see if you see any difference in size.
- Want more proof? Photograph the Moon with the same focal length at any level in the sky and see if there is any difference in size.

Have you noticed that the Moon and Sun look noticeably compressed when they are on the horizon—especially the Sun during the last moments of sunset, when its top appears to be flat? This is due to the greater thickness of the air near the horizon, which distorts the Moon's shape, making it appear smaller top-to-bottom. Earth's air is thicker near the horizon and the air compresses the Moon's image instead of magnifying it. When the Moon is on the horizon, it is a few thousand miles farther away in space than it is when it is overhead. So, it's actually smaller on the horizon than it is when it's overhead.

Ponzo's Theory

Many scientists have tried to explain the full-moon illusion. In 1913, Mario Ponzo, an Italian psychologist, suggested that the mind judges objects' sizes based on familiar backgrounds, which he called reference objects. To prove it, he used pictures of railroad tracks with horizontal lines, like those in the illustration on page 238. The upper horizontal bar may appear to be wider because it spans a greater *apparent* distance between the rails. But if you measure them, they are the same width. This is known as the Ponzo illusion.

PONZO ILLUSION

WHICH LINE IS LONGER?

There's a Bad Moon on the Rise

The Moon looks largest when it appears on the horizon over an ocean or large body of water under a cloudy sky. Lloyd Kaufman, Professor Emeritus at NYU, who has studied the full-moon illusion for nearly 50 years, says it is universally agreed that under these conditions the diameter of the Moon appears to be twice its normal size and its area four times that of normal, so it's tricking the brain.

Professor Kaufman says that viewing the Moon cresting the horizon near hills diminishes the illusion because the hills frame the Moon, giving its size perspective. But the illusion grows when the Moon or Sun are surrounded by clouds, which make the sky appear flatter and infinite. When looking at the Moon near the horizon, it appears to be close. Our brains exaggerate the Moon's size because it appears to take up so much space in the sky.

Our brains may be smart, but they are easily fooled.

FYI *Check out this celestial coincidence: Earth's Sun is 400 times the diameter of the Moon and 400 times the distance, which means it appears to be almost exactly the same size in the sky. What are the odds of that? No one knows for sure, but it's pretty cool.*

30 BAD HAIR DAY—NO ONE IS SAFE

Have you ever played basketball on a sweltering summer day and felt like you took a shower wearing clammy clothes and soggy sneakers? You may feel and say the heat is dragging you down, but it's not the heat—it's the humidity. High humidity (invisible water vapor), not only gives you the much-feared "bad hair day" from the excess moisture in the air, it also accelerates sweating as your body tries to cool itself. This results in feeling weighed down with a palpable sense of atmospheric pressure.

Measuring Humidity

Robert Hooke, a creative chap with an insatiable curiosity about humidity, is credited with inventing the "hair hygrometer," a gadget that measures the moisture content—or humidity—in the air. The hair hygrometer stretches a single strand of hair between two points and measures its length at different levels of atmospheric moisture. Hooke found that hair length shrinks when humidity rises, and it returns to its normal length when it falls. You know how your hair curls up on humid days? It's the same thing.

How to Make a Hair Hygrometer

Here's how to create your own hair hygrometer. You can record trends, using your own hair and become skilled at predicting bad hair days—or, rather, good baseball cap days.

GEAR LIST

- One strand of hair, about a foot long is best, but you can use a shorter strand
- Piece of corrugated cardboard, 9 × 12 inches
- Small piece of flat cardboard, approximately 2 × 8 inches
- Scissors
- Knife
- Pushpin
- Common pin
- Hot-glue gun (This can be purchased at a hardware or crafts store, or you can use epoxy.)
- One U.S. dime

Cut two small slits ¼ inch apart, about 1 inch in from the top left-hand corner of the corrugated cardboard. Cut the small piece of flat cardboard into a triangular-shaped indicator, about 6 inches long. Cut two slits at the base of the indicator, about 1 inch in from the larger end. Use a pushpin as an axis point for the indicator by simply pushing it through the surface, close to the larger side—about ½ inch from the left and 5 inches down the corrugated cardboard base. Slide the strand of hair through both sets of slits and use the hot-glue gun to secure them in place. Fasten a dime as a counterbalance, 1½ inches from the larger end of the indicator. Then push the common pin through the indicator hole to increase the tension on the hair when the indicator is pointing straight across.

To calibrate the hygrometer, place it in the bathroom while you're taking a hot shower—soap is optional. Once you're clean and dry, make a mark on the base where the indicator is pointing. This is your 100% humidity reading. Now use a hairdryer to completely dry the hygrometer, increasing the tension on the hair, and make a corresponding mark for your 0% humidity reading.

Look at all you've learned for nice price of 10 cents and a strand of hair. That's what I call good, clean fun—and learning!

FYI *Leonardo da Vinci built the first crude hygrometer in the 1400s.*

31 HOW TO MAKE A SIMPLE THERMOMETER

Being an adventurer, outdoor temperature often dictates my life. If I'm packing for an expedition in the Arctic, I'm sure to bring a subzero sleeping bag and down pants, while my trips to tropical climates require a rain jacket with a hood and 30+ SPF sunscreen. Even at home, often the first thing I want to know as soon as I crawl out of my cozy bed is What's the temperature? While it may be important to "dress for success" in business and school, knowing the temperature allows proper clothing selection and skin protection, which is critical for safety and survival in the outdoors.

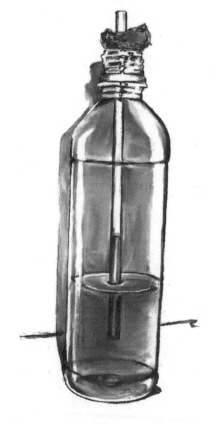

Most of us are familiar with the standard bulb thermometer, like the glass tube with fluid—generally mercury—indicator. You may have one outside your window. The liquid detects temperature change and its molecules contract (get smaller) when it's cold and expand (get bigger) when it's warm. So as the temperature rises, so does the mercury. With proper calibration, liquid reflects temperature.

Here's how to build your own thermometer that's incredibly accurate!

GEAR LIST

- Clear plastic bottle (an 11-ounce water bottle will work)
- Water
- Rubbing alcohol
- Clear plastic drinking straw
- Modeling clay or chalking cork—or even chewing gum
- Food coloring (your choice of color)

STEP 1: Fill the clear plastic bottle one-quarter of the way with equal amounts of water and rubbing alcohol.

STEP 2: Add a few drops of a dye or food coloring to make the liquid easier to see.

STEP 3: Put the straw in the bottle, but do *not* let it touch the bottom (keep it about ¼ to ½ inches away from bottom).

STEP 4: Seal the neck of the bottle using modeling clay or even used chewing gum, keeping the straw straight and stable (keep the straw as vertical as possible and be sure it doesn't touch the bottom).

FYI *If you don't have modeling clay, chewing gum or clear packing tape are great alternatives.*

STEP 5: Put a warm cloth around the bottom of the bottle—your own warm hands will work just as well—and watch the liquid move up through the straw.

FYI *Why does this happen? Just as in a regular thermometer, the liquid in the bottle expanded when it was warmed, and it filled the available space (the straw).*

Calibrating Your Thermometer

Calibrating your thermometer will enable it to report accurate temperatures. It's not difficult to do, but it takes patience, as tweaking it can take a bit of trial and error. Also, because the bulb of this thermometer (the bottle) is somewhat large, relative to standard thermometers, it takes more time to reach the same temperature as the air it is measuring.

To calibrate your thermometer, it is helpful to use a standard thermometer to set a scale for yours. Look at both thermometers every day at the same time of day, and compare the liquid levels. After a few days, you should have a good understanding of your thermometer's readings. Once you feel confident, you can use a permanent marker to note temperature measurements along the straw.

FYI

- *Will my thermometer freeze? Water freezes at 32° F, the mixture of rubbing alcohol and water used in your thermometer won't freeze until the temperature drops below –5° F.*
- *The American Fahrenheit scale, named after its inventor, Daniel Fahrenheit, is somewhat arbitrary as it's based on water freezing at 32° F and boiling at 212° F. The Celsius scale, which is used in Europe and in most scientific communities, makes more sense as it sets the freezing point of water at 0° C and the boiling point at 100° C.*

Although Fahrenheit and Celsius are the most widely used scales, there is nothing to say that you can't create your own scale.

32 HOW TO BUILD A SNOWMAKER

They say you can't fool Mother Nature, but you can
certainly imitate her.

When I was 13 years old, I got really into skiing. Unfortunately, I
lived on New York's Long Island—nice beaches but no mountains.
However, we did have the infamous Bald Hill, with a screaming 302-
foot elevation gain, 155-foot vertical rise, and a tow rope. It was indeed
the Mighty Midget. The problem was, for all its convenience, Bald Hill
took less than 30 seconds to ski down and at least 20 minutes to ride up
on the tow rope. Still, I was committed to shredding suburban snow.

As I wiggled my frozen toes to keep them warm inside my plastic
ski boots on my ride to the top, I often pondered the inner-workings
of the nearby buzzing snow machines. I assumed all a snow machine

did was spray water in a mist that froze when it hit the cold air, thus becoming snow. Man, was I wrong!

While sipping steaming hot chocolate after a day on the slope, I rummaged through my father's tool shed to look for a paint sprayer, so I could do my own snowmaking. The night was cold enough, a brisk 20° F, and much to my excitement, the spraying mist froze into tiny bits in the air, creating frozen ice on my backyard. But it was a far cry from the white fluffy stuff I wanted to ski on. It became my mission to discover the secret of snowmaking. To answer my questions, I turned to the Snow Pros.

The Snow Pros

Ski resorts depend not only on ample snowfall but on the professionals who patrol the mountains, sell the tickets, operate the lifts or tow ropes, and man the snow gun machines—the contraption that makes more snow and thereby offers skiers precious extra days on the slopes. I made quick friends with some of the snowmaking specialists, hoping they would give me the inside scoop on how a snow gun works.

Here's what I found out.

Traditional snow guns produce water droplets by combining cooled water and compressed air. Upon hitting the air, the water shatters into a fine mist, increasing the amount of time it's in the air—the *hang time*. To optimize hang time for wider distribution, many resorts position snow guns in towers.

Alas, snowmaking requires more than air and water. Compressing air pushes air particles together, restricting movement. So, when the air is released, the water particles spread, becoming a misty cloud that needs a nucleating agent to properly form crystals. In nature, snow-flakes form around a single particle.

While industrial snow machines are huge and expensive, you can make your own fairly easily. I made mine following the plans from a leading snowmaking company called Snow at Home, but I have made a few modifications to the design.

Make Your Own Snowmaker

This design works a lot like the large snowmakers at ski resorts do by mixing air and water internally. This machine won't make a mountain of snow, but it is easy to assemble and will be high on the fun factor!

GEAR LIST

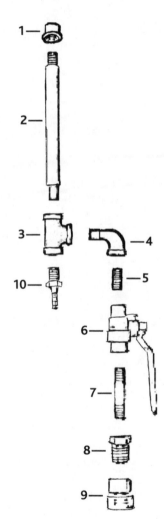

1. ¼-inch cap
2. 6-inch×nipple
3. ¼-inch×tee
4. ¼-inch×90-degree street elbow
5. ¼-inch close nipple
6. ¼-inch mini ball valve
7. 2-inch×nipple
8. ¼-inch female×½-inch male bushing
9. ½-inch female to garden (this will connect to a garden hose)
10. Quick-connect air fitting (this will connect to the compressor)
11. Garden hose

The best place to buy these parts is at a home improvement store or plumbing supply store (the total cost should be about $20).

ADDITIONAL MISCELLANEOUS GEAR NEEDED

- Roll of Teflon tape (used to seal threads)
- 7/64-inch drill bit

Requirements for Operation

- Compressor with a minimum rating of 3 cubic feet per minute at 90 pounds per square inch. Use an oil-lubricated model. The oil-free machines are not designed for continuous use.

Operating Your Snowmaker

STEP 1: Check Weather Forecast—Mother Nature Rules

This may sound obvious, but you need the right weather to make snow. Temperatures below freezing (perhaps as low as 20° F) are ideal for snowmaking. High humidity is death for a snowflake as it is more difficult for a drop of water to form around a nuclei and make a flake. Think: cold and dry.

STEP 2: Use Diagram and Begin Assembly

Use the Snow-at-Home diagram to assemble your snow machine. All your parts are designed for plumbing and thus should fit snuggly together, but the last thing you want is water squirting out of the sides of a loose pipe fitting in freezing weather.

Things to Know

Keep in mind that you need to attach your snowmaker to something secure, such as a ladder, fence post, or tree, because it will vibrate and shake. I have found large wire-ties or metal hose clamps to be best for securing.

You will also need to attach a basic garden hose connected to a water spigot to your snowmaker.

Remember that when your snow gun is not in use, any water left in the hose will freeze, and it will become a real pain to thaw later on.

The height above the ground is important for this model of snowmaker. The best height is around 4 feet. If it is much higher than 6 or 7 feet, your snowflakes will blow all over the place.

STEP 3: Connect Hose

Use the quick-connect fitting to connect the air hose from your compressor to the snowmaker.

This is the most important step. Make sure the ball valve on the snowmaker is closed and then turn on the compressor. Next, turn on the water, which should squirt from pipe cap. There is no backflow mechanism on this model, so if you turn the water on first it may back flow into the compressor. Slowly open the ball valve until a steady spray of water and air is being released. If there is a "pulsing flow," carefully adjust ball valve until the stream becomes steady. You should be able to hear air and see water coming out of the nozzle.

STEP 4: Check Snow Consistency

If the weather conditions are right for snowmaking, go make snow! Keep in mind that this design doesn't make very much snow at a time, so it may take several hours to make a small pile.

As with most of the projects in this book, I encourage you to experiment. In this case, you can adjust the nozzle and spray to find the optimum setting. If everything goes right, you should be able to cover a 20-by-20 foot area in your yard with an inch or so of snow during the night. Your snowmaking will undoubtedly give you a some appreciation for what the big guns on the ski slopes make—and an even greater appreciation for the sheer volume of snow Mother Nature produces during a big dump. Have fun and enjoy!

Why It Works

Snow forms as water condenses into tiny droplets when it comes in contact with tiny particles called freezing nuclei (or ice nuclei), which are created by dust, specks of plant debris, or bacteria blown by the wind.

According to snow-making expert Matthew Pitman, as more water vapor condenses on the droplets' surface, it grows and cold air then freezes the water into an ice crystal. Eventually, the ice crystal falls from the sky, continuing to grow by picking up more water vapor en route. If temperatures are below freezing when snowflakes travel through the atmosphere, they will typically accumulate on the ground. It's possible for snow to fall when surface temperatures are above freezing as long as the air temperatures immediately above the ground are below freezing and the atmosphere contains a minimum amount of moisture.

Wiese Weather Machine

So where did I go wrong with my first paint-sprayer attempt at creating a snowmaking machine? First, I did not ask for my father's permission. More to the point, though, the size of the droplets in the spray were probably too big or too small. Also, snowflakes require nuclei around which to form, and since there were none available at that time, I was out of luck. Although the air is filled with billions of particles, I was atmospherically too low for proper formation. I still think a paint sprayer will make snow if you place it high enough, adjust the nozzle so the spray is just right, and, of course, if the temperature is low enough.

FYI *The water content of snow varies more than most people realize. When I was a weatherman in New York people would always ask me "if that rain was snow, how many inches would we have gotten?" The rule of thumb is 1 inch of rain equals about 10 inches of snow is not always accurate. Ten inches of fresh snow can contain as little as 0.10 inches of water or as much as 4 inches, depending on the structure of the snow flakes, the wind speed, and the temperature.*

Parting Thoughts

Many people are disappointed when their local weather forcaster predicts the wrong amount of snow. Having been an on-air meteorologist, I can tell you that predicting snow is a difficult task. Once you've played Mother Nature with your snow machine, you should have a better grasp of how complicated it is to make snow. In the future, you might show a bit more compassion to your weather forcaster. If you see one in your neighborhood, you might consider buying him a slushy—and be sure to say something nice about his appearance.

33 HOW TO CREATE A RAINBOW

If you have ever dreamed about finding the end of a rainbow, it may be one dream you should give up. Rainbows are an optical effect. As you walk toward its end, the rainbow appears to move further away. Believe me, when my sister Kim (who illustrated this book) and I were kids we tried countless times to find the end of the rainbow. Have you ever heard the expression "chasing rainbows?" It is a metaphor for trying to obtain impossible dreams.

Reaching the end of a rainbow may be impossible, but making one is quite possible and something you can do with a little sunlight and water.

Where Is the Sun When You See a Rainbow?

Rainbows can only be seen by looking in the opposite direction of the Sun. Think about the last time you saw a rainbow. The rain or mist was most likely in front of you and the Sun was behind you.

This allowed the sunlight to bounce off the raindrops and reflect an arch of red, orange, yellow, green, blue, indigo, and violet colors into your eyes. To see a rainbow, your back must always be to the Sun.

Making a Small Rainbow

GEAR LIST

- Glass
- Water
- Sheet of white paper
- Sunshine

The easiest way to create a small rainbow is to place a glass of water in the sunshine and then place a piece of white paper behind it. Adjust the paper or the glass until a rainbow forms on the paper, and notice how the rainbow is only visible when the Sun is directly behind the glass along the shadow line. This is an important principle to remember when you go outside to create your large rainbow.

FYI *It's easier to create a rainbow in the morning or late afternoon when the Sun is low in the sky.*

Making a Large Rainbow

GEAR LIST

- Water hose
- Sunshine

Note: Full sunshine is the most important requirement for this experiment.

STEP 1: Holding the end of the water hose, walk to an open area full of sunlight.

STEP 2: Partially cover the end of the hose with your finger, or use a misting nozzle to create mist. The finer the mist, the better.

STEP 3: Turn your back to the Sun, so that you are facing your shadow, and spray water on your shadow. Voilà! You should see a rainbow!

It's really easy to know whether or not you are doing this right. If you see a rainbow—congratulations! If you see only the left half of the rainbow, move your spray a little to the right or move a little to the left. If you see only the right half of the rainbow, do the opposite.

FYI

- *If the Sun is high in the sky, you should see a slanted rainbow that you will be standing in.*
- *If you get really close to your shadow and wave the water like a mad wizard's wand, you might get to see a full circle rainbow floating right in front of your face. That's right—a full circle! Give it a try.*
- *Photographers love to set up shoots near waterfalls or large agricultural sprinklers.*

PART VII

EXPLORING

34 LORD OF THE TREE RINGS

Tree rings store information about the past such as an area's climate, insect outbreaks, glacial activity, volcanic events, fires, floods, earthquakes, and more. The oldest known tree in the world, believed to be 4,700 years old, is a Bristlecone Pine in the White Mountains of California.

Think about the history and evolution of species surrounding these trees' lives. During their lifetime, religions formed, civilizations were built and destroyed, wars were fought, millions of people were killed, and millions of others like us were born. Trees can be considered the quintessential survivors!

Reading Tree Rings

Tree rings are all around us. Look at the edge of a wooden bench or table or at the center of a tree stump. The thin line you see is a tree ring.

There is an entire science called *dendrochronology* that is dedicated to studying tree ring measurements. Each ring represents one year of a tree's life and can measure a mere fraction of a centimeter. Let's go find some tree rings!

GEAR LIST

- Sheet of parchment paper, 3×3 feet (Wax or butcher paper from the grocery store also works fine.)
- Pencil
- Thumbtacks

STEP 1: Find a Tree Stump

You don't need to cut down a tree to find some tree rings. All you need to do is find a stump, preferably one that is a few feet in diameter. Forests and parks are good places to find stumps, as are graveyards and church grounds (pulling out the stumps would cause damage to what is buried below them).

STEP 2: Count the Rings

Do a quick count of the rings to estimate the age of the tree when it died. A good way to do this is to count how many rings roughly fit between the tip of your index finger and the knuckle. Then turn your hand sideways and count out how many index fingers it is to the center. If it's about seven, that means the tree is probably close to 100 years old. But don't take my word for it; be precise and count each line.

STEP 3: Create a Tree Rubbing

Tack down the parchment paper to the stump's surface. Make sure it's smooth and secure. The paper should cover the entire surface—

including the edges. Rub the pencil over the rings, and they should magically appear on the paper as grayish-black lines. Before removing the paper, remove the tacks and step back to make sure all the areas are completely rubbed; otherwise, it will be difficult to match up the rings.

STEP 4: Locate the Year You Were Born on Your Rubbing

Once you take your rubbing home, you can use a ruler or a sheet of paper to number each ring. Then count each ring inward until you find a particular year, perhaps the year you were born. Mark this ring on your rubbing with a red pen or a sticker. You can also note rings for when your father, mother, sister, brother, or dog were born.

You can also look for notable dates in history, such as 1969, the year Neil Armstrong and Buzz Aldrin became the first humans to walk on the moon. If you're a master at this, you can find a tree ring for 1776, the year the Declaration of Independence was signed.

STEP 5: Reading Past Climates through the Rings

Tree rings become very small during droughts and quite large during years of ample rain, so scientists use them to reconstruct past climates. Assuming the weather affected ancient tree ring growth the same way it does today, scientists count rings from the middle of the trunk and study their width to construct an approximate calendar of wet and dry years. They also note the occurrence and frequency of fires by finding scars that appear in the growth rings.

Check out your stump to see if you can tell which years were dry and which ones had lots of rain. Does it match up with the information from the National Weather Service?

FYI

- *The fastest-growing plant in the world is bamboo, which is not actually a tree, but a grass.*
- *Baobab trees in Africa have the widest trunks in the world, and can grow as wide as 30 feet.*

Note: Notice the thicker rings that correspond to years in which hurricanes saturated the ground with more water than other years.

Parting Thoughts

Trees have been a silent witness to so much of Earth's history. It is amazing to think about trees that were mere sprouts in the time of the Egyptians, some 4,000 years ago, and are still alive today. Being a "Lord of the Tree Rings" can give you a good appreciation for time, history, climate—and the wooden table you may be sitting at right now.

35 A PALM TREE GROWS IN BROOKLYN

One day, after marveling at the Wollemi pine at the Brooklyn Botanic Garden, I noticed, of all things, a palm tree. I thought palm trees only grew in tropical climates. That, as I discovered, is a myth. Palms actually grow in many parts of America, even in areas that have seasonal snow.

Surprisingly, several "tropical" plants, such as banana trees, bamboo, cactus, and palms, can flourish in less-than-tropical places. All of these trees can be easily ordered online or purchased through local nurseries. I prefer to buy from my local nursery, where I have developed a good rapport with an expert, who is able to answer my many questions.

What Type of Palm

There are more than 1,500 species of palms worldwide. Some thrive in the blustery high mountains of Nepal, while others relish the hot, humid rainforests of Brazil. Though there are several "cold weather palms," I will focus on the Chinese windmill palm, which tolerates most climates.

When I noticed the 35-foot palm growing outdoors among pak and maple trees at the Brooklyn Botanic Garden, I asked arborist Chris Roddick how they moved this tree indoors every winter when it was clearly rooted in the ground. He explained that it was a variety of palm that grew in the Himalayas—and in Brooklyn with a little extra care.

If you are interested in gardening or growing plants or trees, it is important to understand the climate of your area and how it changes seasonally. An excellent source for this information is the Plant Hardiness Zone Map produced by the Department of Agriculture (www .usna.usda.gov/Hardzone/ushzmap.html). Zones predict the lowest winter temperatures for a given region in increments of 10° F. For example, Brooklyn is considered to be in between Zones 6 and 7. Zone 6 has a predicted low temperature of –10° F to 0° F, and Zone 7's predicted low is 0° F to 10° F.

The word *microclimates* means an assortment of climates (temperatures and weather conditions) that occur in an area. These regions can be large or small. For instance, there are microclimates in your backyard. You may feel hot and sweaty playing catch with your buddy in the blazing sunshine, but if you move over to the shade, you'll notice that the temperature drops instantly.

Being aware of microclimates is essential to cultivating plants and trees. Some grow better in direct sunshine, while others thrive in shady conditions. Before purchasing and planting a young palm, make sure you select the type that will thrive in your microclimate. Keep in mind that young windmill palms are sensitive to cold, and may defoliate at around 15° F. If that happens, the bud tissues will be severely damaged, and you will need to treat the crown cavity with a little copper fungicide (available at most garden stores) to prevent bud-rot.

Winterizing Is Not Cheating

As a kid, I remember visiting my great grandmother at her house in the Bronx during the winter and seeing her precious fig tree from Sicily, Italy, wrapped in canvas and rope. I didn't think much of it at the time, other than it looked weird, but she was "winterizing" her tree to help it survive the harsh winter.

Every winter, the arborists at the Brooklyn Botanic Garden wrap the palm leaves in plastic to protect them from frost damage. You may want to do the same if you live in a frosty area. But sure to remove the plastic as soon as the sun warms up or it will cook the palm.

In cold climates, experts suggest using supplemental heat, like a heat cable or holiday lights strung around the trunk and through the foliage, and covering the palm with a bed sheet on nights the temperature drops below 10° F. Make sure that the heaviest concentration of holiday lights or heat cable is around the top two feet or so of the trunk and up around every newly emerging spear leaf.

Mulching, or placing loose bark over the ground just above the roots of the palm, is another secret cold-weather-survival weapon. It keeps the ground at a consistent temperature, and protects the underground roots from freezing. Also, make sure your palm is well watered both before and after winter. Snow may seem harmful, but it can actually work as an insulator against harsh winds. You can also use a black plastic tarp—sort of a body bag—to protect your palm tree from wind damage.

36 FINDING FOSSILS—OUR RELATIVES FROM THE PAST

I was once scuba diving in the Cooper River near downtown Charleston, South Carolina, and saw a black triangular-shaped tooth on the riverbed. I knew about ancient Great White Sharks, some reaching 50 feet in length, and soon discovered that this tooth was from the fabled Megalodon, meaning "big tooth." The tooth's owner, a huge prehistoric shark, lived some 16 to 1.5 million years ago. How lucky was I to find it?

Of the estimated 30 billion species created on earth since life began 3.8 billion years ago—from the tiniest single-celled creatures to the giant T-Rex—99.99% are now extinct. With all these dead critters, you would expect to trip over fossils or have a bone pile in your backyard! The truth is, it isn't easy to become a fossil.

About one bone in a billion is thought to be fossilized. To put this in perspective, if you took the current world population of 6.6 billion individuals (each human having 206 bones in their body) and turned the

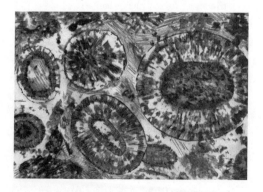

calendar ahead 1 million years, the equivalent fossil record would contain only 1,359 bones. In the end, as most paleontologists say, you have to be extremely lucky to become a fossil. That being said, you don't have to be lucky to find fossils—you just have to know where to look.

How Fossils Are Made

Finding fossils first requires understanding how they are created. In order for a creature's remains to be preserved, not only does it have to die, it must also be buried. It's a two-part process. Most things that die never get buried in a place that's going to stick around for a long time, and most post-mortem creatures are eaten by scavengers. Furthermore, even if bones do get buried, most will erode and never fossilize.

The terrestrial fossils we see in museums typically come from lakes, streams, ponds, and coastlines. But the best place to find fossils is likely to be where the earth has been covered by water and is now exposed, such as an old river bank or the side of a cliff. A sandstone or limestone formed in an ancient river would be a more promising place to look for fossils than a mountain made of granite. The good news for fossil hunters is that nearly all of the United States, especially the Midwest, was once covered by an ancient sea.

Fossils Found in Your Town

Chances are you have fossils all around your town. Many buildings use sandstone or limestone, which contain fossilized remains of a variety of marine animals. For example, the walls of the Maine State Capitol are made from black limestone and have countless marine fossils visible to anyone who chooses to look.

Virtually all of the State of Florida was built upon limestone bedrock, which is essentially fossilized coral reef. Look for fossils in freshly exposed rock along roads or new construction on your next visit to the Sunshine State. In Denver, there are fossil-hunting tours devoted exclusively to certain buildings. Perhaps your city has something similar. In some areas, limestone pinched between shale is often full of ancient fossilized ferns. Shale is commonly used on patios, so check your own backyard. Every time I take a train at New York City's Grand Central Station, I like to examine the limestone walls, which are littered with marine fossils from the Jurassic era. Washington, D.C., also provides many amazing fossil-viewing experiences.

Organize a fossil hunting safari in the buildings of your town.

You can see Jurassic sea fossils embedded in the limestone walls of New York City's Grand Central Station.

Finding Fossils in Nature

STEP 1: Where to go. The best place to find fossils is at your local museum. Jokes aside, a museum paleontologist, a fossil expert, can point you to the best fossil-finding locations in your area. Joining a paleontology club is a good way to meet others who may have already figured out the best places to look, saving you a lot of time. Please note that you need permission to remove or dig for fossils in most areas. Federal laws restrict collecting vertebrate fossils without permission.

That said, there are many places in the United States where you can easily find fossils. You can even go on fossil vacations. One of the top dinosaur diggers in the country, Kirk Johnson from the Denver Museum of Nature and Science, recommended two of his favorite places to find fossils. According to Kirk, Delta, Utah, is a great place to find trilobites, which are hard-shelled, segmented sea creatures that existed more than 300 million ago. Big Cedar Ridge, in Worland, Wyoming, is known for fossilized plants. I like the Cooper River in Charleston, South Carolina, which is where I found the fossilized megalodon tooth. Calvert Cliffs in Maryland and Poricy Park in Monmouth County, New Jersey, are also good places to find fossils.

STEP 2: Get your tools. Fossil-finding tools don't need to be high tech or expensive. If you watch a fossil-hunting show, you will see the hunters using an oddly shaped hammer called a "geo pick." It has a flat side for hammering and a pointed side for prying or making delicate cuts into rock. A butter knife, gardening spade, or shovel will also work well. You'll need brushes to clear the dust and sand off your finds. Toothbrushes are excellent for cleaning up fine details.

STEP 3: What to look for. Assuming you have permission to hunt for fossils, there are a few things to keep in mind. Canyons, river banks, cliff sides are good places to start looking for fossils. Look for unusual shapes, textures, and color variations in the rock. Keep in mind that there are more varieties of fossils yet to be discovered than have been identified by science.

STEP 4: Expose it. Once you find a fossil, take your time to gradually and gently expose it using the proper tools, so you don't damage your precious find. I have spent hours brushing sand and grit away from a bone with a toothbrush and whiskbroom, which allowed me to clear the area around it without disturbing whatever was underneath. It allowed me to see the position and condition of the fossil clearly, so that I could extract it without damaging it.

Handle your discovery with great care as it may be fragile. It is also important to take note of your location as you may have made an important discovery.

STEP 5: Extract it. When trying to remove a small fossil, it's often better to dig wider and then move inward, rather than cutting in too narrowly and running the risk of breaking it. So, if you find a three-inch shell, it's better to start cutting a foot around it, away from the center of the fossil. Most sedimentary rock (the rock that surrounds the fossil) breaks easily, so it's usually not too hard to remove fossils from them. To extract fossils from soft sediments such as sands, silts, and clays, use a flat-faced tool, like a gardening spade or shovel. And remember to use your brushes to clear the surrounding area.

Extracting a fossil from solid rock is usually a long and difficult task, so before you attempt to remove a fossil, make sure you can do so without destroying or damaging it. Before extracting fossils with a chisel and hammer from harder rocks, like shale, practice on a similar type of rock first to see how it breaks. Different types of rocks will break differently.

STEP 6: **The fine details.** Once you have dug out the fossil, you may notice that parts are missing. You can often find them by using a *sieve*, a mesh container that can separate fossils from sands and pebbles and missing bone pieces. Use an ultra-fine mesh that will allow dust and dirt to fall through but will catch large fragments.

How to Make Your Own Fossils

Why wait millions of years and leave everything up to Mother Nature when you can make your own fossil today? You can make several kinds of fossils out of leaves, bones, feathers, shells, and other objects.

GEAR LIST

- Plaster of paris mix (available at most hardware stores)
- Coffee can (to mix the plaster)
- Plastic spoon (for mixing and smoothing)
- Fossils to imprint (choose any from the following list)
    Twigs
    Leaves (stiff bay leaves work well)
    Dead, hard-shelled bugs (like rolly-pollys)
    Seashells
    Fish bones

1. Mix the plaster in a coffee can or a container that can be thrown away (it is also possible to wash the paste from the container before it dries). Most plaster of paris mixes use two parts plaster powder to one part water, but you should read the instructions on the package to be sure.
2. Set up a work area either with newspapers on the ground or outside in an area where you can make a mess.
3. Mix until the consistency of the plaster is smooth and even.
4. Pour the mixed paste into a shallow plastic container (I use recycled plastic food containers).
5. Smooth out the surface either by using your spoon or by gently swirling the container.
6. Wait until the mix dries so that there is very little water on the surface (this may take anywhere from 10 to 20 minutes).

7. Press your object evenly into the plaster and use your finger or spoon to smooth or press down detailed areas.
8. *Carefully* lift the object out of the plaster. Do not wait too long or the object will get stuck.
9. Let the plaster print dry fully. Once it's dry, you can paint it if you so desire.

This is much like the way genuine fossil prints were formed. Thousands, sometimes millions of years ago, plants, bugs, and animals left imprints in soft soil or mud, which eventually dried out, got covered, and eventually became rock.

FYI *Plastering is an ancient art used in the first primitive huts of man thousands of years ago. The walls of the great pyramids have plaster on the inside. The name* plaster of paris *was actually derived from the city of Paris, France, which had abundant supplies of the mineral gypsum, a key ingredient of plaster.*

Parting Thoughts

Fossil hunting is the ultimate detective game, and it can be won by some of the most unlikely participants. My friend Coley Burke, a businessman and adventurer from New York City, stumbled across one of the largest dinosaurs ever found while looking for a place to string his fish during a fly-fishing trip in Patagonia. The dinosaur was a giant soropod, a vegetation-eating dinosaur, that probably weighed 40 to 60 tons and was at least 60 to 70 feet long. The femur Coley found was approximately 7 feet long, and the leg would have been 19 feet long.

Ichthyosaur remains were discovered by a 12-year-old named Mary Anning almost two centuries ago. Although she had no formal training, her lifetime of fossil collecting and selling along the beaches of her hometown of Dorsett, England, inspired the rhyme "she sells sea-shells on the seashore." Neither Coley nor Mary were experts, nor were they even looking for fossils. Imagine what you can find if you actually know how and where to look.

37 CITY WILDLIFE SAFARI

There are roughly 100 million different organisms on earth, and only approximately 1.5 million have actually been identified, according to famed Harvard biologist E. O. Wilson. Every time you stand on a patch of grass, there are countless squirming, unnamed microorganisms beneath your feet. There is still so much left to discover!

You don't have to travel to the Amazon or to Africa to unravel scientific mysteries. The United States is filled with biodiversity. Wildlife can be found in backyards, vacant lots, streams, ponds, fields, gardens, roadsides, and even on apartment balconies. Just walking out your door, you can find hundreds of species thriving in urban and rural areas.

I live in New York City, which is about as urban as you can get. And believe it or not, not too long ago, a coyote wandered into Central Park and avoided capture by park rangers for almost a week. While I was writing this book, a red-tailed hawk flew up to my apartment windowsill. And one time, my friend Stefani Jackenthal was kayaking near Brooklyn, New York, when she saw a harbor seal. Find out what animals await you in your own backyard or city park!

There are several ways to enjoy the richness of the environment around you. Here are some that you and your friends can use to learn about the creatures living your neighborhood.

Zip Code Search for Animals

Visit the World Wildlife Fund's website, www.worldwildlife.org/wild finder/searchByPlace.cfm, to get a list of species living in your area. Click on Wild Finder, type your zip code in the box, and—bingo—a list of hundreds of species will pop up.

When I typed in my New York City zip code, I got 376 species. So, grab a friend and see who can find the most species in one day. Who knows, you may even get lucky and identify a new critter.

Organizing a Bio-Blitz

Central Park Rowing Pond:

In 2002, one of my best friends, Peter Burrow, wrote to me with a seemingly ridiculous idea to "identify every living organism in Central Park." Overwhelmed but intrigued, I took him up on his kooky challenge. Clearly, it was not a two-person job. So we did what every man must do every now and again, and asked for help, enlisting several organizations to help organize the project.

We called our mission the Central Park Bio-Blitz, and it was held June 27–28, 2003. The plan was to spend 24 hours documenting all the living things in the park. Not only was it a kick, but it turned out to be useful to biologists who were looking into the overall health of Central Park. Much to our surprise, there was an outpouring of interest from hundreds of people who consider the park to be their own backyard. More than 500 scientists and students volunteered through various conservation groups, and the event was covered by CNN, ABC, CBS, *USA Today*, *The New York Times*, the BBC, and many others, allowing millions of people around the world to watch.

Our inaugural Central Park Bio-Blitz was not only a huge social success, but a valid scientific experiment. On that warm, sunny summer day, we identified more than 800 species of life, ranging from trees to birds. During our second Bio-Blitz, we concentrated on microbes, and discovered 202 new species of life never before identified.

How to Set Up a Bio-Blitz

Organizing your own Bio-Blitz doesn't have to be complicated. Choose an area, rally your participants, and create a fun but precise plan. You may find species that have never been found or species that are about to become extinct.

STEP 1: Define your Area of Research
Keep it small so you can achieve your goals. I recommend using your backyard or a small section of a local city park.

STEP 2: Have an Idea of "What" you Might Find
Use the World Wildlife Fund Wildlife Finder or speak to a local wildlife ranger to find out which species live in your area.

STEP 3: Divide Responsibilities

While one person or group records birds, have others document animals, plants, and insects. There are no hard and fast rules, so use common sense. Most of all, be sure to keep it fun.

STEP 4: Pick an Exact Time to Start and End the Bio-Blitz

Most large Bio-Blitzes occur in a 24-hour period, but you may want to do yours over a weekend or on an afternoon.

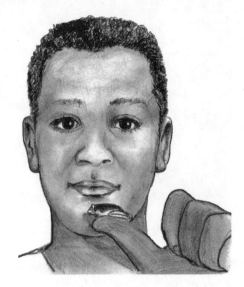

STEP 5: Analyze Your Results

If you find a new species or one thought to be extinct, notify your nearest science or natural history museum and be sure to take credit for your finding—or others will bask in the glory of your discoveries. One purpose of a Bio-Blitz is to look for trends over time, from one season or year to the next, so you may want to make it an annual thing. This is a great way to note an increase or decrease in a species population.

City Safari Contest

For your Bio-Blitz, pair up with friend and make a game out of your discoveries.

GEAR LIST

- Animal identification materials (National Audobon Field Guides are classic sources, but there are many others). Many local parks offer free animal guides. Contact your local park for information.
- A friend
- A pen
- A piece of paper
- Your backyard or a local park

THE GAME

Assign a number of points to birds, mammals, insects, plants, and add bonus points for a species that neither of you has yet identified. Set a time limit, for instance, 1 hour.

SAMPLE POINT BREAKDOWN

1. Plants: 1 point
2. Insects: 2 points
3. Birds: 3 points
4. Mammals: 4 points
5. A new species of wildlife you've never seen before: 5 points

SAMPLE CHART

Wildlife	Points
Wood Duck	2
Red Tail Hawk	5
Cuckoo	2
Sparrow	2
Herron	5
Snow Cricket	3
Fox	5
Total:	22

Bonus: Extinct Creatures

Keeping a Life List

A life list is a written record of all the species you have ever seen. These are often created by bird-watchers (who are also known as "birders"). Birding is a good way to start your list because it is focused and can be easily picked up and shared. Birders are proud of their life lists, and you don't have to be professional birder to achieve birding glory. The ivory-billed woodpecker is the Holy Grail of bird-watchers—even Teddy Roosevelt looked for it. It was long thought to be an extinct species, but credible sources say it was rediscovered in Arkansas by Bobby Harrison, an amateur enthusiast. If you make a cool find, be sure to document it with a high-resolution photograph.

Getting Started

To start your own life list, print a list of birds known to be present in your state by visiting the Bird Checklists of the United States website (www.npwrc.usgs.gov/resource/birds/chekbird), presented by the Northern Prairie Wildlife Research Center.

GEAR LIST

- Binoculars are helpful but not necessary.
- A new notebook in which to start your life list. You may want to list your discoveries by date and location in 3 columns: August 10, 2007—Florida Keys—Flamingo.
- For advanced birders, a Digi-Scope, which is a digital camera, telescope, and spotting all rolled into one, is wonderful thing.

CREATE YOUR OWN BIRD LIFE LIST:

These easy tips will help you begin your own birding adventure:

- Wear subtle-colored clothing that will blend in with the surroundings.
- Walk slowly and quietly.
- Go solo or keep your group small.
- Close your eyes and listen; try to identify sounds from different birds.
- Use binoculars to observe high up in trees.
- Keep a detailed list of your findings.

- Create a bird-finding competition with friends and family.
- Notice birds at random times—as a passenger in a car, walking to school, and so on.
- Never disturb birds or their natural habitats.

Parting Thoughts

Keeping a bird life list or a more comprehensive all-species life list, or going on a wildlife safari is simple no matter where you live. If you pause to take a look, you might see gulls circling overhead, a squirrel scampering across a power line, or ants scurrying along a crack in the sidewalk.

38 PANNING FOR GOLD

When I was 15 years old, I flew to Fairbanks, Alaska, with my father. He was a pilot, and he literally flew us there. It was a fun trip filled with hiking, wildlife viewing, kayaking, and—one of the highlights for both of us—panning for gold.

Feeling like we had stepped back into the era of gun-slinging, horse-riding pioneers, we bought two extra-large tin pans about the size of hubcaps and hiked over to an old gold mine.

After a little coaching from a local old-timer, my dad and I scooped and swirled dirt around in our shiny new tins, eagerly scanning for a glimmer of gold. Grinning like a cat home alone with the parakeet, I stared into the mucky pan with an intense focus that could have bored holes right through the bottom of the pan. And not 20 minutes after starting, I pounded my fist in the air—I struck gold! Mind you, I ended up with just a few flakes that I carefully tucked into a tiny glass bottle, but finding them was so cool! I was so high on the gold rush that I filled a large bag with dirt and took it home with me so I could continue my quest for gold in my own backyard. This obsession is commonly referred to as "gold fever." Unfortunately, the flakes and golden dirt somehow got mixed up with other soil and now resides somewhere in my parents' garden.

Panning

During the California Gold Rush (1848–1855), when gold was first discovered in Sutter's Mill near Columa, California, nearly 300,000 gold-hungry "forty-niners," as they were called, arrived in California from around the world. Did you ever wonder where the San Francisco 49ers got their name? The discovery of that shiny precious metal in El Dorado County, California, started the Gold Rush of 1849.

Every day, hordes of starry-eyed gold seekers waded into bone-chilling streams, wearing just wool pants and leather shoes. Sticking their bare hands under numbing, rushing water, they dragged up fistfuls of minerals from the bottom and placed them in their pans, or "gold dishes," as they were called back in the day.

Panning, as we think of it today, is actually a technique that involves placing a pan underwater, about an inch below the surface, and swirling it to allow the gold particles, which are six to seven times heavier than sand, to settle at the bottom of the pan. In theory, the lighter sand, mud, and gravel washes over the sides of the pan, leaving the gold behind.

Before you grab your mom's baking pan and streak down to your local stream, there are a few things to keep in mind.

GEAR LIST

- Large pan. The standard gold pan that miners used in days of old was typically made of steel and was 16 inches wide at the top, 2¹/₂ inches deep, and 10 inches wide at the bottom. Your pan can be slightly larger or smaller, but it should be in that range. Although traditionalists will insist upon steel, plastic works just as well.
- Turkey baster

STEP 1: Find the Gold

Gold does not occur in every waterway, so research a few prime locations before creating your panning or travel itinerary. A good place to start is www.goldfeverprospecting.com or The Gold Prospectors Association of America (Post Office Box 507, Bonsall, CA 92003; 619-728-6620). Both are good resources for how and where to pan for gold.

In addition to California, which is known as the Gold Rush State, you may be surprised to find gold in North Carolina, Wisconsin, Alabama, and Ohio. In fact, most of the 50 states have naturally occurring gold deposits. Some even offer gold-panning vacations. Try Gold Country Prospecting (3119 Turner Street, Placerville, CA 95667; 916-622-2484). If you want to hit the big time, head up to Alaska's Crow Creek Mine on New Seward Highway in Chugach National Forest, about 45 miles south of Anchorage (907-278-8060). Visitors receive demonstrations, a shovel, and a pan.

STEP 2: Submersion (Panning Technique)

Scoop about four handfuls of soot, silt, and rock-filled sand into the pan. Then submerge the pan in stream water—just below the surface—while moving it carefully in a circular motion so that the lighter materials get carried away by the water flow. Don't move it too rapidly or you may lose gold along with the rocks and sand. Continue swirling the pan until about half of the debris is gone.

Remember that gold is heavier than water, so it stays on the bottom of the stream, and gets caught in sand and slow-moving currents along the shore. It also tends to get wedged in crevices, under rocks, and in wood, so look for places like that along the stream.

Tie a lead fishing weight (1 or 2 ounces) to an inflated balloon with about 10 feet of fishing line, and toss it into the water to see where it settles. That may be a good place to start looking for gold. The weight of lead is similar to that of gold, so in theory, the lead weight will mimic gold's behavior as it moves along the stream and settles.

STEP 3: Panning

Lift the pan out of the water, and swirl it around while tipping it slightly to the side so that water can spill off, carrying along some of the debris. When the water is gone, dip the pan into the water again, bring it back out, and start swirling again. Repeat this pattern until nearly all the material in the pan is gone.

STEP 4: Separation and Retrieval

Use a turkey baster to spray water into the pan and separate any nuggets or flakes of gold from the sand in the bottom. You can also use the baster to suck out small flakes of gold and deposit them into a container.

Parting Thoughts

Don't bum out if you didn't hit the mother lode or find any gold. It takes practice, persistence, and a little luck. Keep trying. It's a great hobby, and the gold you find is worth the memories—and maybe even a few bucks. Good luck!

39 THUMB PIANO, PLEASE

When sitting in your tent waiting out a storm, taking a break after a strenuous hike, or hanging around the fire, it's nice to have a musical instrument. Sometimes, however, even a harmonica is too expensive or unavailable. But did you know that several interesting musical instruments can be made by hand? One of my favorites is the thumb piano.

Thumb pianos are not commonly found in America. Known as "mbiras" in Africa, they have been around for more than 1,500 years and are often used in religious ceremonies and at social gatherings. They are the national instrument of choice in the Zimbabwean culture. Across Africa, it is believed that plucking the keys of a thumb piano will attract your ancestral spirits, and even communicate with them.

Make Your Own Thumb Piano

Thumb pianos usually have strips of metal of various lengths pinched tightly against a hardwood or metal box bearing a hollowed hole.

Sometimes also called a "gwariva," the body of the thumb piano works as an acoustical box. While the box size varies, it always requires that the right thumb and index finger be free to pluck the high notes from above and below the keys.

Bottle caps, shells, or a thick nail are traditionally placed below the keys to give the prongs a buzzing sound when they are tugged. The keys are arranged in three rows: two are on the left and one is on the right. The tried-and-true configuration has the bass keys in the bottom-left row, the middle-range keys in the the top-left row, and a combination of the secondary bass keys and the high keys in the right row.

After you make your thumb piano you may be surprised by the resonating sounds this little instrument can make as well as its nifty portability. Are you ready to make your friends jealous? In no time, you can be making up your own songs or trying to play one of today's little ditties.

While African locals have the benefit of village elders to teach them how to construct a thumb piano, westerners need to improvise. When I made my first piano, I followed the instructions from a kit I obtained from a leading music shop in Stillwater, Minnesota (info@musikit.com). The plan and instructions that are given here, however, are based on my own experiences building the pianos. Allow a full day to make your first thumb piano.

Thumb Piano Kit

GEAR LIST

- 10 × 14 inch oak or cherry wood sheet $1/8$-inch thick. Pine will also work, and it is cheaper.
- $1/2$ × 1 × 24 inch furring strip to be cut for frame. The dimensions are given in the illustration.
- 1 metal clamping rod 5 × $3/8$ inches in diameter to hold the keys down.
- 1 metal bridge rod 5 × 3/32 inches in diameter
- 8 to 12 keys (also called tongues or tines) or street sweeper bristles from a metal rake (I ordered mine.)
- Hardwood, such as cherry or oak, bridge $1/4$ × $1^3/8$ × 5 inches.
- 2 $1/4$ inch t-nuts with 2 machine screws approximately $1^1/4$ inches long

- Paper (for blue prints)
- Saw
- Drill
- 1 ³/₄ inch arbored hole saw
- Hammer
- Tape or clamps
- Sandpaper. Get both medium grit (120) paper and fine grit (180).
- Wood glue

Assembly Instructions

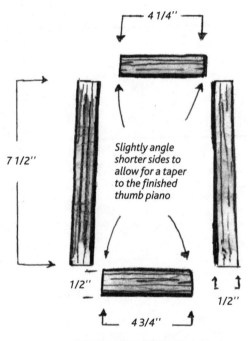

Slightly angle shorter sides to allow for a taper to the finished thumb piano

CUTTING THE 1/2" X 1" FRAMING

STEP 1: The first part of the process is to make an acoustic box (a box that resonates sound). I found it helpful to sketch out a plan to help visualize how the components will be laid out.

STEP 2: Cut your frame from the furring strip, to the dimensions outlined in illustrations. I used a table saw but you can use a hand saw, too.

STEP 3: Note that the top and bottom are slightly different dimensions and are angled to allow a taper to the finished thumb piano.

STEP 4: Glue the frame together. It is a good idea to try to piece it together to make sure all parts of the frame fit together nicely before you start gluing. When you are satisfied with the fit, glue each section of the frame together. Use masking tape or clamps to hold it together and let it dry on a flat surface. Drying times vary, but allow at least half an hour.

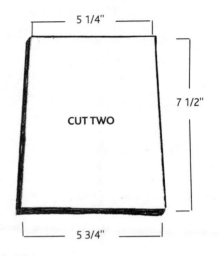

STEP 5: While the frame is drying, cut the top and bottom of the wood sheet.

STEP 6: Once the glue on your frame has dried, remove any clamps or tape. Lay the back panel down and place the frame on top of it. The frame should fit within the bottom panel. If you are satisfied, glue them together, tape or clamp them, and let it dry.

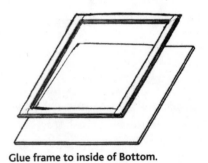

Glue frame to inside of Bottom.

STEP 7: While the frame and bottom panel are drying, work on the top panel. Cut a 1¾-inch sound hole (use a 1¾-inch arbor-hole saw to do this). The center of the hole will be 4½ inches from the top end of the top panel and centered (see the illustration).

> Note: The size of the sound hole affects the overall sound of the instrument and how notes will be emphasized. (A larger sound hole seems to emphasize higher notes, while a smaller hole makes the lower notes seem louder.)

Sand any rough edges, and generally make it look pretty!

STEP 8: Cut a 1⅛×4-inch brace out of the extra wood.

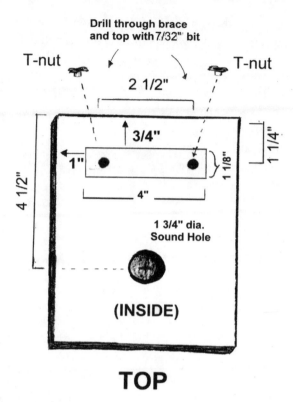

**Drill through brace
and top with 7/32" bit**

T-nut

T-nut

2 1/2"

3/4"

1"

4"

1 1/8"

1 1/4"

4 1/2"

1 3/4" dia.
Sound Hole

(INSIDE)

TOP

STEP 9: Place the brace on the inside of the top, 1 inch from the sides and ¾ inches from the top (opposite the sound hole).

STEP 10: Glue the inner brace to the *inside* of the top piece. Remember that the brace will be on the opposite side of the sound hole. Let it dry.

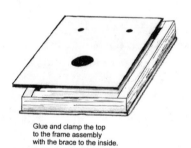

Glue and clamp the top
to the frame assembly
with the brace to the inside.

STEP 11: Measure and mark the two points to drill for the t-nuts on the top panel as shown in the illustration.

STEP 12: Drill holes through the brace and the top panel using a 3/16-inch drill bit. Take care not to split the wood. This is where the t-nuts will be inserted. The holes will be slightly smaller than the t-nut.

STEP 13: Gently tap the t-nuts into place in the inner brace with a hammer.

STEP 14: Line up the clamping rod with the t-nuts and brace. Mark and drill the clamping rod with a 3/16-inch drill bit. Set it aside.

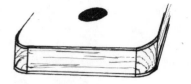

Round corners and sand edges when glue dries.

STEP 15: Assemble the rest of the box by gluing the top to the frame, making sure the brace is on the inside. If you are using a clamp, use a piece of cloth so that you do not mark the wood.

STEP 16: While the box is drying, you are going to create the bridge. This is where your keys will be clamped down. Many successful designs substitute a wooden dowel and a metal rod, but we will be using a wooden bridge. This is the surface that will allow the keys to vibrate and make their various notes.

FORMING THE BRIDGE

Begin with hardwood 1/4" x 1-3/8" x 5".

1 3/8"

5".

BRIDGE

A- Use dado blades to cut out the center, 5/8" wide x 1/4" deep.

B- Chamfer the edges with a router or table saw.

C- Cut a 3/32" groove with veining router bit.

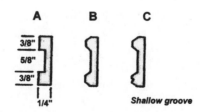

A   B   C

3/8"
5/8"
3/8"

1/4"

Shallow groove

STEP 17: Cut and form the bridge as shown in the illustration.

STEP 18: Mark the center of the bridge with a pencil.

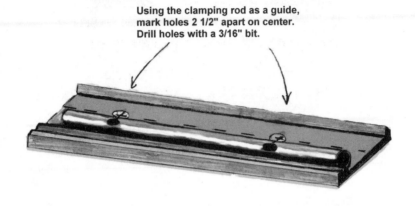

Using the clamping rod as a guide, mark holes 2 1/2" apart on center. Drill holes with a 3/16" bit.

STEP 19: Center the clamping rod on the bridge. Mark and drill the bridge so that it lines up with the holes. Use a 3/16-inch bit.

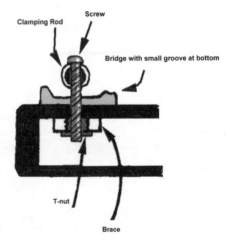

Clamping Rod

Screw

Bridge with small groove at bottom

T-nut

Brace

STEP 20: At this point, you should have your acoustic box assembled. It is a good time to sand and remove any rough surfaces or excess glue. You may also stain the wood at this point, or paint or decorate it any way you choose.

STEP 21: Place the bridge on the top of the box, aligning the holes with the t-nuts. If necessary, trim the bridge so that it does not hang over the sides of the box.

STEP 22: Apply a small amount of glue on the bottom side of the bridge. Be careful not to apply too much or it will seep out onto the box surface. Place the bridge.

Be sure that the bridge does not slide around or move while it is drying. I use the clamping rod and two mounting screws to hold it in place.

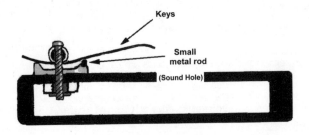

Keys

Small
metal rod

(Sound Hole)

STEP 23: Once the glue has dried on the bridge, loosen the screws on the clamping rod, because you will need some wriggle room to place the keys.

STEP 24: Place a small metal rod in the groove of the bridge.

STEP 25: Insert one key in the middle and tune it roughly to C. Place the other keys as indicated on the illustration and tighten the bridge firmly. You should feel or hear a buzz when the keys are plucked or pressed.

Don't worry if it sounds horrible—the keys are not tuned yet.

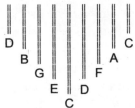

D   C
  B   A
    G   F
      E   D
        C

STEP 26: Tuning the keys was difficult for me. I have always considered myself quite musically challenged, so I enlisted the aid of a friend who knows a lot more about music than I do. She helped me tune the notes correctly by sliding the keys in or out. The notes will not be tuned to absolute pitches but rather relative to one another.

STEP 27: When you are satisfied with your tuning, tighten the screws a little more so that the keys will not slide.

> Note: I found that bending the metal rods slightly downward at the ends helped make it feel smooth to the touch.

STEP 28: I marked letters or notes on my instrument to help me play while reading notes off of sheet music. Many thumb piano songs are available and sometimes use numbers to indicate which keys to play, which is helpful if you don't read music. My first song was *Twinkle, Twinkle Little Star*.

Playing

You can learn to play songs that already exist by researching bass songs online. The bass instrument is popular and also typically plucks only one string (note) like the thumb piano. When you are playing it, hold the instrument like a Gameboy, placing your thumbs over the instrument keys, leaving your right thumb and index finger free to play the keys. The right thumb is used to play the first three keys on the right. The remaining keys on the right are played with the right index finger. You can use either thumb to pluck the middle three notes.

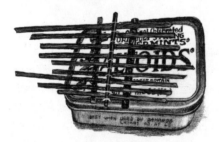

If you are feeling especially creative, you can make a great make-shift piano from an Altoids tin. In some circles, they are even collector's items (see Chapter 1, Altoids Survival Kit).

40 LIGHTNING IN YOUR MOUTH

Ever bite into a Wint-O-Green Lifesaver and get a tingly feeling that screeches down your spine? It's a pretty funky feeling that gives me a quick adrenaline pump. The next time you have a roll with you at night, give one to a friend to bite between his front teeth and watch for sparks. Really! It's sort of like lightning in your mouth.

The exact way lightning forms is still under debate, but it is always the result of charge separation between a cloud and the ground (or another cloud). This means there is a build-up of electrons in one place and a lack of electrons in another. Because electrons have a negative charge, this creates an "electric potential" between the two places. Eventually, the extra electrons move toward the place with less charge. We can't actually see electrons moving, so the bright bluish bolts of light, followed by a tremendous crash, is actually the result of the interaction between the moving electrons and nitrogen gas in the atmosphere.

Atoms, which are made up of positively charged protons and electrically neutral neutrons that are surrounded by negatively charged electrons, emit light when they get excited with energy. The color (wavelength) of the light that is discharged depends on the type of atom being stimulated. For instance, nitrogen emits light in the blue region of the spectrum, and that's why we see lightning as bluish in color.

Back to our mints: Using only our hole-in-the-middle wintergreen candy and a mirror, we can create a little lightning in your mouth. This effect is called *triboluminescence*. Here's what you need to make it happen.

GEAR LIST

- One roll of Wint-O-Green Lifesavers
- A dark room such as a closet
- A mirror

Stand in a dark room for about five minutes, until your eyes have adjusted to the dark (See Chapter 15, Tracking). Face a mirror and take a Wint-O-Green Lifesaver from the roll. Trying not to moisten the candy, put it in your mouth and quickly bite down hard. You should see a spark of light from the Lifesaver every time you chew until it becomes moist.

Here's why it works. When the crystalline sugar and wintergreen oil in the Lifesaver is fractured by your teeth, several types of particles are released, including electrons. These electrons are not evenly distributed between the two halves of the fractured candy, and this imbalance creates an electrical potential. As the electrons move between the halves to reduce the potential, they create an electric current. This in turn, excites nitrogen atoms in the atmosphere within the fracture. The excited nitrogen atoms then emit photons in the blue region of the spectrum, and this is the visible spark that we observe. Here, the addition of wintergreen oil changes the final wavelength to a somewhat different color of blue light than lightning, but the two phenomena are quite similar.

You can also do this experiment using two large quartz crystals. Keep in mind that these crystals must be smashed during the experiment and will therefore be damaged. The quartz crystals may be taken into a dark room as before and smashed against each other or with a hammer on a prepared surface to create a spark.

41 STAR TRAIL AND MOON PHOTOGRAPHY

As digital technology continues to improve, photography is becoming more popular than ever. But I still prefer to gaze into the night sky as the ancient Greek philosophers did long ago. It took thousands of years of looking at stars to figure out that Earth isn't the center of the universe.

Digital versus Film Photography

When I do shoot, I'm a big fan of digital photography, although sometimes 35-millimeter film cameras are better for nighttime exposures.

One downfall to shooting outside with a digital camera is the noise. The longer the exposure, the more buzzing (essentially, pixilation) is heard.

Shooting Your Own Images

GEAR LIST

- Digital SLR camera (I recommend the Olympus E–520)
- Tripod or bean bag
- Photoshop
- Timer device (I recommend Pclix)

Moon Photography

Photographing the Moon can be difficult because the surrounding night sky can cause glare or overexposure. The best times to shoot the Moon are morning, afternoon, or around sunrise and sunset, when the contrast is minimal and there is ambient light in the sky.

Helpful Hints

- If you are using a telephoto lens, you will need a tripod or some-thing sturdy to brace the camera, like a wall or tree. When taking the picture, it's important to slow your breathing and gently squeeze the trigger, much like a marksman fires a rifle.
- If your camera has a light sensor or built-in light meter, play around with the settings. I frequently toggle between the digital ESP/ Center-Weighted Average to Spot.
- Keep your ISO setting on auto or a low setting (below 400).
- For exposure, you should think in terms of fractions of seconds, not minutes.
- If the sky is bright enough, leave your exposure on auto. I find the best Moon to photograph is a sliver of a new moon.
- Use a telescope to photograph the Moon up close to see the sharp, beautiful, crater edges on the sun's shadow. If you have a large eyepiece, you can carefully place your camera's lens up to the eyepiece and take a photo.

Star Photography

Star photography is one of the most artistic and innovative ways to capture the rotation of the earth on its axis. In photographs, it appears as if the stars are forming circles around the earth.

Here are some tips to help you get the best photos.

Helpful Hints

- Choose an evening with clear skies. The best conditions for clear skies are cold nights, when the atmosphere contains less moisture. Snowy regions tend to contain less dust in the air, and being far from big cities ensures there is less light pollution in the atmosphere.
- Professional star photographers debate whether it's better to have the Moon in the night sky to provide contrast against the stars, which are points of light. Most suggest that having the Moon in the sky is a good thing because it illuminates the foreground of the picture, such as trees or mountains.
- Finding the right exposure is tricky, and it depends on the quality of your lens and the ambient light in the sky. It's best to take a few test frames to get the correct settings. Start with short exposures and gradually increase them.
- While a typical film photographer takes a minutes-long exposure of stars, digital cameras are too noisy to use this technique. Use a timing device with digital cameras that automatically take a single

shot at preset intervals (I use Pclix). I often set up my camera on a tripod and preset my Pclix to take one exposure every 5 minutes for 6 hours. That means my camera takes 72 photos over 6 hours. I then have 2 options. I can import the photos into Photoshop or create a movie.

Importing Photos into Photoshop

Here is how renowned star-trail photographer Sam Javanrouh integrates his images into a single, fantastic star-trail image. This method only works with Photoshop version CS3 or later.

- Go to FILE MENU SCRIPTS and choose LOAD FILES INTO STACK.
- Depending on how you saved your images, select FILES or FOLDER from the drop-down menu and then BROWSE to find your photos.
- Check the CREATE SMART OBJECT AFTER LOADING LAYERS checkbox and click on OK. After a while, Photoshop will create a SMART OBJECT layer in the Photoshop Layers window.
- Select the layer and go to menu LAYER SMART OBJECTS STACK MODE MAXIMUM (You can also try different items under STACK MODE to experiment. You might be surprised by the results).
- Voilà! You're done! If you want, you can right-click on the layer and select RASTERIZE LAYER to minimize your file size (but if you do that, you won't be able to change the STACK MODEs later).

Making the Best Picture

Here are some tricks you can use to take good pictures and turn them into great pictures.

Helpful Hints

- Pick an interesting foreground such as trees or mountains, which offer night sky perspective. Some of the best shots use the mountains illuminated by moonlight or the reflection of snow off the ground.

- More than 2,000 years ago, the Greek philosopher Aristotle wrote that great art is divided into "the rule of thirds." For us that means the foreground should be the bottom third of the photograph and the sky should fill the remaining two thirds.
- Use a wide aperture setting of approximately f4. This will allow more light to come through more quickly, minimizing the exposure time and amount of noise.
- If you have an ISO setting, use a value of less than 400. Higher settings will be too grainy.
- If you are using a timer device, put your focus on manual and have it slightly below infinity. If you are using an object in the distance as a focal point, such as a tree, use a flashlight to get the tree in focus.
- If you don't have a tripod, use a bean bag or a bunched up jacket to stabilize your camera, but remember to use a cable or auto-timer because your finger will shake the camera.
- Use a wide-angle lens instead of a telephoto lens. Your shot will be more in focus, and the perspective will be more interesting.
- High-elevation areas will reveal more stars than low-elevation areas.
- Avoid cities or artificial light sources. Nothing ruins a star photo more than light pollution.

Creating a Movie with Photos

Remember that a movie is just a series of still frames sped up, roughly 29 frames per second for video. To create a movie with all 72 frames, use editing software, such as Premier or Final Cut. Keep in mind that frame dimension, such as 720×480 pixels, is quite specific. Just as important, the resolution needs to be at least 72 dpi, so you may have to reduce the size of your file. Again, I would use a timing device so the photo intervals will be even and the frames will show seamless continuity.

Special Bonus Points

The Northern Lights, or Aurora Borealis, are one of the most spectacular sites in the sky. It looks as if the gods gently waved a sheet of multicolored lights over Earth. The best way to photograph this effect is to open your aperture as far as you can, say f2.8, and put your ISO around 400 and have an exposure of less than 30 seconds. Don't try to take too long an exposure of the Borealis or it will start to lose its shape and distinct coloration. Instead, use a timer, take a series of pictures, and don't be afraid to experiment—there are no hard and fast rules.

Parting Thoughts

Star-trail or meteorite photography can be very rewarding and result in some inspiring additions to your photography repertoire. It can open up new ways of expressing the beauty of a subject and excite those looking at your cool pictures. It's not difficult, but the logistics and preparation needed to get a great shot require time, thought, and patience.

> *"Why not look at the sky?"*
> —Ben C. Oppenheimer

42 COLLECTING METEORITES

On October 9, 1992, a sudden hush came over a lively crowd of high-school football fans when a freakish fireball flashed over Peekskill, New York. The flashing rock, the size of a bowling ball, bolted through the sky, screeching to a thunderous boom as it pierced the trunk of a parked Chevy Malibu and dented the driveway below. Residents rushed out of their suburban homes to the crash site, awed by the meteorite embedded in the driveway, still steaming and reeking of sulfur.

Meteorites are the ancient leftovers from the formation of planets. They are much older than our minds can comprehend and hold great significance as extraterrestrial messengers from the solar system's distant past. Meteors and comets built our planet's geology, and scientists think that it is likely that they supplied much of our water. They have even been connected to the origin of life on earth as some meteorites contain large quantities of carbon compounds, the basic building blocks of life.

Scientists rely on these special rocks for information about the history of our Solar System. There are several mammoth meteorites from Greenland on display at the American Museum of Natural History in New York City. At 34 tons, Ahnighito, which was originally 200 tons before it broke apart in the atmosphere, is the largest meteorite on display in any museum in the world. Just as fascinating are the 7-ton fragments of the Cape York Meteorite.

To hunt, gather, and study meteorites, museum scientists from various organizations periodically visit Antarctica and Greenland. Since 1976, the Antarctic Search for Meteorites Program, ANSMET, has found more than 10,000 meteorites among the bright snow and ice. They are easily spotted, owing to the stark contrast and debris found on top of the frigid surface, and the researchers believe they fell from space.

Because a plane ticket to Greenland or Antarctica is pretty pricey and mounting an expedition is a serious endeavor, I suggest another, cheaper way to collect souvenirs from the solar system's humble beginnings.

Every year, tons of meteorite dust falls to Earth, and there is most likely plenty in your neighborhood. While some meteorites are the size of cars and can be seen streaking across the sky, most are about the size of a grain of sand. But they do fall to Earth, and it is possible to collect them. Keep in mind that most are probably metal-bearing rocks of Earth origin, which makes our meteorite mission all the more worthwhile.

GEAR LIST

- Beach or backyard
- Magnet
- Zip-lock or other type of plastic bag
- Magnifying glass or microscope (optional)
- Creative license or a plausibility certificate

STEP 1: Using a magnet, it's easy to comb the ground along a beach or in a desert. The beach is one of the easiest places to hunt for meteorites. Any magnet will work, but the more powerful, the better.

STEP 2: Place the magnet in the plastic bag and drag it along the beach. Meteorites contain a lot of iron, so tiny metallic particles will collect on the outside of the bag. Beaches naturally possess high levels of iron, so you may probably attract a lot of terrestrial material.

STEP 3: Examine the space dust you've collected with a magnifying glass or microscope, noting the molten glassy surface and twisted melted metal. Upon entering Earth's atmosphere, meteorites get bombarded by billions of molecules, causing friction that heats the surface to 3,100° F (Your oven only goes to about 450° F). Most meteorite material gets melted or vaporized. So, what are your chances of finding a real meteorite? It's not likely, but it's also not impossible.

STEP 4: For folks who think they have found a real meteorite, Arizona State University offers a free identification service. Each week, two or three meteorites arrive there via mail, but only about five a year turn out to be the real thing—but yours may be one of them!

Option 2

If you don't live near a beach, you can use your backyard. Lay out a big tarp or sheet on the lawn. Make sure it is centered away from trees or bushes and open to the sky. After a few days, tap the sheet to shift all the dust to the center, forming a pile, and run a magnet along the sheet. Some of those black specs that stick to the magnet may be meteorites or volcanic dust! There is a very big sky, and so much is out there. Why not make a tiny piece of it yours?

PART VIII

GIVING BACK

43 GROW A JURASSIC TREE

"We are all living fossils."
—Charles Darwin

In the movie *Jurassic Park* scientists re-created Jurassic era dinosaurs by extracting DNA from amber-locked mosquitoes that existed 200 million years ago. To create your own Jurassic life, you can just dig and plant your own primitive tree.

In 1992, David Noble, an Australian park ranger for the National Park Service was on a hiking trip in the Blue Mountains in Australia. He and his buddies noticed an odd-looking pine tree that none of them had seen before. With their curiosity peaked, they hacked off a branch and toted it to their local botanic garden, hoping an expert could identify the perplexing pine.

The tree was ultimately recognized as the Wollemi pine, part of an ancient Coniferous family whose fossil record dates back more than 200 million years to the time of the dinosaurs—meaning a T-Rex could have used one for shade. "This was the major botanical find of the century," according to Josh Schneider, Director of the Wollemi Pine Project in North America. "Some people even said it was the equivalent to finding a small dinosaur alive in the forest." In its day, the Wollemi pine covered the entire southern hemisphere, a time when continents were stuck together in one supercontinent called Gwandanaland. The pine most likely provided food and protection for thousands of species of dinosaurs.

Habitat and Growing Conditions

Growing as tall as 100 feet, Wollemi pines are majestic evergreens that look a bit like ferns. Their soft leaves and branches grow in two or more rows of needles, with lush green apple foliage that resembles a fireworks plume.

It's a hearty breed that can survive in temperatures of 10° F, but it prefers warmer temperatures of between 23° F and 113° F. With ample light and soil, they can grow about 3 feet per year. As it matures, the bark turns bubbly, as if coffee beans had been glued to its trunk and branches.

What Makes a Wollemi Special

Wollemi pines, similar to Boston ferns and other leafy indoors plants, detoxify their surroundings, so they make great house plants and offer many health benefits. To contain their potentially mammoth growth in domestic settings (they can grow to about 4 or 5 feet), plant pines in small containers and consistently cut them back. Just like goldfish, a Wollemi grows only as much as its environment allows. Although it is a rare breed, the Wollemi is hardy and will flourish in a variety of soils and light conditions.

Many Wollemi pine owners keep their trees outside in the spring, summer, and fall and bring them inside during the winter. Some even decorate them, creating little fossil Christmas trees.

FYI

- *Wollemi pines have been called the supermodel of the plant world. Their wild locations are kept secret, and the Australian government has set a $130,000 fine for disturbing one.*
- *The first Wollemi pines were auctioned off at Sotheby's in 2006, and a lot of 15 trees went for $135,000.*

What You Can Do to Help

Experts believe there are less than 100 Wollemi pines left in the wild. The Wollemi Pine Project aims to breed as many plants in as many places as possible, to proliferate this rare pine and make it less vulnerable to a catastrophic event in its limited natural habitat.

Check with your local botanical garden gift shop about getting involved. I saw my first Wollemi pine at the Brooklyn Botanic Garden, in New York. I was amazed to see a Jurassic-aged tree in an urban place like Brooklyn. I got so excited that upon returning home, I immediately wrote to Wollemi Pine of North America, which is based in San Diego and partners with the National Geographic Society, to find out how I could buy my own tree.

For about $100, you can help to conserve the species and advance science by purchasing and planting your own prehistoric tree. Check out the sources listed here to find out more about Wollemi pines and how you can bring this dinosaur-era tree into your living room. A portion of the proceeds of the sale of every tree goes toward conservation of the Wollemi pine and other threatened and endangered species.

Wollemi-Friendly Links

- www.nationalgeographic.com/wollemipine
- www.usna.usda.gov/Hardzone/ushzmap.html
- www.ancientpine.com/
- www.wollemipine.com/USA_link.php

44 BUILDING A BAT HOUSE

Bats are among the most misunder-
stood creatures on earth thanks to a few Dracula
movies and the Bram Stoker novels. Contrary to
popular belief, they will not suck your blood, get
tangled in your hair, or give you rabies. In fact, bats
are vital to controlling insect populations. A single
Brown Bat can eat up to 1,000 mosquitoes in an hour.
It's pretty nasty to think about, but a few hundred of
these little winged guys can do a lot to prevent that
itchy feeling. Also, many insects can hear bats up to 100 feet away, so
they will avoid bat-occupied areas, which lessen the need for pesticides.

Abundant in North America, even in cities and suburbs, bats may
live in your own backyard! Getting an up-close-and-personal glimpse
of these amazing creatures is another good reason to build your own
bat house.

Bat houses can be installed year-round, but they are more likely to
be used if they are erected in early spring before the bats return from
their winter dwellings.

Building a Bat House

GEAR LIST

- 2×4 foot×1/2-inch outdoor-grade plywood. Do not use pressure-treated wood.
- 8 feet of 1×2 inch pine furring. The actual dimensions will be 3/4×11/2 inches.
- 20–30 exterior grade screws 1" in length
- 1 pint dark, water-based stain, exterior grade
- 1 pint of water-based exterior-grade primer
- 1 quart of flat water-based exterior-grade paint or stain
- 1 tube of latex caulk and a caulk gun

If adding a roof (highly recommended)

ADDITIONAL GEAR

- 1×4×28 inch board for roof (optional, but highly recommended)
- Black asphalt shingles or galvanized metal (optional)
- 6 to 10 7/8-inch roofing nails (optional)

TOOL LIST

- Table saw and handsaw, or circular saw
- Caulking gun
- Variable speed reversing drill with Phillips screwdriver bit
- Paint brush
- Phillips bit for drill
- Tape measure or yardstick
- Rags

EXTERIOR FINISH

- 1 pint of exterior latex primer and 1 pint of flat exterior latex paint or 1 quart of exterior water-based stain

STEP 1: Overview of the Bat House Design

Although this design, inspired by Bat Conservation International, is a single-chamber bat house, it can be modified to be multichambered, which bats prefer. Keep in mind that bats like tight spaces where they can stay warm and be safe from predators during the day. Be sure to elevate your bat house 12 to 15 feet off the ground to keep it away from hungry intruders and place it in a sunny, warm spot.

The actual house should be two feet tall, and the inside chamber should be 20 inches high and 14 inches wide. The landing area, which extends below the entrance, should be at least 3 to 6 inches deep. The landing needs to be roughened, scratched, or grooved horizontally in ¼-inch to ½-inch intervals, to allow the bats to easily climb in and out of the house. Landings can also be covered with durable square-plastic mesh.

Open-bottom houses are great for reducing problems with birds, mice, squirrels, and parasites, and it prevents guano (bat droppings) from accumulating inside.

The exterior plywood should be at least 4 plies and at least ½ inch thick. Cedar plywood or a combination of cedar and other wood is preferable. Do not use pressure-treated wood because it contains chemicals that may be harmful to bats, and its offensive smell will discourage them from inhabiting the house. You can use plastic or fiber-cement board instead of plywood to extend the useful life of the bat house.

All screws, nails, and staples must be exterior grade (galvanized, coated, etc.). To increase durability, use screws instead of nails wherever possible.

STEP 2: Exterior Painting and Color Selection

Selecting the exterior color is important to maintaining the proper temperature of the bat house. In areas where the average high temperature in July is less than 85° F, use black. Where the temperature is between 85° F and 95° F, select dark colors, such as dark brown or dark gray. If the July highs are between 95° F and 100° F, go for medium colors like light gray or green, and for areas with temperatures that reach 100° F and above, use light colors or white.

Sun exposure also plays a big role, so adjust to a darker color for less exposure and a lighter color for heavy exposure.

STEP 3: Cutting Sections

To make front and back walls, measure and cut the plywood into three sections:

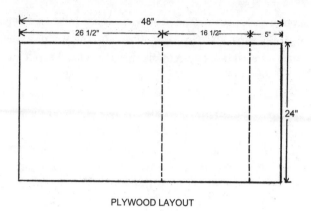

PLYWOOD LAYOUT

Backboard: 26^1/$_2$ × 24 inches
Upper front: 16^1/$_2$ × 24 inches
Lower front: 5 × 24 inches

- Measure and cut the furring into one 24-inch and two 20^1/$_2$-inch pieces.
- To allow bats to land and climb into the bat house, cut shallow horizontal grooves on the interior side of the plywood's back wall, parallel to the 24-inch dimension of each section.
- To groove the landing, use a handsaw or set the depth of circular saw to a minimum of ^{1}/$_{32}$ inches deep. Another alternative is to attach a durable plastic mesh with a staple gun after the interior has been stained.

STEP 4: Interior Wood Treatment

Apply two coats of a dark exterior water-based stain to the inside of the wall sections and on each of the furring strips. Allow the stain to dry between coats. Wipe off any excess stain with a rag. Do not use paint on the interior because it will fill the grooves, making it difficult for the bats to land.

STEP 5: Assembly

- Start by attaching the 24-inch furring strip to the top of the interior of the back wall with wood screws. Attach the remaining strips to the sides as shown below. Then caulk interior of the seam formed by the wall and furring strips.
- Attach the upper front plywood section to the top of the bat house with wood screws, sandwiching the furring strip in between the front and back.

- Attach the lower front plywood section leaving a $1/2$-inch gap between the upper front for ventilation.
- Caulk all the exterior seams and allow them to dry.

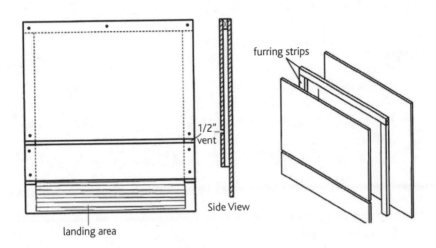

furring strips

$1/2$" vent

Side View

landing area

STEP 6: Exterior Finish

If you are finishing your bat house with paint, prime all the exterior surfaces and then paint the surfaces with two coats of flat latex paint, allowing each coat to dry between applications.

If you are staining it, apply three coats of stain to the unprimed exterior, allowing each coat to dry between applications. Wipe off the excess stain with a rag.

STEP 7: Optional Roof

Center the board on top of the bat house and secure it with wood screws. If you plan to mount the bat house to the side of a building, mount a roof board on top of the bat house, keeping the back of the board flush with the back wall and let overhang toward the front. Caulk the seams and finish the rooftop with shingles or galvanized metal, and then paint or stain it.

STEP 8: Finding the Best Location for Your Bat House

Now you are ready to find a home for your bat house. If you live near water, set it up near the body of water. Most bats prefer to roost within $1/4$ mile of a lake or stream (bugs tend to breed near swampy areas).

Place the bat house at least 30 feet from the nearest tree branches, wires, or other perches for hawks and other potential predators. Single-chamber houses work best when they are mounted on buildings, so you may consider mounting it on a building with good sun exposure.

STEP 9: Mounting Your Bat House with Predators in Mind

You can also mount the bat house on a wood or metal pole as long as it's at least 15 feet high and is not near bright lights at night.

FYI

- *Bat houses mounted on trees or on metal siding are seldom used by bats.*
- *Metal predator guards are helpful in warding off predators. To make your own, buy metal flashing—it's usually made of thin tin—and wrap it around the base of the bat house to prevent clawed creatures from climbing inside.*

Congratulations! You have built your first bat house and you are helping improve the ecology of your town. As you enjoy your new guests, keep an eye out for unwanted invaders like wasps or bees that can take over a bat house if not monitored. If you see wasps or bees lingering, remove them during the winter using a high-pressure hose (do not use pesticides).

FYI *The largest bat house in the world is in Gainesville, Florida, and has more than 100,000 bats.*

Sick bats occasionally carry rabies, but the likelihood of coming into contact with them is very small.

45 RESLER REEF

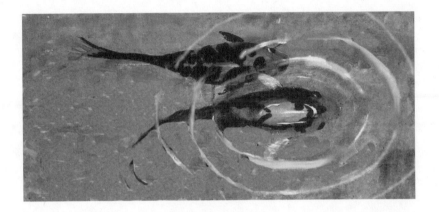

The summer I was 15 I met Steve Resler, a young biologist who was creating an artificial reef off the shore of Smithtown, Long Island, a couple of miles from where I lived. Just hanging out with Steve sent my mind rocketing with dreams of diving with Jacques Cousteau, the great French oceanographer and TV star of the 1970s, or of exploring Australia's famous Great Barrier Reef. Needless to say, I was excited about Steve's project.

At the time we met, I was practicing for my scuba diving certification in my parents' pool, when one of my sisters brought him home on a date. It was 1975, the summer *Jaws* came out and the movie made being a marine biologist very cool. Steve Resler was unquestionably a driving force in my mission to pass my scuba quest. He also was a major influence in my continued interest in exploration.

I joined Steve and his team in creating his artificial reef. I was fortunate to have a leader like Steve engaging me, explaining things in detail, and taking an interest in my thoughts and curiosity. He taught me how to create and maintain a reef and, to this day, there are still fish swimming around the reef we created. So, how did we make his reef?

Making Your Own "Resler" Reef

Before building an artificial reef, it's important to understand how real ones function. Reefs are a uniquely biodiverse portion of our seas. They provide places for fish to rest, feed, and hide from predators, and they are integral to sustaining marine life. They also support the diving and fishing industries.

Unfortunately, reefs are eroding at an unprecedented pace due to global warming and pollution. Artificial reefs are human-made simulations created from nearly every imaginable material. Some artificial reefs have been made from used automobile tires, old ships, retired subway cars, and discarded Christmas trees sunk into water with cement blocks.

Here's how to make your own reef.

GEAR LIST

- Permission from adults and governing bodies
- A dead tree with lots of branches (Christmas trees work great)
- Rope or chord
- Cinderblocks, rocks, or bricks

STEP 1: Getting Permission

Before you start tossing things into your local lake or seascape, keep your legal record clean and check out the laws pertaining to water use. A good place to start is by contacting your local department of conservation or parks. Know what your city, county, town, or village governments will and won't allow.

For artificial reefs built in saltwater, government agencies require permits, and they can often be obtained from local or state natural resources, conservation or fisheries agencies, or from the offices of the U.S. Army Corps of Engineers.

Some bureaus require that paperwork be filed, while others may help you build your artificial reef or put you in touch with others who would like to help build one. SCUBA diving shops, SCUBA clubs, and fishing or boating club members are often eager to pitch in.

It may take more than one try to get proper approval, but don't be discouraged by naysayers. Steve was turned down a few times before he made it happen.

STEP 2: Collecting Reef-worthy Material

I like to think of collecting bits and pieces for a reef as recycling with a twist. One of my favorite methods is to traipse through my neighborhood after the holidays, collecting discarded Christmas trees and hauling them off to a lake or ocean. (The habitats of freshwater fish are very similar to its salt water cousins.)

Essentially, you want items that are environmentally safe for the water. They should be biodegradable and provide protection for small species. A properly designed and built artificial reef will attract fish where they wouldn't typically be found without the artificial reefs.

Most fish are *thigmotropic*, meaning they are attracted to objects in the water. If you watch a lone fish in an aquarium filled only with water, it will invariably swim into the glass instead of swimming in the center. But if you put a rock in the aquarium, the fish will swim near and around the rock.

STEP 3: Creating Your Reef

There are several ways to create a reef, but only a few hold up over the long term.

Trees float and can drift underwater. You therefore want to submerge them with cinder or cement blocks; hammer a few thick nails at an angle into the tree base so that the cement has something to catch on.

Once weighted, haul your tree into the water with a boat, or wade it out if it's shallow enough. If you are sinking more than one tree, pile them close together to simulate a coral reef. You can also use a heavy wire or thin cable to tie them together, but avoid plastic-based ropes because they degrade in sunlight.

FYI

- *Freshwater fish, such as largemouth bass, bluegill, and crappies are attracted to submerged trees.*
- *Small fish will congregate for protection because larger fish will chase the small fish around this area.*

Parting Thoughts

Reefs are one of the most biodiverse places on the planet. Create your reef where you are likely to see fish, perhaps your local pond or bay. Your artificial reef can be used as your own private fishing hotspot or diving hole. It also may simply leave you with the knowledge that you gave Mother Nature a helping hand. Steve Resler taught me that one person with a lot of determination can make an eco-difference and so can you! Build wisely, and help marine life flourish.

CONCLUSION

I wish I could give each of you an explorer's badge. Unfortunately, that's not going to happen, so get over it. What I hope you have taken away from *Born to Explore* is greater confidence and a greater desire to expand your world.

With the skills you have picked up by doing some of the activities in these chapters, your outdoor options are endless. Dream big and take risks. Not risks that put you in physical danger, obviously, but do try things that excite and challenge you. Build upon the experiments you tried in *Born to Explore*, take them further, and create new opportunities.

I am passionate about my adventures and equally passionate about sharing my experiences, enthusiasm, and curiosity—if only to offer an inside scoop of what is possible. My exploration has taken me to physical and mental places beyond my wildest dreams. The more I see, the more I realize there is to see, hear, feel, and taste.

Nature Is Nourishment

The more time I spend doing things outdoors, the more I realize how critical nature is to my survival—how it nourishes my overall mental and physical health. There are numerous entertaining books and TV shows about outdoor survival. To be sure, navigating the wilderness can be an exciting challenge. However, I don't look at nature as something to be survived; rather, nature helps *me* survive and is a treasure to respect, embrace, and enjoy. I hope *Born to Explore* has motivated you to put down the clicker, pick up your compass, and create your own adventures.

Embrace Experimentation

After reading *Born to Explore* and completing some of the projects, you will look at familiar surroundings in a novel way. And if you embrace experimentation, you might discover a talent you didn't know you had. One of my favorite projects was building the 6-hour canoe with my father and nephews. Whenever I walk past the canoe, I marvel at its craftsmanship and remind myself that we actually built it. I often think of it when I'm facing a daunting task and think to myself, If I can build a boat that floats, then I can build or figure out nearly anything.

What Makes an Explorer?

Perhaps the most important part of being an explorer is to think like an explorer by questioning the status quo, feeding your curiosity, and applying a can-do attitude to everyday challenges. Here are nine questions I ponder when evaluating what truly makes an explorer and how I can improve my explorer skill set. I have left the tenth slot open for you to fill in your own topic.

1. Are Leaders Born or Made?

William Shakespeare said, "Be not afraid of greatness; some are born great, some achieve greatness, and others have greatness thrust upon them."

Until you get outside and get intimate with the dirt and the trees, you may not realize how the skills and strengths you call on in your daily routines can serve you well in the outdoors. Further, I am convinced that the qualities and skills you develop during outdoor activities and nature exploration will then increase your confidence in other areas of your life. The experiences you have outdoors, be it in your local park or on top of mountains, will undoubtedly lead you to accept and conquer other rewarding challenges.

2. Whom Do I Admire?

I don't have enough paper or time to write down all the names of the people I admire. A few in particular, however, have played key roles in my life as an explorer. Former president Teddy Roosevelt is one for sure. He was a tough, no-nonsense, persuasive individual who got things done. In addition to the people I have mentioned in this book there are also many other public figures I admire, such as Steven Colbert and Craig Fergusson for their laser-sharp wit; Geraldo Rivera for his fierce loyalty to friends; Jim Whittaker, the first American on Mount Everest, for his enthusiasm and drive to get people into the outdoors; Buzz Aldrin, part of the first expedition to the Moon, a true hero who kept the dream alive in space; Jonathan Kaplan, a top surgeon who devotes much of his time to missions with Doctors without Borders; Oprah Winfrey, who is just about the most outstanding woman I have ever met; and biologist E. O. Wilson, whom I respect for his modesty and tenacity when solving perplexing problems. Joan Connelly is an archaeologist who happens to be the best expedition leader that I have explored with, and Steve Resler, my "reef man," a marine biologist and environmentalist, was my earliest mentor and has been a mentor to many others. I suspect there are many Steve Reslers throughout the country.

I have taken bits and pieces of the teachings, approaches, and styles from the individuals I most admire and have incorporated them into my own activities as a nature investigator and expedition leader. Ultimately, though, no one is better at being you than you are, so develop your own style and be true to yourself.

3. Can You Adapt to Changing Circumstances?

The quintessential leader is thought to be Ernest Shackleton, who became a legend among explorers for his leadership and survival skills when his ship, *The Endurance*, became helplessly trapped in ice and smashed in Antarctica in 1915. Despite extraordinary hardships lasting nearly two years, he saved all 27 of his crewmen. It's ironic that in "failure" (his goal was to transverse the continent of Antarctica), he is remembered as a hero. Shackleton abandoned one prized goal to survive unanticipated conditions. In other words, his heroism lay in his flexibility and willingness to shift goals when events dictated another scenario.

4. Is a Victory "At All Costs" a Victory?

As far as I'm concerned, victory at all costs is not a victory at all. When winning requires one to step over others, to cheat, lie, or destroy friends and family, there is no victory. Winning is about working hard and maintaining your focus. There are plenty of admirable champions. Be one of them!

5. Why Should I Try Something New?

If an organism or species does not continue to thrive and evolve, it becomes extinct. It eventually dies. It may sound a bit harsh, but I like to apply this concept to life. Look for new things to try, new ways to do the same old thing. Keep improving. Always try to take your "game" to the next level. Stay hungry. Never stop learning and improving. Your experiences in the outdoors and your skills as an adventurer will surely benefit.

6. Who Wants Me to Succeed?

Wanting others to succeed is an important part of being a good outdoors leader. I wish I realized how many people wanted me to succeed when I was a teenager. There were so many more than I realized at the time. I encourage you to ask for advice and seek out at least one mentor. Write to someone you admire. In turn, share your knowledge with and encourage others. In no time, you will you have an intimate group of nature-enthusiast friends with whom you can lead journeys to the great beyond.

7. How Are My Fears Limiting Me?

Ask any leader or sports champion if they have ever failed, and most will tell you they have failed spectacularly. Do not be afraid to fail. Understand that *not* achieving your goal on the first attempt can often be a powerful tool. You will learn from your pitfalls and difficulties and be victorious the next time.

The easy road is safe and predictable. Sticking your neck out and caring about something is difficult. But on those occasions when you have put every ounce of energy and passion into a goal, the exhilaration of success will be well worth the fight.

8. Do I Have the Skills to Accomplish the Mission?

There is no fast-food solution to honing skills. Sylvia Earle, a famous oceanographer at National Geographic, tells young people, "If you hang around the action long enough you will become part of the action." She advises them to do the tasks that no one else wants to do, like washing boats, cleaning gear, or wrapping rope. It all goes into a database called your head. Olympians and top-flight athletes like Tiger Woods did not become "overnight sensations." Be proactive and remember that Rome was not built in a day.

9. Do I Volunteer?

Besides having the opportunity to help others, I have met some of my best friends and explorer colleagues while volunteering. When I first joined The Explorers Club, I volunteered for as many activities as possible because I was psyched to be a member and enjoyed meeting people with similar interests. Expanding your friend network while also helping others is what my wife Nicci calls "doing well by doing good."

These are some of my favorite "do-good" organizations:

- Boy Scouts of America, http://www.scouting.org/
- Earth Watch, www.earthwatch.org
- NOLS, www.nols.edu
- Big City Mountaineers, www.bigcitymountaineers.org
- National Audubon Society, www.audubon.org
- Nature Conservancy, www.nature.org
- Appalachian Mountain Club, www.outdoors.org
- US National Park Service, www.nps.org
- Your local museum of natural history
- Students on Ice, www.studentsonice.com
- Outward Bound, www.outwardbound.org

What are you still doing here? Go out and explore!

SOURCES CONSULTED AND SUGGESTIONS FOR FURTHER READING

I: Explorer Tool Box

CHAPTER 1: Altoids Survival Kit

McCann, John D. "Build the Perfect Survival Kit." *Field and Stream Magazine.* http://www.fieldandstream.com/fieldstream/photo gallery/article/0,13355,1225788,00.html.

CHAPTER 2: Your Knife, a Point of Pride

The American Knife and Tool Institute. "Knife Safety, Sharpening and Maintenance."http://www.akti.org/PDFS/AKTIKnifeSafetyCare .pdf.
Buck Knives, "Knife Sharpening." http://www.buckknives.com/index .cfm?event=about.sharpening.

CHAPTER 3: Backwoods Bow and Arrow

U.S. Army Survival Manual FM 21–76. "Equipped to Survive, Field Expedient Weapons, Tools and Equipment." http://www.equipped .org/21–76/ch12.pdf.
Wiseman, John. *SAS Survival Handbook.* New York: HarperCollins Publishers, 2004.

CHAPTER 4: Miracle Material: Duct Tape

Duct Tape Guys. http://www.ducttapeguys.com.

CHAPTER 5: Fire

Angier, Bradford. *How to Stay Alive in the Woods.* New York: Black Dog & Leventhal Publishers, 2001.
———. *Basic Wilderness Skills.* Guildford, CT: Lyons Press, 2002.
Beard, Dan. "Fire Lighting." http://www.inquiry.net/outdoor/skills/ beard/light_fire.htm.

Berkun, Scott. *The Myths of Innovation*. O'Reilly: Sebastopol, CA, 2007.

Boy Scouts of America. *Fieldbook: Boy Scouts of America*. Irvington, Texas, 2004.

———. Boy Scouts of America Handbook, Sports & Recreation. Mineola, NY: Dover Publications, 2005.

Fisher, D. "The Secrets of War." Interview, Documedia group, 1998 (TV documentary). http://www.sas.upenn.edu/~nmiller0/dung.html#ww2.

Needham, William. "Hiker's Notebook." http://www.mwrop.org/W_Needham/ClinkerPolypore_Chaga_051216.htm.

Seton, Thompson Ernest. "Fire: Rubbing-Stick." http://www.inquiry.net/outdoor/skills/seton/rubbing_fire.htm.

Seton, Thompson Ernest, and Powell Robert Baden Powell. *The Boy Scouts of America Handbook*. BSA, 1910.

Storm. "The Usefulness of Polypores in Primitive Fire Making." http://www.stoneageskills.com/images/the_usefulness_of_polypores_pdf_article.pdf.

———. "Wildwood Survival." http://wildwoodsurvival.com/survival/fire/tinder/tinderfungus/spolypore/part2.htm.

Watts, Steve. "Stone Age Skills." http://www.stoneageskills.com.

CHAPTER 6: Chopping Down a Tree

Beard, Daniel. *The Field and Forest Handy Book*. New York: Charles Scribner's Sons, 1906.

———. "Axe Skills." http://www.inquiry.net/outdoor/skills/beard/axe.htm.

Little, Elbert Luther, Sonja Bullaty, and Angelo Lomeo. *National Audubon Society Field Guide to North American Trees*. New York: Knopf, 1980.

National Arbor Day Foundation. http://www.arborday.org.

Picariello, Gary. "The Art of Chopping Down a Tree," December 12, 2006. http://www.associatedcontent.com/article/97428/the_art_of_chopping_down_a_tree.html.

Reames, Richard. Arborsmith Studios. http://www.arborsmith.com/treecircus.html.

Roddick, Chris. *The Tree Care Primer*. New York: Brooklyn Botanic Garden, 2007.

CHAPTER 7: Floating Art: The Six-Hour Canoe

Boating Safety. http://uscgboating.org.

Butz, Richard. *Building the Six-Hour Canoe*. St. Michaels, MD: Tiller Publishing, 1994.

Nautilus SSN 571. "Naval Terms." United States Navy. http://www
.nautilus571.com/naval_terms.htm.

Skorucak, Anton. "How to Measure the Speed of a Ship." http://www
.physlink.com/Education/AskExperts/ae400.cfm.

United States Navy. "Origins of Naval Terminology." http://www
.navy.mil/navydata/navy_legacy_hr.asp?id=280#ahoy.

CHAPTER 8: Build a World War II Foxhole Radio
To purchase radio kit and parts:
Borden Radio Company
138911 Kensington Place
Houston, TX 77034
http://www.xtalman.com

II Safety

CHAPTER 9: How Not to Be a Victim of Insects
Insects on the Web, http://www.insects.org.

CHAPTER 10: Avoiding Becoming Wildlife Food
Animal Behavior Society. http://www.animalbehavior.org.

CHAPTER 11: Taming an Electric Fence
Alliant Energy Kids, "Fun Facts about Electricity." http://www
.alliantenergykids.com/stellent2/groups/public/documents/pub/
phk_eb_ae_001470.hcsp.

CHAPTER 12: Ninja T-Shirt Sun Hood
Reid, Vern. "How to Do Stuff." http://how2dostuff.blogspot.com/
2005/11/how-to-make-ninja-mask-out-of-t-shirt.html.

CHAPTER 13: Rumble in the Jungle: Avoid Mr. Poopy Pants
Boulware, David R., M.D., William W. Forgey, M.D., and William J.
Martin II, M.D. "Medical Risks of Wilderness Hiking." *American
Journal of Medicine.* http://www.amjmed.com/article/PIIS000
2934302014948/abstract. Center for Disease Control and Infec-
tion. "Travelers' Diarrhea." http://www.cdc.gov/ncidod/dbmd/
diseaseinfo/travelersdiarrhea_g.htm.

Hiking Dude. "Giardia and Friends," http://www.hikingdude.com/
hiking-giardia.shtml.

Sol Aqua. "Solar Still Basics." http://www.solaqua.com/solstilbas.html.

Yates, Johnnie, M.D. "Traveler's Diarrhea." American Family Physi-
cian. http://www.aafp.org/afp/20050601/2095.html.

III Navigation

CHAPTER 14: Maps

Bellis, Mary. "The Compass and other Magnetic Innovations." About .com. http://inventors.about.com/od/cstartinventions/a/Compass .htm.

Charity, M. "Your Body Ruler—A User's Manual." http://www. vendian.org/mncharity/dir3/bodyruler.

Compass Dude. "How to Read a Map." http://www.compassdude .com/map-reading.shtml.

Compass Store, "How to use a map and compass." http://www .thecompassstore.com/howtousemapa.html.

"Finding Your Way with Map and Compass." *United States Department of Geological Survey (USGS).* http://erg.usgs.gov/isb/pubs/ factsheets/fs03501.html.

Rocky Mountain Mapping Center. http://rockyweb.cr.usgs.gov.

Seton, Ernest Thompson. "A Home-Made Compass." http://www .inquiry.net/OUTDOOR/skills/seton/home_compass.htm.

Solar Navigator, "Navigation," http://www.solarnavigator.net/ navigation.htm.

United States Department of Geological Survey (USGS). http://www .usgs.org.

Wilderness Survival. "Field Expedient Direction Finding." http:// www.wilderness-survival.net/chp18.php.

CHAPTER 15: Tracking

Brown, Tom. *Tom Brown's Field Guide to Nature Observation and Tracking.* Tom Brown's Field Guides, New York: Berkley Publishing, 1977.

——. *Tom Brown's Science and Art of Tracking.* New York: Berkley Publishing, 1999.

Cabrera, Kim A. "Tracking Activities with Kim A. Cabrera." http:// www.bear-tracker.com/teachers.html.

Elbroch, Mark. "Tracking Wildlife in North America." http://www .wildlifetrackers.com.

International Society of Professional Trackers (ISPT). http://www .ispt.org.

Kays, Roland W., and Don E. Wilson. *Mammals of North America.* Princeton, NJ: Princeton Field Guides, 2002.

Massachusetts Wildlife Guide. http://www.cityofmelrose.org/ departments/Conservation/files/tracks/tracks.jpg.

National Audubon Society. *National Audubon Society Field Guide to North American Mammals*. New York: Knopf, 1996.

Noyoun, Sam. "Improve Your Night Vision with Sam Noyoun." http://www.metacafe.com/watch/576933/improve_your_night_vision.

Reid, Fiona. *Peterson Field Guide to Animal Tracks*, Fourth Edition. New York: Houghton Mifflin Harcourt, 2006.

Udvardy, Miklos, and John Farrand. *National Audubon Society Field Guide to North American Birds*. New York: Random House, 1994.

Worsley School. "Casting Animal Tracks." http://www.worsleyschool.net/science/files/casts/oftracks.html.

CHAPTER 16: Sky

Angier, Bradford. *Basic Wilderness Skills*. Guildford CT: Lyons Press, 2002.

Boy Scouts of America. *Fieldbook: Boy Scouts of America*. Irvington, TX, 2004.

———. Boy Scouts of America Handbook, Sports & Recreation. Mineola, NY: Dover Publications, 2005.

Dickinson, Terence. *Exploring the Night Sky*. Richmond Hill, ON: Firefly Books, 2007.

Hunkin, Tim. "Hunkin's Experiments." http://www.hunkinsexperiments.com/pages/height.htm.

Kjernsmo, Kjetil. "Kjetil Kjernsmo's Illustrated Guide on How to Use a Compass." http://www.learn-orienteering.org/old/nocompass1.html.

Lambert, John V. "Viking Sun Compass." http://members.aol.com/jvlambert/Norman/SunCompass.htm.

National Atlas, "What is Latitude." http://nationalatlas.gov/articles/mapping/a_latlong.html#two.

Olesik, S. "How to Make a Simple Sextant." WOW Project. Ohio State University. http://wow.osu.edu/experiments/measurement/sextant.html.

Sanford, Walter. "Me and My Shadow, Making the Sun-Earth Connection." http://www.wsanford.com/~wsanford/exo/sundials/shadows.html.

Vardner, Diane. "Making a Simple Sextant to Find Latitude." NASA. http://www2.jpl.nasa.gov/files/educator/sextant.txt.

IV Shelter

CHAPTER 17: Levitation Station

Fairley, David. "History of Hammocks." http://www.ecomall.com/greenshopping/hammock.htm.

CHAPTER 18: How to Build an Igloo

Yankielun, Norbert E. *How to Build an Igloo and Other Snow Shelters.* New York : W.W. Norton & Company, 2007.

V Food

CHAPTER 19: Your First Meal Outdoors

Best Camp Recipes. http://www.bestcamprecipes.com.

Boy Scouts of America. *Fieldbook: Boy Scouts of America.* Irvington, TX, 2004.

——. Boy Scouts of America Handbook, Sports & Recreation. Mineola, NY: Dover Publications, 2005.

Brill, Steve. *Identifying and Harvesting Edible and Medicinal Plants.* New York: HarperCollins Publishers, 1994.

Crazy Crow. "Outdoor Cooking & Recipes." http://www.crazycrow.com/resources/cooking-outdoors.php.

Dutch Oven Dude. "Great Recipes for Camping." http://www.dutchovendude.com/dutch-oven-recipes.asp.

Hale, Vincent. "Exciting Scout Craft, Boy Scout Recipes in a Paper Bag." http://www.e-scoutcraft.com/activities/fun_cooking.html.

Make Stuff. "Coffee Substitutes from Plants Around Us." http://www.make-stuff.com/cooking/coffee.html.

National Geographic. "Coffee Beyond the Buzz." http://www.nationalgeographic.com/coffee.

Quiet Journey. "Camping Recipes by and for Campers who Paddle." http://www.quietjourney.com/recipes.

Reid, Jim. "Hassle-Free Campsite Recipes—Quick and Easy Meal Ideas." http://www.coleman.com/coleman/colemancom/news release.asp?releasenum=63.

ScoutORama. "Camping Food & Dutch Oven Recipes." http://www.scoutorama.com/recipe.

Seed Head. "Plant Intelligence." http://www.seedhead.com.

Storm Lake. "Heritage Tree Museum Map." http://www.stormlake.org/city/Pages/heritagetreemuseummap.htm.

CHAPTER 20: The Paper Bag School of Cooking

"French Chef Cooks Delicious Food in A Paper Bag," *The New York Times*, August 20, 1911. http://query.nytimes.com/mem/archive-free/pdf?_r=1&res=9B0DE0DC1531E233A25753C2A96E9C9460 96D6CF&oref=slogin.

Hale, Vincent. "Exciting Scout Craft, Boy Scout Recipes in a Paper Bag." http://www.e-scoutcraft.com/activities/fun_cooking.html.

"How to Make Bread in a Bag." *Explore*. July/August 2007, 64.

Scott, Juliet. "Easy on the Washing-Up." *Bint Magazine*. http://www.bintmagazine.com/bint_stories/925.php?story_id=822.

Witmer, Denise. "Camping Recipes." http://parentingteens.about.com/od/recipesforkids/a/camping_recipes.htm.

CHAPTER 21: Fishing

Beaufort, South Carolina. "Crabs and Crabbing in Beaufort and Hilton Head Island." http://www.beaufortusa.com/crabs.htm.

Crabbing for Hard Shell Crabs. http://www.bluecrab.info/crabbing/hardcrabs.html.

Girls Gone Grabblin. "Catfish Grabblers—Girls Gone Grabblin'." http://www.catfishgrabblers.com.

Hall, Yancey. "Using Hands as Bait, 'Noodlers' Stalk Giant Catfish." *National Geographic*. http://news.nationalgeographic.com/news/2005/09/0908_050908_noodling.html.

Jeff's Captivating Guide to Crab Fishing. http://www.heff.net/crabbing.

Kohlsaat, Peter. "Fishing in Baja." http://www.shelterpub.com/_baja/fishing.html.

Sea Grant. "Steaming Blue Crabs." http://www.vims.edu/adv/ed/crab/steam.html.

CHAPTER 22: Eat Like the Rest of the World

Bailey, C. T. P. *Knives and Forks*. London: The Medici Society, 1927.

Diners Digest. "Chopsticks." http://www.cuisinenet.com/glossary/chopsticks.html.

Handwerk, Briann. "Chopsticks Tax to Target China's Hunger for Timber." *National Geographic News*. March 22, 2006.

Harrison, Molly. *The Kitchen in History*. New York: Charles Scribner's Sons, 1972.

Norman, Jerry. *Chinese*. Cambridge, UK: Cambridge University Press, 1988.

Tribole, Evelyn, and Elyse Resch, *Intuitive Eating*. New York: St. Martin's Press, 1995.

CHAPTER 23: Mining for Iron in Your Food

O'Hare, Mick. *How to Fossilize Your Hamster.* New York: Holt Press, 2007.

VI Weather

CHAPTER 24: Weather—You Know More Than You Think

Christians, Spencer. *Spencer Christian's Weather Book.* Upper Saddle River, NJ: Prentice Hall, 1998.

Patton, Darryl. "How to Forecast by Nature." http://www.wwmag .net/forecast.htm.

Williams, Jack. *The Weather Book.* New York: Vintage Press, 1992.

CHAPTER 25: Reading the Wind

Lehr, Paul E., Burnett R. Will, and Zim Herberts. *Weather a Guide to Phenomena and Forecast.* A Golden Guide Series. New York: Golden Press, 1957.

CHAPTER 26: Mountain Weather

Nova. "Volcano Above the Clouds." http://www.pbs.org/wgbh/nova/ kilimanjaro/weather.html.

Royal Meteorological Society. "Mountain Hazard." http://www .rmets.org/activities/schools/mountain_hazard.php.

CHAPTER 27: Weather Animal

Patton, Darryl. "How to Forecast by Nature." http://www.wwmag .net/forecast.htm.

Schlanger, Vera. "Environmental Science Published for Everyone Round the World." Short Range Forecasting Using Plant and Animal Behavior. http://www.atmosphere.mpg.de/enid/3sn.html.

CHAPTER 28: Why Is the Sky Blue and Sunsets Red?

Nave, R. "Blue Sky and Rayleigh Scattering." http://hyperphysics .phy-astr.gsu.edu/Hbase/atmos/blusky.html.

Science Made Simple. "Why the Sky is Blue." http://www.sciencemade simple.com/sky_blue.html.

CHAPTER 29: The Mystery of the Full-Moon Illusion

Kaufman, Lloyd, and James H. Kaufman. "Explaining the Moon Illusion." http://www.pnas.org/content/97/1/500.full.

Museum of Unnatural Mystery. "Experiment in Perception: The Ponzo Illusion and the Moon." http://www.unmuseum.org/ exmoon.htm.

Science at NASA. "Summer Moon Illusion." http://science.nasa.gov/headlines/y2005/20jun_Moonillusion.htm.

CHAPTER 30: Bad Hair Day—No One Is Safe

Doherty, Paul, and Linda Shore. "Better Hair through Chemistry, How to Build a Hair Hygrometer." http://www.exploratorium.edu/exploring/hair/hair_activity.html.

Franklin Institute Science Museum, *The Ben Franklin Book of Easy and Incredible Experiments*. A Franklin Institute Science Museum Book. Jossey Bass: San Francisco, CA, 1995.

Jack, Williams. "How Humidity Is Measured." http://www.usatoday.com/weather/whairhyg.htm.

CHAPTER 31: How to Make a Simple Thermometer

Brannan Thermometers and Gauges. "Who Invented the Thermometer." http://www.brannan.co.uk/thermometers/invention.html.

Franklin Institute Science Museum. *The Ben Franklin Book of Easy and Incredible Experiments*. Jossey Bass: San Francisco, CA, 1995.

CHAPTER 32: How to Build a Snowmaker

Libbrecht, Kenneth. *The Snow Flake Winter's Beauty*. Stillwater, MN: Voyageur Press, 2002.

Snow at Home. "Make Real Snow at Home with a Home Snow Machine." http://www.snowathome.com.

CHAPTER 33: How to Create a Rainbow

Humphreys, W. J. *Weather Proverbs and Paradoxes*. Baltimore, MD: Williams and Wilkins Company, 1923.

Stern, Fred. "Finding and Making Rainbows." http://www.rainbowmaker.us/content/making.php.

University Corporation for Atmospheric Research. "About Rainbows." http://eo.ucar.edu/rainbows.

VII Exploring

CHAPTER 34: Lord of the Tree Rings

Grissino-Mayer, Henri D. "Ultimate Tree-Ring Web Pages." http://web.utk.edu/~grissino/references.htm.

Museum Link Illinois, "Tree Rings: How Do We Know?" http://www.museum.state.il.us/muslink/forest/htmls/how_tr.html.

CHAPTER 35: A Palm Tree Grows in Brooklyn

Francko, David A. Palms Won't Grow Here and Other Myths:

Warm-Climate Plants for Cooler Areas. Portland, OR: Timber Press, 2003.

Gary's Nursery. http://www.garysnursery.com.

National Association of Agriculture. http://www.nasda.org.

United States Department of Agriculture. "USDA Plant Hardiness Zone Map." http://www.usna.usda.gov/Hardzone/ushzmap.html.

Plant Delights Nursery. http://www.plantdelights.com.

Plant Purchasing Links for Cold Hardy Palms.

Southeastern Palm Society. http://www.sepalms.org.

Triple Oaks Nursery. http://www.tripleoaks.com.

Woodlanders. http://www.woodlanders.net.

CHAPTER 36: Finding Fossils—Our Relatives from the Past

Bryson, Bill. *A Short History of Nearly Everything*. New York: Broadway Books, 2003.

Johnson, Kirk. *Crusin' the Fossil Freeway*. Fulcrum Publishing, Golden, CO 2007.

CHAPTER 37: City Wildlife Safari

Bull, John. The National Audubon Society Field Guide to North American Birds: Eastern Region. New York: Knopf, 1995.

Farrand, John. The National Audubon Society Field Guide to North American Birds: Western Region. New York: Knopf, 1994.

Griggs, Jack L. *All the Birds of North America*. New York: Harper Collins Publishers, 1997.

Groombridge, Brian. Global Biodiversity: Status of the Earth's Living Resources. Chapman and Hall, 1992.

Hogan, Kathleen. *Eco-Inquiry*. Dubuque, IA: Kendall/Hunt Publishing Company, 1994.

Little, Elbert L. The National Audubon Society Field Guide to North American Trees: Eastern Region. New York: Knopf, 1998.

Snedden, Robert. *Yuck! A Big Book of Little Horrors*. New York: Simon and Schuster, 1996.

Spellenberg, Richard. The National Audubon Society Field Guide to North American Wildflowers: Western Region. New York: Knopf, 2001.

Thieret, John. The National Audubon Society Field Guide to North American Wildflowers: Eastern Region. New York: Knopf, 2001.

U.S. Department of Agriculture, "Backyard Conservation Tip Sheet." http://www.nrcs.usda.gov/Feature/backyard/wildhab.html.

Whitaker, John. The National Audubon Society Field Guide to North American Mammals. New York: Knopf, 1996.

The World Wildlife Fund, "Wildlife finder," http://www.worldwildlife .org/wildfinder/.

CHAPTER 38: Panning for Gold

Kirkemo, Harold. "Prospecting for Gold in the United States." *United States Department of Geological Survey (USGS).* http:// pubs.usgs.gov/gip/prospect2/prospectgip.html.

CHAPTER 39: Thumb Piano, Please

To purchase the thumb piano kit, contact:
MUSICMAKER'S KITS, INC
P.O. BOX 2117
STILLWATER, MN 55082–3117
(651) 439–9120
info@musikit.com

CHAPTER 40: Lightning in Your Mouth

Dickinson, J. T., L. B. Brix, and L. C. Jensen. "Electron and positive ion emission accompanying fracture of Wint-o-green Lifesavers and single-crystal sucrose." *Journal of Physical Chemistry* 88 (1984): 1698–1701.

Sweeting, L.M. 1998. "Scientific Experiments at Home: Wintergreen Candy and Other Triboluminescent Materials." http://pages .towson.edu/ladon/wg/candywww.htm (accessed August 2, 2007).

Zink, J. I., G. E. Hardy, and J.E. Sutton. "Triboluminescence of Sugars." *Journal of Physical Chemistry* 80 (1976): 3, 248–249.

CHAPTER 41: Star Trail and Moon Photography

Edens, Harald. "Weatherscapes, Star Trail Photography." http://www .weatherscapes.com/techniques.php?cat=astronomy&page= startrails.

Groenhout, Chris. "Star Trail and Moonlight Photography." apogee magazine.com. http://www.apogeephoto.com/mag7-6/stars_ moon.shtml.

Hemming, Mark. "Star Trail Photography." Mark Hemming's Blogspot. http://markhemmings.blogspot.com/2007/04/star-trail-photography.html.

Javanrouh, Sam. "Sam Javanrouh Daily Dose of Imagery." http://wvs .topleftpixel.com.

Novikov, Oleg. "Oleg Novikov Photography." Star Trails Photography Tips. http://www.olegnovikov.com/technical/startrails/ startrails.shtml.

PCLIX, "Time Lapse Photography." http://www.pclix.com.

CHAPTER 42: Collecting Meteorites

American Museum of Natural History, "Meteorites." http://www
.amnh.org/exhibitions/permanent/meteorites.
University of Missouri Department of Geology. "Meteorite Identification." http://geology.missouri.edu/rockid.html.

VIII Giving Back

CHAPTER 43: Grow a Jurassic Tree

Ancient Pine. "The Wollemi Pine Tree," http://www.ancientpine.com.
National Geographic Society. http://shopsearch.nationalgeographic
.com/?sp_sr=rank&q=wollemi+pine.
United States Department of Agriculture. "USDA Plant Hardiness
Zone Map." http://www.usna.usda.gov/Hardzone/ushzmap.html.
Wollemi Pine Society. http://www.wollemipine.com/USA_link.php.

CHAPTER 44: Building a Bat House

Bat Conservational International, "How to Build a Bat House,"
http://www.batcon.org/home/default.asp.
Graham, Gary L., and Fiona A. Reid. Bats of the World. Golden
Guide. New York: St. Martin's Press, 2001.
National Parks, "Bat Facts." http://www.eparks.org/wildlife_
protection/wildlife_facts/bats/bat_house.asp.

CHAPTER 45: Resler Reef

Gruson, Lindsey. "Artificial Reefs Helping to Replenish Fishing."
The New York Times, September 11, 1984.
Piedmont National Wildlife Refuge. "Artificial Fish Habitat." http://
gf.nd.gov/multimedia/ndoutdoors/issues/2004/feb/docs/both-
sides.pdf.

INDEX